Lesbian Couples

D. Merilee Clunis
&
G. Dorsey Green

Seal Press

Cover design by Clare Conrad
Composition by The Typeworks
Printed in the United States of America
10 9 8 7 6 5

Library of Congress Cataloging-in-Publication Data
Clunis, D. Merilee.
Lesbian couples
Bibliography: p.
1. Lesbian couples--United States. 2. Lesbians--United States--Life skills guides. 3. Interpersonal relations. I. Green, G. Dorsey. II. Title.
HQ75.6.U5C58 1988 306.7'663 88-3178
ISBN 0-931188-59-8

Acknowledgements

We are very grateful to the many people who encouraged us in writing this book and who helped us in different ways over the past five years.

There are the therapists in Seattle, Washington and in San Francisco, Oakland, Berkeley, and Sebastopol, California who generously gave us their observations and reflections on the issues which lesbian couples bring to counseling. Many thanks to Ruth Baetz, Lilian Bern, Laura Brown, Rita Cahn, E. Kitch Childs, Deborah DeWolfe, Jan Hesslein, Nan Jervey, Barbara Johnstone, Pat Kalafus, Dan Kelleher, Patti McWilliams, Flora Ostrow, Vickie Sears, Nikki Sachs, Margaret Schonfield, Sara Sharratt, Adina Tarpley, and Pamela Weeks.

There are a number of women to whom we wish to extend a very special thanks:

Ruth Baetz, Laura Brown, and Vickie Sears for their sensitivity in giving us such loving and gentle feedback on some early versions of the book.

Ginny NiCarthy and Sharon Carson for their enthusiasm and encouragement during our informal writers' group.

Margaret Schonfield for her ongoing support and feedback about our ideas and plans, from conception to completion. Margaret Sorrel for the solid grounding of her clarity and objectivity. Rosemary Powers for her sense of what was needed to make segments come alive.

Our clients, our friends, and our partners for all that they have taught us about relationships.

All those who have asked us how the book was going. They helped us believe that we could finish it, even when we weren't sure.

Sandra Heindsmann educated us about writing and about the pleasures of working with a talented editor. She taught us to let go and to enjoy the writing process. We credit the acceptance of the manuscript by Seal Press in part to Sandra's skills in helping us integrate our two very different writing styles.

Vickie Sears worked with us to identify content for the chapters on racism and disability. We relied heavily on her unpublished manuscripts in the preparation of these chapters. She also helped us incorporate awareness of race and disability issues throughout the book.

A number of people gave us information and feedback on specific topics. We are indebted to these individuals not only for their comments and suggestions, but also for their patient clarification: Molly Barnett, Karen Bosley, Ana Mari Cauce, Betty Conkling, Jerry Evergreen, P. Catlin Fullwood, Ruth Gundle, Patricia Hunter, Dorothy Marie, Fran Miller, Laurel Robinson, Marilyn Smith, Ilene Stein, Nan Stoops, Mavis Tsai, Evelyn White, Frances Wood.

DeeDee Evergreen, Teresa Mathis, Will Elliot, and Carolyn Stevens rescued us by typing various versions of the manuscript onto the computer. We are also indebted to Rosemary Powers who monitored the printer and interpreted the Macintosh manual when things got rough.

Laura Brown read our "almost final" draft and gave us feedback about the book as a whole. We thank her for believing in us and for reminding us that being in a couple is play as well as work.

We are grateful to the staff of Seal Press for their early interest in this book. We cannot thank our editor, Barbara Wilson, enough. She challenged everything: our ideas, our selection of material, our language, our organization, and our politics. And she managed always to challenge with respect and caring. Whether we initially agreed with her or not, her instincts were accurate. Both of us learned a great deal from her and feel privileged to have had her as our editor. We want to thank Faith Conlon for her editing comments and for guiding the manuscript through the final copy-editing and production stages. We are also grateful to Sue Davidson for her gifted copy-editing of our final manuscript.

Dorsey thanks Ethan and Brendan for not putting up with her always saying she was too busy to play. Thanks also to Margaret for five years of listening, babysitting, and love while we were writing this book. Most of all I am grateful to Merilee for wanting to do the project in the first place and, finally, for always being willing to talk about whatever wasn't working and what was. I cannot think of a better person to write my first book with, or my second.

Merilee wants to thank Margaret, Lise, and Noah for their acknowlegement and acceptance, and for living through this process with me. I know it wasn't always easy. And to my co-author, Dorsey, I am grateful for the opportunity to explore and savor the joys and challenges of collaboration. Her optimism, vision, and unfailingly good humor made working together truly a pleasure.

Contents

For our partners
Margaret Schonfield
and
Margaret Sorrel

Preface

Five years ago we started talking about writing a book about lesbian couples. There were many books for and about heterosexual couples but little that referred to healthy lesbian couples. No single source validated the specific experiences of lesbian couples, offered help and suggestions to lesbians who had questions about their relationships, or described the imaginative ways lesbians had found to create family.

Both of us worked as therapists with lesbian couples; we were both in long-term lesbian relationships (and still are), so we knew that there were things that lesbian couples had in common, as well as ways in which they differed. In spite of this, it took us months to identify what these commonalities were, and even longer to make an outline that we felt adequately covered most lesbian couples' experiences. And even so, we know that we have not covered everything that makes up the lives of individual lesbian couples, nor have we covered all of our various topics in depth. We would be happy if each of our chapters were to stimulate books by other authors on that topic alone.

We have written this book for lesbians. Anyone who has been part of a lesbian couple, is now, or wants to be in the future, should find the book particularly useful. Therapists who work with lesbians in counseling settings should also find the book helpful in gaining an understanding about lesbian couples.

Apparently, co-authoring a book is much like being a couple. We found ourselves going through the stages we outline in Chapter 2. Our first experiences were much like the prerelationship stage, as we spent time figuring out whether we wanted to work together. Once we had decided to go for it, our relationship looked much like the romance stage. Eventually we had conflict, as we learned we did not have to agree about everything. Then, Dorsey got pregnant, and we had to deal with the shift in her availability and energy. Luckily, Merilee was willing to write on her own until Dorsey had stopped feeling nauseated. This was one of the hardest tests of the writing team; we didn't know whether we could work so unevenly and still feel like partners. Acceptance and stability did come, however, and both of us began to feel sure of our ability to work together. Finally, we knew we were committed to finishing the project. The publication of the book represents the final product of the collaboration stage. Within the context of producing this book, we have been a couple. It has been quite an experience!

Since we are both psychologists, we tend to place issues in an individual perspective, rather than in a broad, societal framework. However, both of us are also concerned with the political realities in our society. This meant that the book needed to reflect the interplay of personal and political. We are also both white, come from middle-class backgrounds, and have similar views of the world. We knew this meant that we shared blind spots and so we interviewed a number of therapists in the Seattle and San Francisco Bay area to help clarify our thinking and identify areas we might have missed. We also asked colleagues with different backgrounds, of different races, and of different ages to read early drafts, to help us identify our blind spots.

Most of the book draws on experiences that one or both of us has had personally, knows of through friends, or through our contact with clients. However, we realized that there were areas where our direct and indirect experience was inadequate to the tasks of the book. We therefore asked Vickie Sears, a writer and a therapist, to help us identify appropriate content for the chapters on disability and racism. A Native American, Vickie has worked with many women of color; she is also a diabetic, with a grasp of chronic illness issues. Her insights, experiences, and written material provided us with a framework for these chapters. We asked qualified readers to give us feedback about the chapters on racism, disability, and aging. We are deeply indebted to these readers who told us how our writing did and did not speak to their lives. They have given us a gift of themselves that has deepened our understanding and has helped us know ourselves better.

This book is not the final and complete guide for lesbian couples. It does, however, offer information and problem-solving suggestions for many of the issues lesbian couples face. However, we do not see the book or our suggestions as substitutes for counseling or therapy. Some women will use our ideas to improve their relationships on their own, and others will use them as indicators that they need professional help. We hope readers will use the book in whatever ways best meet their needs.

At times this book may give the impression that a good relationship as a couple means all work and no play. Actually, in our experience, it is when couples do both that the relationship thrives. We hope that lesbians use our suggestions for playing and relaxing as well as our guidelines for tackling the harder aspects of being a couple.

We are also not under any illusions that our book is *the* book for everyone. Some people may read the book and find that it does not speak to them or their situations. This reflects the diversity of the lesbian community. It would be exciting if those readers were to write books that speak to their particular experiences.

Publishing a book means committing to print ideas that really represent only one stage in the authors' thinking. We expect our ideas to go on developing. For us, this book is at once the end product of five years of work, and also the starting point for new ideas and new ways to work with clients. We hope the book will be as stimulating to read as it has been to write.

Merilee Clunis and Dorsey Green
Seattle, Washington 1987

Lesbian Couples

Chapter 1

What is a Couple Anyway?

Our relationships are what define us as lesbians to the world and to each other. And in large measure it is in our relationships that we learn who we are. It is here that we discover the joy and the exhilaration of loving women; here that we experience the magic and rightness of being lesbians. It is here, also, that we confront some of our greatest challenges. Will she still love me when she sees me at my worst? Can I keep my heart open when she disappoints me? Can we be different from each other and both be okay?

Couple relationships aren't for everyone. They are not a necessity nor a requirement for being happily lesbian. Some women decide that they never—or never again—want to be part of a couple. Others find that at certain times in their lives, other interests, goals or activities are more important than being in a relationship. Still others prefer to be involved in multiple relationships, rather than being with one primary person. And sometimes a woman may not know anyone with whom she wants to have a relationship, and so may choose to put her energy elsewhere, rather than to get into "just any" relationship.

On the other hand, many of us live in couple relationships or would like to. We want to know how to choose our relationships well and make them work successfully. And relationships do take work. We know that some people don't like to hear the words *relationship* and *work* in the same sentence. We have been told that relationships shouldn't take work. We do not agree. But work does not mean endless drudgery. Many goals and pleasures in life involve work.

Raising children is work; so is gardening, and working on one's racism, and meditation, and running a marathon and resolving conflicts with our partner. But it can be joyful work, done in a spirit of loving kindness for oneself and one's partner.

One of the questions we asked ourselves as we worked on this book was " Just what is a lesbian couple, anyway ?" Lesbian couples don't follow the same rules and have the same rituals as heterosexual society. So how do we know when a couple is a couple? We finally decided that the answer to this question is that lesbians are in a couple relationship when they say they are. Generally, a couple is two women who are committed to being with each other more often, or more intensely, or for a longer continuous period, than with others. The partners usually profess love for each other and a desire for intimate contact. The two may live together or not; they may have other sexual involvements or not; they may have a formal contract or commitment ceremony or not.

Why are relationships so important to us?

For most of us, our personal relationships have a significant role in our lives. We focus a lot of time on them: fantasizing, analyzing, daydreaming, writing in our diaries/journals, worrying, and talking to our friends. And this doesn't even count the time actually spent with our partners.

So, why are relationships so important to us? As human beings we have a desire for intimacy, and we look to our couple relationships for much of this. Because we are women, most of us received strong cultural messages about the value of coupling, and we learned to prize couple relationships. As lesbians in a homophobic world, we live with oppression. We give and gather strength from the couple partnerships which validate our identity and nurture our self-esteem.

Intimacy

The desire for intimacy is a major reason for wanting a

couple relationship. Intimacy is being close, sharing, feeling loved, understood, accepted, known, and appreciated. Being part of a couple makes it easier to have intimacy. For one thing, it takes less planning to get together—especially if the partners live together.

Intimacy grows with time. It takes time to get to know and to trust another person. Time together does not *guarantee* intimacy, but closeness over the years does mean that a couple has the opportunity to share experiences and changes. "We grew up together" is one expression of this shared history. Often the women in a couple come to know one another more fully than they are known by anyone else.

On the negative side, stress can arise from too much togetherness, too little separateness. While distance can also cause trouble, for lesbian couples, too much merging is more likely than too much separateness.

Some of us have difficulty with intimacy because we are afraid that we have to be close all the time, or that our partner will be hurt if we pull back at all. We may think that being close means we have to do what our partner wants, or take care of her, or be taken care of, or always stay the same, or never want what she doesn't provide.

We all have our own fears about intimacy, but that does not mean that we are afraid of intimacy itself. Rather, we are afraid of being hurt, or of not doing it right, or of the price we think we have to pay for being close, or that we cannot choose how close or how far away we need to be at any particular time. Out of our fears about giving and receiving intimacy, we may put up barriers to being close. We may push our partner away at exactly the moment that we feel closest to her.

There is a flow in relationships that includes separateness, making contact, and merging. Being separate is being apart, focusing on different things. Contact is being together, focused on the same thing; and merging is focusing intensely on each other. Intimacy is a combination of all three states, as they move and flow from one to another and back again.

Knowing that there is this natural flow, and that no one phase of it is permanent, can help partners give each other the space each needs to be separate, and to be together. Trusting the flow and recognizing what part of the process they are in helps to calm such fears as, "I'll never get enough time to myself," or "I'll never get enough of feeling close."

Some people want more separateness than others, while some want more contact and merging. These differences may change over time, as well. Although couples often seem to be polarized, with one person wanting more closeness and the other more space, it is important to remember that both wishes exist in both partners. When partners fail to recognize that they each want some separateness *and* some togetherness, they may feel stuck, and unable to resolve their differences.

Cultural messages

Because of the way our society treats girls, as compared with boys, women are more vulnerable to a sense of feeling incomplete—of having a gap to fill. Boys are generally told to "go for it," to be all they can be. Many girls are encouraged to stay closer to home, to curtail their own development in order to support someone else's, to be careful of the male "ego," not to develop independence, and so on. By the time little girls are six or seven, they know that they are eventually supposed to find someone and settle down for life. Career or talent is secondary to marriage, and not to be taken seriously. As women, our lives are full of messages that we need someone—a man—to feel complete. Long before we reach our twenties, it is likely that we will have started to look for our "other half." Much of what we do is designed to make us more desirable to that "someone else" who will complete us.

How does this translate to lesbians who have chosen women as lovers? Quite directly. We all begin as girls who are assumed to be heterosexual. We all receive similar messages. So instead of looking for a man to provide the completion, lesbians may look for a woman: Prince Charming becomes Princess Charming.

There are both advantages and disadvantages to this cultural training and emphasis on relationships. The disadvantage is that we may neglect ourselves by overfocusing on our couple relationship. We may put a partner's wants and needs first, and neglect our own. We may put too much energy into making the relationship a good one, and not enough into personal growth and development. On the other hand, there are advantages. Because women value couple relationships highly, both women in a lesbian couple feel a responsibility for making the relationship work. Both expect to give as well as get nurturing and support. Lesbian couples have the advantage of both partners' expecting and being willing to invest a good deal of time and emotional energy in the relationship.

Support in a homophobic world

It is a fact of life that we live in a society in which we may be disliked, feared, and even hated because we are lesbian or gay. These negative attitudes are called *homophobia*; when we ourselves believe them, they become internalized homophobia.

We think Suzanne Pharr, a feminist writer and activist, articulates well the bind that lesbians and gays are in as we live our lives. "When we talk about homophobia, we are talking about that particular blend of... fear, dread, and hatred that works to keep homosexuals as a hidden (closeted) underclass of society, discriminated against, treated as deviants, sinners, maliciously perverted, sick and abnormal. From those who hate us most, we receive the messages that we should be cured or killed; from those who are liberal and tolerant, we receive the messages that we must be quiet and invisible."

In our daily lives we are faced with subtle and not-so-subtle oppression. Our couple relationships can be a place where we give and get support and energy to deal with the homophobia of the outside world. This need to support each other can pull a couple together, leading to the closeness and security of "you and me against the world." However, it can also strain a relationship. Partners can become emotionally drained. Or they may avoid expressing differences and working through conflicts because it feels too dangerous to risk losing the partner's support.

Our desire for intimacy and support, and our values about relationships, all come into play in the course of creating and maintaining quality couple relationships.

Being part of a lesbian couple provides opportunities both for learning and for satisfaction. The chance to become more fully oneself while also being in a loving couple relationship is one of the most delightful of these opportunities. Differences between partners can provide excitement and challenge while similarities can offer warmth and comfort. In many ways, creating a successful couple relationship is like an art. It takes time and motivation; it requires learning and refining specific skills; and, it takes patience. Like good art, a couple relationship can bring pleasure to those who create it and to those around them.

Chapter 2

Stages of Relationships

Like individuals, couple relationships go through changes over time. Individuals move through infancy, childhood, adolescence, and then through the developmental stages of adulthood. Each stage has its characteristics, its tasks, and its particular problems. Couples, too, move through different stages in their relationships. Each of these stages also has its own particular characteristics, tasks, and difficulties.

However, we know more about stages of individual development than we do about the stages of relationships. This is especially true of lesbian relationships. So, one way to think about the model of the relationship stages that we will present is that it is a rough map. Like early pioneers, we have only a general sense of the territory, but even a general sense can be useful. While every relationship is unique, different couples cycle—and recycle—through similar stages. Having even an incomplete roadmap can be reassuring. Some of the issues that couples face are to be expected at particular stages in their relationship.

The following outline of six stages of relationship development for lesbian couples blends ideas from Susan Campbell's (1980) model for male-female relationships, and David McWhirter and Andrew Mattison's analysis of male couples. In applying these stages to any relationship—past or present—several cautions are in order. The first caution is that relationship development is a process, and the stages blend into each other. No buzzer sounds to annouce passage from the *prerelationship* stage to the *romance* stage, or from the *conflict* to *acceptance* to *commitment* and *collaboration* stages. However, even though the stages do overlap, and even though features of one stage can be present in another, each of the stages does have its own special features, developmental tasks, and problems. Also, class and race, as well as other factors, may drastically affect the degree to which these stages apply to a particular couple relationship.

Other cautions have to do with how couples move through the stages:

- No couple moves through the stages without hitches.
- Not every couple starts with the first stage.
- Some couples never go through all the stages, and certainly not in the order they are presented.
- There is no rule about how long a couple is supposed to stay in a stage.
- There is no rule about how many times a couple re-experiences any of the stages.

1. Prerelationship stage

This is the "getting to know you" stage. Some people refer to this process as dating; others describe it as "spending time." The prerelationship stage for lesbian couples is typically short. It may be a matter of weeks, or days (or sometimes even hours). No matter how long it lasts, our primary task in this stage is making choices.

Maria met Lucille at a friend's party. She was pleased when Maria called her to go out for coffee. They ended up talking nonstop for hours. Lucille had a wonderful time and wondered if maybe this could develop into something. She didn't want to get her hopes up too high, and she worried about whether she should make the next move.

So, the first choice after meeting someone is deciding whether to invest time and energy into getting to know her better. And she, of course, has to make the same decision. This first step is similar, whether Maria and Lucille are exploring friendship or something more. In our example, it might be useful for Lucille to look at her attraction to Maria.

Is Maria attractive because she is different, or because they have a lot in common? Does she remind Lucille of someone else? Does the attraction include a sexual attraction? Is Maria a solution to a current boredom, dissatisfaction, or emptiness? Might she be a way out of a current relationship that is over, but not ended?

Attractions usually combine a mixture of motives. The decision to pursue a new relationship depends on a combination of what we like about the other person and how well she seems to meet our needs. The important task for Lucille at this prerelationship stage is to find out more about who Maria is, and to share honestly who she is with Maria. The problem is that at this initial stage, each woman tends to try to look good to the other. Each tries to create a good image, a positive impression. Since, as women, we are encouraged to be whatever someone else wants us to be, we are especially likely to hold back information about ourselves, our wants, and our expectations, for fear that the other person may not like us.

Another choice at this stage is deciding whether, or when, to include being sexual in the getting-to-know-you process. The guidelines women learn about sexual behavior usually have to do with relationships with men. "Don't let him kiss you before the third date"; and "Save yourself for marriage"; and, "The best birth control pill is an aspirin held between your knees" are examples. These rules are based on a heterosexual (and possibly out-of-date) model. They do not apply to lesbians. Thus, particularly if a woman is newly lesbian, she may be confused about what rules to follow. This is quite understandable—since there really are no rules. The best plan, therefore, is for each woman to be clear about her own values about sex, and to follow those. For example, some women believe in sex only within a committed relationship; others regard being sexual as a way to break the ice in a new relationship. In the situation of Lucille and Maria, Maria may want a "fun" physical relationship until she leaves for the West Coast in two months. Or she may want an ongoing sexual relationship, with deepening intimacy over time. The key here is for both women to be honest with themselves and with each other about their values, intentions, and expectations. If Lucille and Maria decide to invest time and energy in getting to know each other better, they need to deal with a number of issues. They have to make choices, such as how much time to spend with each other, how often to see each other, and whether they will be sexual and/or monogamous. Often, these choices do not feel like choices. One or both women may just slide into a "relationship" without being clear with herself or with the other person about what she wants, expects, and intends in that relationship. There are at least three things that may get in the way of being clear: making assumptions; mind reading; and being unsure about what is reasonable.

Making assumptions

Often a woman makes assumptions about what "dating" or a new relationship should be like. She neglects to share these assumptions with her new friend, and then feels hurt and betrayed when the other person violates the assumptions. For example, instead of asking herself whether or not Maria will be sexually "faithful" to her during their dating period, Lucille just assumes that this will be the case. Maria has no such expectation for herself. Unless they are clear with each other, Lucille will be very disappointed when she finds out that Maria is being sexual with someone else. Maria may be irritated that Lucille had that expectation, because she never promised anything of the sort. Lucille is acting as if she knows what Maria thinks. She assumes that they agree about monogamy, without checking it out. Making assumptions can extend to beliefs about behavior, about attitudes, clothing styles, whatever. We may figure that if we "know" the right way, or the correct thing, or the best solution, our partner will also "know" it. Then, if she does something counter to our assumptions, we may believe that she is deliberately trying to hurt us.

Mind reading

Mind reading is another barrier to clear communication. In this society, women have been taught that mind reading is a loving communication. The lesson goes like this: if we really love someone, we know what she wants and needs without her having to tell us. If she does have to tell us, we have failed, somehow. On the other side is the belief that, "If you really loved me, you would know what I want. If I have to ask for it, it's not as good." This tendency to mind read, or to expect our partner to read our mind, is not at all helpful. In fact, it most often leads to misunderstanding, disappointment, and resentment.

Am I being reasonable?

Finally, as women we sometimes hesitate to mention our expectations and wants, because we are not sure that they are reasonable:

- Is it reasonable to expect a partner in a new relationship to move across the country after you have known each other for eight weeks?
- Is it reasonable to expect that she will stop seeing her old lover because you are jealous of the time they spend together?
- Is it reasonable to expect that you will share expenses equally, even though she makes a lot less money than you do?

The issue here is not what is reasonable so much as what it is that we want. There are no objective rules. What is reasonable is a matter of opinion. What is reasonable to one person is unreasonable to another. So the best strategy is to be clear about what we want, and to share that information with the other person. Wanting is not the same as getting. Because we want something does not mean that our partner is obliged to do it—no matter how reasonable we think our request is. But we do have the right to ask for what we want.

After both women state what they want, they can negotiate for what will work for them both. Or, they may realize in this process that their wants are too divergent. Discovering that they don't want the same things allows them to change their expectations and plans for this relationship. Whatever they decide, both women are ahead in the long (and short) run, because they are free to pursue a relationship that will meet each of their needs. Most women have been taught to believe that if we just give enough, we will get what we want and need. This belief reinforces the idea that we do not need to ask, or that we shouldn't ask. So we continue giving and depleting our energies while not getting what we really want and need. We just keep hoping—we go on. Eventually, we burn out and feel betrayed. It is much more effective to acknowledge these needs and wants as early as possible in the relationship.

2. Romance stage

Merging and fusion are both the goal and the reality in this stage. There is a feeling of oneness, of being completely understood, accepted, loved, and appreciated. There is also a lot of exciting sex. The new lovers focus on each other while neglecting friends. The lovers feel made for each other. Each woman puts her best foot forward, and potential irritations are overlooked or minimized, as the lovers bask in the glow of perfect harmony.

Rosie and Yvonne met during their summer vacations from college. Both were working as counselors at a camp for disabled children. Rosie was immediately attracted to Yvonne's sense of humor and her playfulness. Yvonne was taken by Rosie's warmth and confidence in dealing with even the most difficult kids. Needless to say, both were thrilled to discover another lesbian at the camp. Before long, they were spending almost all their free time together. And that was not nearly enough. Yvonne cancelled plans to meet friends on her weekends off. Rosie's drawing projects went untouched.

They were delighted to find that they had so much in common. They liked the same sports, the same music, the same books, and so on. "We just seem to be on the same wavelength. We feel so relaxed together." Both felt wonderful about themselves, each other, and their relationship. Rosie could easily overlook the fact that Yvonne tended to be a little more dramatic and emotional than Rosie found comfortable. Yvonne decided not to mention that Rosie was sometimes more serious and bossy than Yvonne would have liked.

They spent the summer blissfully involved in their work and in each other. They talked endlessly about their fantasies for the future, including how they would meet on the weekends and vacations. Eventually, they would attend the same college, so that they could be together.

The romance stage is a gift. It shows the possibilities, the visions of what could be. Shared dreams and fantasies, and this sense of oneness, harmony, and happiness hold a couple together long enough for them to imagine what the future really might be. The merging and togetherness of the romance stage are typically very intense for lesbians. In heterosexual relationships, the differences between men and women help to set limits on this kind of fusion. Just being physically different helps to establish boundaries. With lesbian couples it is easier for the partners to assume that there are no differences, because both are women. Another difference between men and women which helps limit the fusion of this stage for heterosexuals is cultural conditioning. Men are trained to have lives independent and separate from their relationships—at least, more so than women. Women are encouraged to involve themselves fully in their relationships—i.e., to merge.

Women are encouraged to want more intimacy, and men to want more space. These differences tend to create tension and distance in heterosexual relationships which lesbian couples do not experience to the same degree. Another factor which contributes to lesbian couples' merging at this stage is that there are no rituals of courtship. There is no "going steady," or engagement, or legal marriage. Without the pacing that these rituals provide, lesbian relationships can move quickly.

Women are encouraged to view love, sex and marriage, or commitment, as chain-linked. In the clear absence of other rituals for lesbians, sex can become the sacrament, and living together the marriage vows. Many lesbians want the security of a commitment as soon as possible. Couples are house-hunting after they have known each other for four weeks. Or they start living together when one woman leaves her current lover and needs a place to stay. She moves in with her new lover, and instantly they are in a "Relationship."

Our primary suggestion for lesbians in the romance (or the prerelationship) stage is to slow down the process of commitment. Get to know the other person, and be clear about wants and expectations, even though it takes time. In the rush to be in a relationship with a capital R, we run the risk of not giving ourselves the time we need to assess whether the vision we have can become a reality.

Yvonne describes Rosie as being "the answer to my prayers, and my reason for living. No one has ever loved me like she does." When the vision is not as easily attained as she hoped, or when Rosie does not seem so loving, Yvonne may feel discouraged, disappointed, and disillusioned. She may be angry with Rosie for "ruining everything." Her vision of what could be may not be wrong. What *may* be invalid is the idea that it will all come to pass as easily and quickly as she had hoped.

Another danger of the romance period is that in putting her best foot forward, Rosie may end up trying to maintain an image, rather than being herself. She may pressure Yvonne to keep up Yvonne's image, as well. Rosie may pressure herself and feel pressure from Yvonne to be fun and carefree. Yvonne may be trying to be confident and "have it all together," with never a moment of doubt. Honesty is essential to reverse this tendency to cling to images. Each woman must allow herself to be fully herself. Yvonne sometimes feels inadequate. She needs to share that with Rosie. And Rosie needs to share the parts of herself that are worried, or serious.

Let us follow Rosie and Yvonne into the next stage.

3. Conflict stage

Rosie and Yvonne continued their relationship after they each returned to college. There were frequent letters, high telephone bills, and all too few chances to see each other. So Yvonne decided to transfer to State, where Rosie had a scholarship that she would lose if she changed schools. They planned to rent a small apartment together the following quarter. In the meantime, Yvonne moved into the house that Rosie shared with two other women.

The move proved to be a difficult transition for Yvonne. She missed her friends; she couldn't get the courses she wanted that quarter; and, the house was small for four people. She felt lonely, disappointed, and unappreciated. She was still very much in love with Rosie, but she wondered if the move was worth it, especially since Rosie seemed to be working or studying much of the time. When Yvonne complained about how little time they spent together, Rosie responded that there was nothing she could do about it. Her courses were demanding, and she had no control over the schedule for her part-time job. Rosie was not pleased that Yvonne moped around and wasn't much fun to be with. In fact, Rosie felt somewhat guilty that Yvonne had moved to be with her, and that things were not going well. However, she had her own problems. She felt a real loss of privacy in sharing her room. Also, her grades had slipped since Yvonne's arrival, and she was worried about losing her scholarship. It seemed to Rosie that there were just too many demands on her: too many demands on her time, her energy, her limited resources.

Rosie and Yvonne have arrived at the conflict stage in their relationship. Each has discovered that the other is not the person she thought her to be. Neither is getting what she wants, and what she expected to get from the other. Each sees her partner as flawed and imperfect. Both feel hurt, disappointed, and resentful.

Rosie discovers that Yvonne is not always the caring, attentive, and warm person she had been at the beginning. In fact, Yvonne is moody and demanding. Rosie expected that living with Yvonne would be fun and easy. It is not.

For her part, Yvonne feels betrayed. She had expected that Rosie would provide her with all the emotional support and attention she needed after the move. To her, Rosie's being unavailable and studying so much of the time seems selfish and rejecting.

Of course, not all lesbian relationships have such difficult struggles as Rosie and Yvonne's. However, some relationships do not survive the conflict stage. One reason for this is that the women did not spend enough time getting to know each other at the beginning of the relationship. They may be poorly matched. So the differences in temperament, values, goals, or lifestyles that emerge at the conflict stage are too great to be resolved in a mutually satisfactory way.

Another reason is that the partners may not be skilled at dealing with conflict. One or both women may end the relationship rather than face conflict. Or their styles of dealing with conflict may be so destructive and painful that breaking up seems to be the only alternative.

How might Rosie and Yvonne try to deal with their failure to meet each other's expectations? A number of responses are possible.

First, either woman could ignore the fact that her partner is irritating or disappointing her. This choice usually results in building resentments which may simmer and boil over into sudden fights over trivial issues—the "straw that breaks the camel's back" pattern.

A second option is for one partner to mention her disappointment or grievance, discuss it a bit, decide that it's not really that important (when it is), and smooth over the conflict. For example, Yvonne shares her disappointment about having so little time with Rosie. Rosie initially responds defensively: she is swamped, and has no time to give. As they continue to talk, Yvonne starts to feel that she is demanding too much, that she should be more understanding of Rosie's school pressures, that she is being childish and dependent. Yvonne convinces herself that she is being unreasonable, especially after Rosie expresses her fears about losing her scholarship. They both smooth over the conflict and avoid confronting the problem of how their relationship will work on a day-to-day basis. When differences are minimized in this way, they resurface again and again.

A third possibility is that Rosie (or Yvonne) decides that this relationship is just not working and wants to end it. If there has been little or no discussion or attempt to resolve differences, such a decision is premature. Unless they clarify what they want and expect of a partner, they don't really know whether the relationship could work successfully.

A fourth option is that Rosie and Yvonne can negotiate their differences. It may be that they will discover in this process that they want very different things from a relationship. Rosie may want to spend a good deal of time pursuing individual activities and leading a life separate from her relationship with Yvonne. Yvonne may prefer that they do almost everything together, that they share as fully as possible in each other's lives. They may not be able to work out an arrangment that suits them both. But at least they can be clear and honest with each other. If they do decide to end the relationship, each has a better chance of feeling good about herself and her partner. They acknowledge their different needs and expectations as just that—as differences, rather than as right versus wrong.

Finally, Rosie and Yvonne may find that they are able to agree on ways of addressing the needs of each. For example, Rosie might be willing to set aside a certain amount of time each day or week to spend with Yvonne, doing enjoyable things. Since she has more time, Yvonne might agree to look for an apartment for the two of them. A new place would allow each of them to have her own room—and more privacy. Rosie and Yvonne need to realize that having wants and expectations that the other person does not or cannot meet is normal. It happens to everyone. It is also normal for it to happen over and over again in the course of a relationship. We are always growing and changing. As we change, what we want of a partner also changes. Thus, conflicts and negotiations are ongoing. Rather than being afraid of conflict, Rosie and Yvonne can see it as a sign of growth and change, and as an opportunity to negotiate agreements that are satisfactory to them both.

Out of the struggles of this stage come basic ground rules and communication patterns for the relationship. The couple tests out and establishes conflict styles, decision-making processes, communication channels, and relationship goals. And then they move on to the next stage.

4. Acceptance stage

This stage can be described as the calm after the storm. There is a sense of stability—even of contentment and deep affection. At this stage each partner has accepted that the other is a separate human being with shortcomings and faults. In our example of Rosie and Yvonne, Rosie realizes that Yvonne's neediness and tendency to dramatize are not to blame for all of their problems. Yvonne recognizes that Rosie is not always confident, even-tempered, and nurturing: sometimes she is moody, unsure of herself, and unwilling or unable to meet Yvonne's expectations.

The conflict stage usually involves a lot of finger-pointing and blaming the other person for the problems. Yvonne often thought (and sometimes accused Rosie out loud), "If only you would spend more time with me, then everything would be fine." And for her part, Rosie responded, "If only you would stop nagging at me and exaggerating everything, we would do much better." Instead of accusing and blaming each other, partners at the acceptance stage look at themselves and try to see the ways they contribute to the conflict. Disagreements and discomfort are seen as opportunities to learn about themselves and each other, rather than as an opportunity to keep score. A couple at this stage starts to recognize patterns. As the same conflict, or the same pattern, arises again and again, the couple learns to resolve the issues faster. The experience of negotiating and resolving problems sucessfully builds their confidence. They no longer are afraid that the relationship is in danger of ending each time they disagree or have an argument.

Rosie and Yvonne illustrate the conflict theme of dependence and independence. Faced with a totally new school and living situation, Yvonne feels isolated and dependent on Rosie. She feels scared and needy, and wants Rosie to take care of her. When this does not happen, Yvonne is hurt and angry. She accuses Rosie of being cold and uncaring. While Rosie does feel a lot of responsibility toward Yvonne, she is also very worried about her grades. She is afraid she won't be able to take care of herself and Yvonne, too. She thinks, "It's Yvonne's fault that I'm so drained, she's so selfish and demanding." Her response is to pull back and try to be more separate and independent from Yvonne.

In the acceptance stage, both Rosie and Yvonne look at their own contributions to the conflict. Rosie realizes that part of her reaction to Yvonne's wanting attention and nurturing arises out of her experience with her own mother. Rosie was the oldest in a family of six. Her father was away from home a lot, working two jobs to support his family. Rosie's mother had severe bouts of depression and lacked confidence in her ability to do anything. She leaned heavily on Rosie for advice and help in raising the younger children and in managing the house. Rosie had felt overwhelmed by the responsiblity of taking care of the children and her mother. She resented her mother's depression and inability to cope with life. Rosie felt trapped in her responsiblities and longed to have fun like other kids.

When Rosie sees Yvonne getting depressed, she panics. Without making the conscious connection with her childhood experience, she becomes fearful that she will have to take care of Yvonne as she had her mother. She does not want to do that. Rosie's survival instinct takes over, and she decides that she needs to be separate from Yvonne and not get trapped. So she is in a state of conflict, feeling both responsible and resentful. When she understands how this present situation triggers a reaction based on her early experience, Rosie is able to see the differences between Yvonne and her mother. The situation is not the same as it had been when she was a child. Yvonne is not her mother, and there are not six children. She can talk to Yvonne, and they can get clear about what Yvonne actually wants and what Rosie is willing to provide.

For her part, Yvonne comes to see that Rosie's behavior reminds her of a previous lover of hers. Before her relationship with Rosie, Yvonne had been involved with a woman who was ten years older than she. This woman had been very dedicated to her work. After a fun-filled courtship, in which Yvonne was wined and dined, the relationship turned into something that resembled a traditional heterosexual marriage. Yvonne was expected to cook, provide emotional support, and an ever-available listening ear to her lover's hard-day-at-the-office stories. Yvonne had been very frustrated about not having attention for herself and her needs. The whole focus of the relationship was on her lover and her demanding job. Memories and resentments from this previous relationship are what Yvonne brings to her conflict with Rosie.

Thus, in the acceptance stage, each partner acknowledges the history she brings as her contribution to the conflict or power struggle. The couple can then examine and understand how their individual past experiences connect to their pattern as a couple. They are then in a position to change the pattern, and create the kind of partnership they want, based on the here and now.

5. Commitment stage

What does commitment in a relationship mean? To some it means a guarantee of forever, or the security of "there won't be anyone else as special to you as as I am."

In our view, commitment is the decision to make choices about the relationship and be responsible for them. It means letting go of the search for the perfect partner, of the guaranteed future, of the happy-ever-after. Commitment cannot come before the power struggle of the conflict stage, or before the understanding of the "me" in the "we" patterns of the acceptance stage. In commitment, partners accept the reality of change. They accept their partners as basically trustworthy; and they do not experience differences as threats, or changes as losses. A stability and familiarity have developed, so that the rough spots aren't so frightening. "This, too, shall pass" is easier to believe during the hard times.

This does not mean that couples at this stage never have doubts. Even with a sense of commitment, a couple may feel doubt, uncertainty, or regret at a *particular* moment. They intend to stay on the bus until the end of the line, but that does not mean that they won't experience bumps along the way. Sometimes they may even want to get off altogether.

In the commitment stage, the couple must come to terms with individual wants and needs that seem to be opposites. These apparent contradictions turn out to be part of a larger whole. One example is being separate and being together. Often these needs appear to be opposite—freedom versus security—and seem to be housed exclusively in one or the other partner. Particularly in the conflict stage, partners can become polarized. One wants more freedom and separateness. The other wants the security of more togetherness. If the woman who desires freedom gets her needs met, her lover's wanting togetherness is frustrated, and vice versa.

During the acceptance stage, the partners recognize that each of them has needs for space as well as for togetherness.

In the commitment stage, the couple realizes that separateness does not exclude togetherness. Each partner recognizes that she needs both, and that the relationship requires a balance of the two. This issue can arise in various ways.

Mary Ann loves to go camping and mountain climbing. Her partner of three years, Dora, does not enjoy these activities. Mary Ann has to decide whether to encourage Dora to go, or whether to find other people who share her interest. If she puts pressure on Dora, there may be conflict and stress. If she goes with others, she meets her needs, but spends time and energy outside the relationship that she could be putting into it. She knows that she can't expect Dora to meet all of her emotional and social needs, but she is torn, because she would rather be with Dora than with anyone else.

Ideally, Mary Ann and Dora can negotiate some kind of arrangement so that they are both satisfied. If they can talk about the issue openly, a resolution may be easier to reach than they think. It may be that Dora is a city person who has had very little experience of the outdoors. She doesn't enjoy camping because she has never really tried it. She may be willing to go camping under certain conditions. Or, Mary Ann may decide that it is the climbing more than the camping that she likes. She may do less camping and spend that time with Dora, doing things they both like to do, while retaining her climbing friends. The key to working out a satisfactory agreement is for both women to be clear about their own wants and concerns, and to express those. Then they can move toward a creative solution that will address the needs of both.

Whatever they work out about the camping/climbing question, Mary Ann and Dora are working on finding a balance between togetherness and separateness. Choosing the togetherness option all the time can burden the relationship with too many expectations and get in the way of each woman's individual growth. Choosing the separateness option all the time may lead to drifting apart.

When one partner is identified as being the one who always wants to be separate—or accused of it—and the other as always wanting togetherness, both are backed into a corner. It is much easier to negotiate getting needs met when the couple recognizes that each wants some of both, and that the relationship benefits from a balance.

Commitment means choice. It implies an expectation about the future, but does not guarantee the future outcome. Partners make agreements with each other. They know that these agreements can be changed, and may even be broken. They don't plan on that happening, but they are aware that it might.

Sharon and Rita agreed to be monogamous. Then Sharon went to visit an old lover in another state, and was sexual with her. She felt guilty about not abiding by her agreement, but also knew that as far as she was concerned, this incident was not a threat to her relationship with Rita. If—or more likely, when—Rita found out about it, she might feel hurt, disappointed, and angry. She might question Sharon's trustworthiness about any agreements they had with each other.

Many relationships grow stronger in the process of dealing with broken agreements. Others do not survive even one violation of an important understanding. If an agreement is broken over and over again, there are serious consequences for a relationship. The woman who does not abide by her agreements may lose respect for herself, and her partner may cease to trust her at all.

In the commitment stage, partners need to seek out and create what Susan Campell (1980) describes as liberating structures. This term refers to arrangements that couples make so that they can each meet their individual needs, as well as enhance their relationship.

Faith and Sheila lived together for 10 years. Then Faith got a promotion at work. The new job brought with it a one-year rotation to a city 350 miles away from their home. Their careers were very important to both women, but so was the day-to-day contact they had enjoyed for the past ten years. Fortunately, they had enough financial resources to support a solution that was a liberating structure for them. Faith rented an apartment in the new city and travelled home to be with Sheila at least every other weekend. This allowed for a balance between freedom for Faith to accept the new job, and security for them both in the relationship.

Another example of a liberating structure is provided by Adele and Fran. For the six years they had lived together, it had been important to them that they split household tasks fifty-fifty. This arrangement worked well until Adele took a second job to pay off her bills. Adele then had less time and energy to keep up her end of the bargain. Without talking about it with Adele, Fran did more than her agreed-upon share of housework. Adele felt grateful, but guilty; and Fran felt resentful.

These women needed to acknowledge that their situation was changed as a result of Adele's additional job. The old fifty-fifty agreement no longer met their needs. After discussing various options, Adele and Fran decided to try a short-term agreement. They changed their split to seventy-thirty and reduced the number of household tasks. For example, instead of sweeping the kitchen every other day, they settled on once a week. This agreement provided a liberating structure.

Other liberating structures may be rituals or activities that couples use to maintain or recapture passion and excitement in their relationship. After the romance stage, partners often settle into familiarity and comfort. Variety and excitement are missing. Liberating structures might include asking and taking their partner on a date, going away for a weekend, or changing the lovemaking routine.

Couples in the commitment stage are working on balancing opposing needs. These include the needs for freedom versus security, for familiarity versus variety, and for stability versus change. The partners have come to a basic trust, and each acknowledges that there are no guarantees. They continue to deal with getting clear about their needs and figuring out ways to meet these needs, both within and outside of the primary relationship.

Some couples in the commitment stage decide to have a ceremony of commitment or marriage to celebrate their relationship. At the 1987 National Gay and Lesbian March on Washington, for example, hundreds of couples participated in a mass marriage ceremony. Society and religions in general have excluded lesbian couples from the heterosexual privilege of a legally recognized marriage. More recently, some couples have been asking their religious groups to hold these celebrations as a way of marking their commitment.

6. Collaboration

Collaboration is the stage of a relationship where the women focus on something bigger than the two of them to share with the world. They have found that they can have conflict without ending the relationship; each recognizes her own piece of the "we" patterns; and they have both made their commitment to the relationship. Now the couple has energy available to direct beyond the two of them, into some kind of joint project.

Yolanda and Tess took the lead in organizing a Gay/Lesbian Pride March in their city.

Melinda and Sue decided to have a baby together.

Grace and Joan had known each other for twelve years, and had been in a couple relationship for ten. Their dream was to open a bed-and-breakfast inn together.

Each of these couples is involved in creating something together—a political event, a baby, a business. This collaboration usually enhances the relationship, but the main purpose is to create something in the world outside of the relationship. Even though lesbians continue to experience oppression in the outside world, we still seem to move toward doing some work together that brings the relationship into a broader context. We may choose to be in the gay and lesbian world, or in the larger community. For example, Grace and Joan's bed-and-breakfast inn may cater to a gay and lesbian clientele only, or may not. The point is that the couple is creating something together that extends beyond the relationship.

As the women shift from an exclusively "us" focus to collaboration, they may go through "miniversions" of the earlier stages of the relationship. They may re-experience romance, conflict, acceptance, and commitment as they work on their project. Collaboration, then, can be like starting the relationship anew. However, this renewed relationship has a history of survival and is usually more resilient and stable than it was the first time around.

Chapter 3

Separateness and Togetherness

Most of us wonder, "What is a healthy intimate relationship? How do I find one? How do I know if I have one?" Janet Woititz, an authority on adult children of alcoholics, provides one of the clearest answers to these questions in her book *The Struggle for Intimacy*. She says that we have a healthy intimate relationship if we have created an environment where:

1. I can be me.
2. You can be you.
3. We can be us.
4. I can grow.
5. You can grow.
6. We can grow.

To have intimacy, each of us must allow her partner to be herself. To do this, we must respect and value her as she is. Our acceptance cannot be conditional on her being who we want her to be, or on her doing what we want her to do. Acceptance, however, does not necessarily mean liking everything about our partner's behavior. For example, we may not like it that our new partner hates concerts and never wants to go to hear music with us, but we can acknowledge and understand her feelings and attitudes, without judging her or putting her down for having them. To meet our own needs, we can arrange to go to these events with other people or by ourselves. In accepting our partner for who she is, we give her understanding, and freedom and support in being herself. We can encourage our partner to grow and change—but in ways she chooses for herself, rather than in ways that we might want. We need to resist trying to make our partner behave and be the way we want her to be.

During the first year of Louise and Pam's relationship, Louise felt more loved, understood, and cared for than she ever had in her whole life. For her part, she had never loved anyone as much as she loved Pam. So it was very confusing to her when she found herself being critical of Pam. She never mentioned anything out loud, but she found herself thinking that Pam didn't take good enough care of her appearance. She also thought that Pam sounded awkward when she tried to express herself in conversations. Louise was afraid that other people would think that Pam was sloppy and not too bright. Louise had also discovered that she and Pam had very different ideas about what things were important. Unlike Louise, Pam was not interested in saving her money, and the idea of having a family no longer seemed to excite her. Louise felt disloyal and guilty for being critical of her partner. But she also felt deeply disappointed, and even betrayed, because of their differences about saving money and having a family.

Personal boundaries

What has happened here? One way to look at this situation is in terms of personal boundaries. Our boundary is that intangible bubble that surrounds each of us at our core. This bubble contains our sense of self, and separates what is "me" from what is "not me."

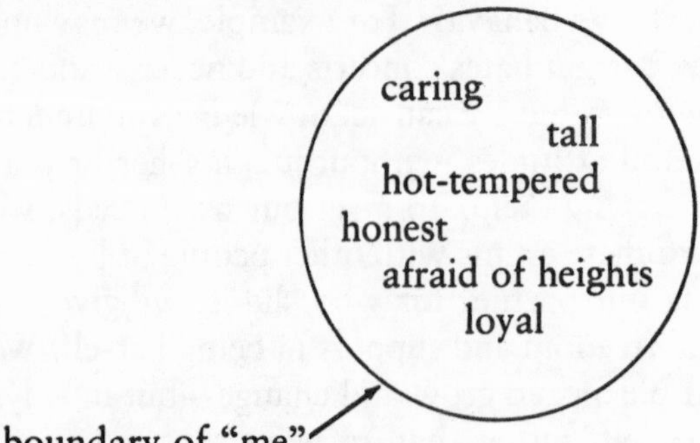

The outside world, other people, and skills and traits I don't have are all examples of "not me." Someone who is *not* afraid of heights is different from me—not me.

In her relationship with Pam, Louise has blurred the boundaries between herself and her lover. Initially, Louise was unaware that Pam had different ideas than she did about saving money, for example. She assumed that they agreed on the important things— and that Pam, in fact, shared her values. She is also very concerned about how Pam appears to other people. If others think Pam is sloppy or stupid, Louise feels vulnerable and devastated. It is as if Pam is an extension of Louise, rather than being a separate person. In Louise's eyes, what Pam says and what others think of her is a reflection and comment on Louise, rather than on Pam.

If a person has not developed a strong sense of self and clear boundaries, it is as if her boundary bubble has a gap, or weak spots. We might imagine this bubble as a "C" shape. In the illustration below, the boundary that separates this person from others is not complete. There is a gap. When a person with a "C" shaped boundary gets involved in a relationship, the boundaries between the two individuals in the couple may become blurred. This is what happened for Louise in the relationship with Pam.

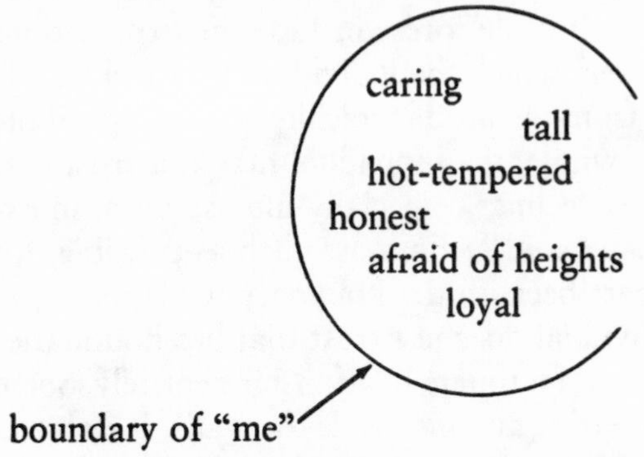

When two people are involved in a couple relationship, it is rather like two bubbles moving through the flow of contact, merging, and separateness. One complete bubble contacts the other, edge meets edge, differences are recognized and appreciated. In the merging experience, there is often the wonderful feeling of "losing oneself." However, the boundaries of the individual bubbles remain intact, rather than becoming blurred, even when the couple is in the merging phase of the relationship.

Separateness looks like this:

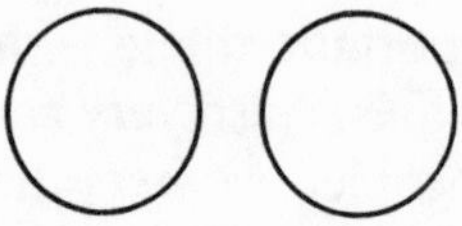

Contact looks like this:

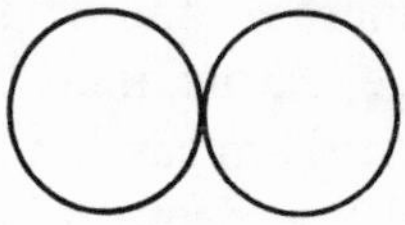

And Merging looks like this:

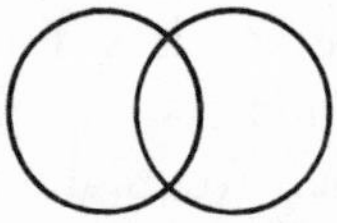

Boundaries and the sense of self begin to develop early in life. A child's healthy development of boundaries is interfered with by experiences such as physical abuse, sexual abuse, having to parent her parents, or being treated as an extension of a parent. When boundaries are not well developed, the person feels vulnerable to pressures both from the outside and from the inside. Outside forces include the expectations and demands of others which the individual may feel unable to resist. Pressures from the inside typically are feelings. If the boundaries are not whole, the individual may not trust that they will contain her feelings, especially intense ones. In extreme cases, she may avoid feelings as much as possible, for fear of blowing apart because the boundary walls may give way. When an individual does not trust that her boundaries will hold, she may avoid intimate relationships entirely. Some do not want to risk letting anyone inside the walls. It feels too risky, too vulnerable, too exposed. At the other extreme, a person may move quickly to try to complete her boundary by joining up with a partner and blurring the boundaries between them. The partnership allows the person with incomplete boundaries to feel whole. But the wholeness is an illusion, in the sense that the person can only feel whole in the relationship when the boundaries are blurred. This kind of wholeness involves being fused, rather than being able to move from merging to separateness. If partners are fused in this way, what one feels is experienced by the other as her feeling, and what one does is regarded by the other as a reflection on her, and so on. As with Pam and Louise, the partners become extensions of each other. They are not able to allow the flow of contact, merging, and separation without being afraid of losing their lover, or themselves.

Creating intimacy

Shared intimacy also requires an equitable power balance. If one partner makes all the decisions; or controls such important aspects of the relationship as money, conversations, or sex; or is put on a pedestal by the other, the balance of power is not equitable. In every relationship, there are ways in which the partners may feel one-up or one-down to each other. One partner may be perceived as more powerful because she makes more money, or is more talented in music, or more fragile, or is white, or has more experience, or is more "normal." A partner may have power because she has a temper, or because she is the one who is trying hard, or because she withholds emotional support. When the power balance is not equitable, resentments build. In addition, the relationship is ripe for the development of unhealthy dependency. Power balances in relationships are continually changing. One person may be more powerful than her partner at different times and for different reasons. There is an ebb and flow in the power balance. An unhealthy dependence is indicated by feelings such as "I cannot live without you," "You are my whole life," or "If you ever left, I might as well kill myself." As is the case with incompletely developed boundaries, power imbalances interfere with the natural flow of intimacy—the contact, merging, and separateness phases.

Healthy intimacy requires both individual and combined effort, because partners are each growing as individuals, as well as in their relationship. Our individual efforts are needed, because few of us are completely comfortable with ourselves, or with others, without some significant work on ourselves. A close relationship often seems to bring out the best—and the worst—in us. This is because an intimate relationship evokes two major fears that we all carry with us.

These are the fear of being close and the fear of being alone. Many, if not all of our problems in intimate relationships are related to these fears. Luise Eichenbaum and Susie Orbach, in their book *What Do Women Want,* describe these as the fear of engulfment and the fear of abandonment. When we get close to another, we may fear being overwhelmed and losing our identity and sense of self. This may lead us to withdraw from our partner. We may also pull back from our "intimate other" because feeling close activates our fear of being alone. Realizing how close and attached we are can frighten us. We worry about being left, about how we could not survive without her, about the possibility of being devastated by rejection and abandonment.

But by definition, intimacy means opening ourselves up, sharing all parts of ourselves, exposing our dreams, our feelings, our weaknesses. So intimacy means vulnerability and risk. This can cause different reactions.

Rosa avoided getting close because she was afraid that a partner would find out who she "really was," and would reject her.

Glenda held herself back from sharing very much with her lover, Trudy, because she didn't trust that Trudy wouldn't use it against her sometime.

Dawn knew intimacy was linked somehow to her sense of control. She was not sure how it worked, but she knew that she felt very uncomfortable and tense in a close relationship. It was as if she were "out of control."

Each couple creates their we-ness from shared experiences, interests, values, and goals. When partners do connect closely, their energies are combined and enhanced. The potential for the relationship to reach new heights of intimacy increases as partners learn to handle this positive energy. In intimate relationships we offer, and are offered, validation, understanding, and a sense of being appreciated intellectually, emotionally, and physically. This closeness is that almost magical connection where we trust that we can say anything and still feel valued and respected.

Diana and Jenine worked very hard on what they described as the "wonderful, terrible feelings of intimacy." They were convinced that the rewards of intimacy—mutual understanding, appreciation, and acceptance—were worth facing their fears.

Samantha was very pleased with herself. Her lover, Erin, had just gotten a promotion at work, and Samantha was whole-heartedly excited and pleased for Erin. At their celebration dinner, Samantha felt full of appreciation and pleasure at what Erin had achieved. Samantha knew that even a year ago, she would have compared herself to Erin and felt inadequate, thus missing the intimacy they were sharing.

Charlie felt disappointed and discouraged. Newly launched in real estate, she thought she had sold her first house, and had been sure her career change was going to be a success. Then the deal fell through, and all Charlie could think about was going back to selling shoes, nine-to-five. But when she got home that day, she was touched and reassured by her partner Sue's reaction. Sue sat and listened to Charlie talk about her disappointment and fears. She didn't try to fix anything, or change the subject. She just allowed Charlie to talk out her feelings.

What do we need to do to develop and enhance intimacy in our relationships?

Trust and openness

Possibly the hardest part of building intimacy is developing trust, and risking openness. Intimacy requires that we risk revealing our thoughts and feelings, and that we be fully open to hearing about our partner's ideas and emotions. We need to say honestly what we feel and think—sharing the range of our thoughts and feelings, not just the positive ones.

In trying to be honest with her partner, Joan, Ling was not sure just how honest to be. Should she tell Joan every one of her thoughts and feelings, even the negative ones that might upset them both?

Ling faces a dilemma. She wants to be honest, but she is afraid of hurting Joan's feelings and losing her trust. One guideline that Ling can use in this situation is to ask herself, "How persistent is this thought or feeling?" If it is persistent, she had better express it. To fail to do so could damage the relationship. But the key factor is the word *persistence*. Infrequent, fleeting memories about good times with an old lover may not qualify as persistent. Dissatisfaction with things that Joan cannot change, and which only bother Ling on rare occasions, may also not fit the persistence criterion. By using this as a guideline, Ling can be honest without abusing Joan's feelings.

Any sharing or openness that creates even a little bit of vulnerability is a risk. In the process of learning about our partners and helping them understand us, we risk being criticized or not having our positive feelings returned. Particularly if we are sharing a fear, insecurity, or weakness, we may feel extremely vulnerable. It helps us to take these risks if we trust that our partner will not hurt us on purpose, that she will keep our confidences, and will try to understand, rather than judge. If we feel judged or punished when we disclose our thoughts and feelings, we will probably withdraw.

Francie remembered an incident that was the beginning of the end of her relationship with Ellen. When Francie got the teaching job she had always wanted, she was very pleased and excited. However, she soon began to feel frightened, inadequate, and confused. When she tried to talk to Ellen about her feelings, Ellen dismissed it all by saying, "You're making a big deal out of nothing. Your fears are childish. You'll do fine at the job." Francie felt so hurt and belittled that she vowed she would never share important feelings with Ellen again. As Francie distanced herself, Ellen also withdrew—and eventually they broke up.

This story could have had a very different outcome. Ellen could have responded with acceptance and understanding instead of putting Francie down for her feelings. Francie could have confronted Ellen about how hurt she was by Ellen's response and requested different behavior from her. Either partner could have enhanced their intimacy, rather than damaging it.

Signs of caring

In addition to trust and openness, intimacy requires that each partner understands what the other needs to feel valued and appreciated. Then it is easier to provide what is most important. These signs of caring do not have to be expensive, or on a large scale, but they do need to be personal and frequent. Feeling close is enhanced by showing we care—often, and in a variety of ways.

Sometimes we do not recognize the signs of love and caring given by our partner, because we have a different way of expressing them. And the signals of appreciation and respect we offer may go unnoticed, because they do not fit our partner's ideas of intimacy.

Angelina and Peggy both felt frustrated. Each felt that she was not getting what she needed, was not feeling valued and supported. Neither knew quite what was going wrong. When Peggy was upset about something, she wanted Angelina simply to listen to her express her feelings. Instead, Angelina offered suggestions and gave advice. Then Peggy felt criticized and cut off. Typically, she got angry with Angelina for not listening; and then Angelina felt hurt, because her efforts to show Peggy that she cared were unappreciated. The problem was that Angelina's signs of caring were what she herself would have wanted to receive if she were upset. Angelina liked to get advice and suggestions when she was upset about something. She, in turn, got frustrated with Peggy's response to her. Instead of helping her to solve the problem, Peggy worked at getting Angelina to talk about her feelings.

These two really cared about each other. But they went about showing it in exactly the wrong way. When Peggy got upset, she wanted "feeling talk," so that was what she provided for Angelina. However, Angelina wanted "action talk" when she got upset, and offered that to Peggy. In this example, neither woman got what she wanted, and each felt rebuffed and invalidated in her attempts to show she cared. Eventually they may stop trying to get support from each other. This, of course, will just make things worse, because the less we offer, the less we usually get back.

Peggy and Angelina each made the mistake of assuming that her partner wanted the same thing that she herself wanted. Like many of us, they give what they wish to receive, not what the other wants. When it comes to showing we care, the Golden Rule needs to be changed. Rather than treating our partner as *we* wish to be treated, we need to treat her the way *she* wants to be treated. If we don't know, we'll have to ask.

Because no one is a mind reader, we have to learn to ask clearly for what we want for ourselves. In turn, we need to listen respectfully to our partner's requests and to notice which of our behaviors pleases or displeases her. Because our previous lover liked to be left alone when she was angry does not mean that our current partner wants the same response from us. It is essential to share and check out what makes each of us feel loved, cared for, and appreciated. Peggy and Angelina could resolve their frustration by talking with each other about how they want the other to respond to them. If Angelina learned just to listen to Peggy's feelings, and if Peggy responded with practical suggestions and advice for Angelina, this issue would no longer be an issue.

Quality time

Another way to build intimacy is to spend quality time together. Some women complain about being so busy that they have to make appointments to see each other. If this is what is required, then do it. Make these times into "dates"—and keep them. We can lose intimacy by taking the relationship for granted and by putting our energy everywhere else. Work, chores, kids, and other demands on our time too often get complete priority. Some couples make sure they check in with each other, even briefly, about the events of the day. Quality time is also needed for relaxation together. This includes time for entertainment as well as time for communicating deeper thoughts, feelings, and concerns.

Shared goals and interests

Shared goals and interests can also increase intimacy. They help create the "glue" that gives a sense of continuity and purpose to the relationship. This "glue" enables us to keep the periodic hassles and the boredom of daily routines in perspective.

When we know that our efforts are directed toward mutually agreed upon goals, it is easier to tolerate occasional neglect from a partner.

Jesse found it easier to bear Andrea's long overtime hours, because she knew that the situation would last only until their bills were paid off. It was important to both of them to get out of debt.

Alinda and Mary found that having shared vacations to plan and look forward to helped counteract the boredom of their daily routine.

Valerie and Roberta tried to take a class together, or to be involved in some kind of political action work together, each year. Last year, for example, they started a support group for women of color. They found that while their separate interests added variety to their relationship, they also needed common activities and interests to enjoy together.

Shared goals and projects are a sign of commitment. They provide a feeling of stability and a shared future. Each investment of time, money, and energy that benefits both partners is a contribution to the future of "we."

However, too much togetherness can be as destructive to healthy intimacy as too little. A couple can overdose on togetherness, and feel smothered. Both partners need to be able to be separate people, with their own interests, lives, and identities. In order to feel connected, partners have to be able to feel their separateness.

Aretha felt much more positive about her relationship with Myra than she had about any of her previous relationships. She was sure that this was because she had forced herself to live alone after her last relationship, in order to become more self-sufficient. She always used to feel that she was missing something in herself. She needed someone else to feel complete. Now, having lived on her own, she could feel like an equal in her relationship with Myra. She had become less needy, less dependent, and less controlling.

As we work to build and enhance intimacy in our relationships, some questions to ask ourselves are:

- Do I share my thoughts and feelings openly and honestly with my partner on a regular basis?
- Do I ask my partner questions, express interest, and encourage her to share her thoughts and feelings?
- Do I judge or criticize my partner's feelings as unreasonable, overreactions, or just plain wrong?
- Do I undermine my partner's trust by lying, by revealing her confidences to other people, or by using her disclosures against her in a hurtful way?
- Do I look for ways to foster my own personal growth?
- Do I look for ways to foster our growth as a couple?

Lesbian couples need to find a balance between individual and couple time. When both women nurture themselves individually, their couple relationship benefits as well. Intimacy is affected by the different pressures in a couple's life, and the quality and depth of intimacy changes as a couple moves through different relationship stages. But generally, when women feel distinct from their lovers, they can enjoy each other more, allow themselves to feel close emotionally, and trust that their boundaries can tolerate both the internal and external stressors that being a couple generates. In this way, separateness enhances intimacy and togetherness.

Chapter 4

Living Arrangements

When a couple is trying to figure out the best ways to develop intimacy, their choice of living arrangements is key. Historically, our society has not admitted to very many variations on the theme of being a couple. Two people sharing a residence has been the norm. However, it may be that separate living quarters can best serve each partner's individual growth and the health of the couple as a unit. While some couples live together in a studio apartment or in a cooperative household with friends, others choose to live in separate apartments in the same building or in different parts of a town.

There are a number of reasons a couple might decide to live apart. They may choose, or for periods of time be forced, to live in different cities, states, or even countries. The women might want their own living spaces for decorating as they please, or for the control they can have over their time and their activities. They may prefer to live separately as a way to keep people from assuming that they are lesbians. Some women like to live apart from their lovers because they enjoy feeling separate and whole all by themselves. Some couples who have chosen to be nonmonogamous find it easier to live separately, so that they are free to be with other women without having constantly to negotiate their comings and goings with their partner. Sometimes couples may live together for a while and then apart, because of special circumstances. One may have chosen to take care of a sick family member in another city, while the other cannot or does not choose to go with her. Some couples live apart because their jobs are in different communities. Many live apart only temporarily, until living together becomes possible; and some much prefer living apart permanently.

Living apart

When partners live in different dwellings, but in the same town or city they are usually able to see each other frequently. At the same time, each can make living arrangements to suit her individual needs and wishes.

Sara and Melanie lived three miles apart. Sara lived in a big house with two other women, three cats, one dog, and a lot of clutter. Melanie had a one-bedroom condo that was neat as a pin. They saw each other virtually every day, spent many nights together in one or the other of their places, and were very happy. Melanie was a graphic artist who liked to work late, and to be noisy when she felt like it. Her solo living arrangement allowed her to sleep at the hours she chose; and she didn't have to fight about it with Sara, who was an early-to-bed, early-to-rise type. One disadvantage was that Sara constantly had to explain to people that she was not available, even though she did not have a live-in lover. Sara and Melanie were beginning to talk about having some sort of public ceremony, or wearing rings, to make their relationship completely clear to everyone.

Sara and Melanie are a good example of a lesbian couple who are not very compatible as live-togethers, but whose relationship is solid. Their frustration about not being seen as a couple is not unusual. The lesbian community lacks recognized conventions that the heterosexual community takes for granted: dating, engagement, and marriage agreements. The lesbian community often has difficulty knowing when a couple is a couple; it can make it harder when they do not live together. Sometimes these couples are nonmonogamous. This may further confuse people who also equate being a couple with being monogamous. Nonmonogamy can also cause confusion for the couple themselves, if they do not have clear agreements (see Chapter 7).

Advantages and disadvantages

One advantage of maintaining separate quarters is that two people do not have to agree about day-to-day matters such as bedtime and housekeeping standards. Melanie goes home when the clutter at Sara's house gets to her. She doesn't argue about it. Because the couple does not have to cope with mundane issues, they have more time for being romantic or for dealing with bigger issues, such as their common interests. These can easily get lost when a couple lives together. Living apart can also offer some protection against homophobic speculation about the sexual orientation of two women living together. Homophobic comment is especially likely when two people of the same sex live together for a long time. While not all lesbian couples want or need to hide their relationships, living apart may offer some cover, for women who want it, especially with homophobic, out-of-town parents. On the other hand, if two women are frequently seen going back and to each other's homes, neighbors may become suspicious of the nature of the relationship.

Another disadvantage that living apart may bring is the constant coming and going. This can get tiring, especially if animals have to be transported as well. Trivial issues may take on exaggerated proportions. For example, one woman we know laughs at how resentful she gets when the milk in her refrigerator goes bad because she spends too much time at her partner's house.

When two people do not live together they may not have the luxury of a lot of time to talk about problems; it is a good idea to set aside some time on a regular basis that is for discussing the difficulties of the arrangement the couple has chosen. At the very least, this offers the comfort of talking it out together; at best, some creative solutions may come out of the talk.

Long distance relationships

The members of a couple can also live farther away from each other than across a town.

Kim and Marsha had been lovers for twelve years; they had lived most of that time in New York City. Kim was fluent in Korean, Japanese, and English, and worked as a United Nations translator. For a number of years, Marsha had been a computer programmer, then she went back to school and took a Ph.D. in mathematics. When she was offered a university job as an assistant professor, Marsha moved to the Midwest, and the two women began living apart. They had huge phone bills, as they called each other almost every night. They had agreed to be open to having affairs, if they were careful about sexually transmitted diseases and made it clear to other women that they already had a primary relationship. Every time Kim thought about taking someone home to the apartment, she realized she didn't really want to do it because there was so much there to remind her of Marsha. They both knew that some day they would need to figure out something better than indefinite separation. Meanwhile, they arranged to visit each other as often as they could.

Sometimes living far apart is the first choice of a couple; and sometimes it is a make-do solution. It can be exhausting spending a lot of time travelling back and forth, trying to maintain enough contact to keep a relationship alive. The expense is prohibitive for some couples, and the wear and tear may drain and eventually destroy the relationship.

However, there can also be benefits to this arrangement. Kim and Marsha were pleased with the side effect of a renewed sex life. Now that they saw each other infrequently, their lovemaking had increased in intensity and quality. Marsha also noticed that they fought very rarely, and it was usually over not getting enough of each other, instead of over getting too much of each other. Another advantage to living apart is the quality of time spent together. Both Marsha and Kim think of their time together as vacations, so they plan their visits carefully to make sure that they get as much free time together as possible. Kim buys new clothes, gets as much work out of the way as she can, plans exciting activities for the two of them when she expects Marsha in New York.

Marsha finds new restaurants, looks up women's events, and buys lots of flowers when Kim comes to visit her. It is easy to see how this might feel like courting all over again.

Marsha and Kim are good examples of how a dual career couple may be faced with living separately, at least for a while. Whenever two partners have jobs that they enjoy, or are tied to for other reasons, they run the risk of following the job at the expense of living together. This situation does not arise only in the case of professional and white collar jobs. A woman may live with her lover in Seattle eight months out of the year, and go fishing in Alaska the other four months. There are increasing numbers of women in the military, and many of them are lesbians. The military will not treat a lesbian couple as a unit, and will not help them stay together when one or both of them is moved around the world. Thus, military lesbians may spend a lot of their time away from their partners. Someone else may be a musician and need to travel to available jobs, while her partner is a school teacher tied to one place for most of the year. Whenever layoffs occur, workers may be forced to move to a location where they can get a job. Since they cannot always guarantee work for their partner, she may stay where she knows she can support herself. When only one member in a couple works, they are freer to move together when the job forces relocation. However, both women in lesbian couples usually work to support the household(s). This increases the possibility that they may have to live apart at some time in their relationship, in order for both to maintain jobs. When couples live apart for any of the above reasons, the individual women need to have supportive communities that both honor the relationship and care for the individual. The woman who sees her partner infrequently needs to develop a circle of friends to provide companionship, and who can be understanding if she drops out of sight for a while when her absent lover comes to town.

Living apart in different countries

Some couples live very far away from each other, across

the ocean, and cultures apart. These women may see each other perhaps two times a year, for a prolonged period of time.

Maggie and Fanchette had known each other for four years when they became lovers. Fanchette lived in France, and Maggie in the United States. Neither woman wanted to move from home, but each wanted the other as her primary lover. They also agreed to be nonmonogamous, except when the two of them were in the same town; at such times, they existed for each other alone. The two women had much in common. Both were published writers, and both needed to live alone in order to work best. They had sex that was very intense and exciting the entire time they were together, usually two to four weeks twice a year. They wrote several times a week and talked on the phone once a month. During visits, each was treated like an honored guest in the other's house. Eventually, they would get into spats after a couple of weeks together, but they could always talk things out. Both women were pleased with their arrangement and hoped it would last forever.

This kind of relationship demands patience and the willingness not to see a lover for long periods of time. There has to be enough contact to keep the relationship alive, but also long periods of time apart, that allow the two women to carry on freely the work they do in the world.

Fanchette and Maggie had agreed that both were free to have other ongoing sexual relationships. They both did. Fanchette had a lover she saw weekly for dinner, theater, and sex. Maggie had a friend she slept with twice a week; sometimes they made love and sometimes they did not. But the arrangement gave Maggie someone to cuddle, because she got lonely. Obviously the women were taking care of their needs, and both felt secure in the arrangement. However, this couple runs the risk of one of the secondary relationships becoming more important than the primary one. The lover Maggie has in California is much more available to her than is Fanchette; if Maggie needs someone and Fanchette cannot be there, or the time zone differences eliminate a telephone call, the balance in the relationship could shift in favor of a lover closer to home.

Couples do not have to live together to be happy. Sometimes their living separately is a temporary solution; at other times, it is their preferred choice. Communication is more awkward and difficult when women have to rely on letters and shouting across transoceanic phone calls. Travel time, money, exhaustion from going back and forth, and the periods of separation are all potential liabilities of living apart. Intense time together, prolonged romance in the relationship, the sense of being on vacation when with each other, and the opportunity to pursue chosen work are all potential advantages. The main point is that couples do not have to live together to be a couple. The two women concerned must decide what living arrangement suits them best.

Living with others

There is another way in which some couples have broken the traditional mold of living together. They live with other people who are not a part of their biological or legal families. They may call their household a collective, a commune, an extended family, or a convenient arrangement. These households can include just lesbians, heterosexual women, children, men and women, or any combination that the lesbian couple chooses.

Sharon and Valerie had lived in a large old Victorian house with five friends for three years. All seven of them owned the house. They were all companions, who often went places together. While there was one other couple in the household, the emphasis was on each woman's individuality. All seven housemates agreed that they should not fall into assuming that the couples would always want the same thing.

In this situation, the couple may not be easily identified. The partners may or may not share a bedroom, for example. This kind of setup usually saves money for the couple. It allows the partners to have day-to-day intimacy (not necessarily sexual) with more than one person. There are more people with whom to share talk, activities, and tasks. Many couples have lived happily for years with friends, and feel that group living has added a richness to their relationship that would be missing if they lived alone as a couple.

Living alone with a partner

In spite of all these options, most couples choose to live together alone. This choice has some advantages and disadvantages, and we recommend that couples think carefully before setting up housekeeping together. Typically, a couple moves in together when they are in the romance stage and so have few realistic ideas of what the other person is like to live with. Unless the two women have been friends for a long time before they fall in love, they may be very surprised when the inevitable conflicts arise. Eventually, the magic of the partially-known gives way to the almost-taken-for-granted. Then the problems that earlier were obscured because of the romantic glow come into focus. If there are unresolved issues about money, commitment, monogamy, or time together, then sharing living space will bring them out. On the other hand, if the relationship has a solid beginning, then living together will enhance it.

Being out and living together

When a lesbian couple lives together, how out each woman is affects her partner more than if they live separately.

Anna was very closeted at work; she was the only woman in a construction crew working on the new freeway. She loved her work, and knew she would suffer if her co-workers found out she was a lesbian. Dru, her partner, was as out at work as you can get; she was one of the bartenders at a lesbian bar. When they moved in together, Anna insisted on getting a two-bedroom apartment so people at her work would think they were roommates, not lovers. She also refused to have any explicitly lesbian literature in view at their home. Dru was upset, but kept it to herself.

Dru and Anna could have serious problems later on in their relationship, unless they can agree about how out to be. They can maintain different degrees of outness for years without trouble, but if each partner expects the other one to change how out she is, then they could have difficulty. Dru and Anna could misinterpret the friction over how out to be as not loving the other or not respecting her limitations. Before they move in together, partners need to talk about their expectations of the other's outness, how out each can realistically be, would it be better to stay apart, what are each woman's fears about being more out of (or in) the closet, and are they realistic. They need to agree to keep talking about this as a problem of outness, not love.

Rent, buy, or whose house is this anyway?

Most couples rent their first home together. But sometimes they have to decide whether to rent a new place, or live in a place already occupied by one of them. Moving into a lover's place is fine, so long as it becomes home to both after the move. This may involve repainting, changing furniture, or whatever else it takes to make the new occupant feel at home. If the place is owned by one of the women, it will still be her house; and her lover is a renter of sorts. This needs to be out in the open, and there has to be clear discussion about what rights are held by each of the parties. Some couples choose to have the new occupant buy into the home, if she can afford it, so that the partners are on an equal footing. If the women cannot commit the same amount of money for a mortgage, they need to agree to a percentage ownership that both feel comfortable with, and re-evaluate the agreement at some later point.

Possessions

Couples sometimes move in together with very few possessions, and enjoy buying things together. But women who have been on their own for a while are likely to have their own furniture, dishes, and so on. The couple has to decide whose things they will use, and who will pay for what is needed. If they buy jointly, they should have an agreement about how to divide their posessions if they break up. If they buy separately they need to decide whether both have equal access to what each buys. If they already have more than they need, the couple should negotiate carefully whose couch goes in the living room, and whose dishes go into the cupboards.

Anna had been married before; she had dishes, tableware, and some furniture brought from her marriage. Dru hated using Anna's "straight" dishes, because they were a strong reminder of an institution—marriage—that Dru disliked. Anna loved the dishes and would not give them up. They talked, and finally decided that because Dru's discomfort was so strong, Anna would put the dishes away and use them when Dru was out—or maybe not at all. They would buy new dishes together; Dru could have them, if the couple ever broke up.

Possessions can be very tricky for couples. Often people are more attached to something than they realize, and give it up for a partner's sake before they really know they want to keep it. Or, a partner will agree to live with something she dislikes because she is so in love with the woman who owns/wants it. Where possible, we encourage couples to keep as many of their individual possessions as they can, until they have lived together for a couple of years. If, after that time, they still want to live together, they can make decisions with a partner they have already practiced disagreeing with.

What do we do about friends and family?

Just because we love someone does not mean we will like all her friends and family. Once people begin to live together, they are likely to see more of one another's visitors than formerly. Usually, partners can tolerate these other folks, especially when each acknowledges the other's right to be her own person. However, when a partner really does not like someone her live-in lover cares for the couple may need to negotiate how to manage that conflict. The important thing is to bring the problem out into the open.

Dru found herself completely ill at ease with Anna's sister, whom Anna saw every week. When she first told Anna, Anna was angry and hurt. Anna wanted both her sister and her lover in her life. After talking it over, Anna and Dru agreed that Dru would go out half the times that Anna visited with her sister; and Anna and her sister would meet elsewhere the other half.

If a couple finds that they do not like *any* of one another's friends, they may want to live apart, as it is likely that any visitors will be a source of friction.

Cleanliness is next to . . .

When a couple lives together they have to deal with each other's standards of cleanliness and neatness. They also have to make decisions about household chores. These two areas often overlap.

Anna did not think that bathrooms needed cleaning more than twice a month. Dru thought every week was minimal. Dru liked cleaning bathrooms and thought Anna should do the living room/dining room as her share of the chores. Anna thought these areas needed even less attention than the bathroom. They solved their dilemma by listing all the chores, chose the ones each wanted, and divided up the rest evenly according to time requirements. Finally, they negotiated minimum cleaning standards that were approximately halfway between their individual preferences. Dru reserved the right to put some of her time into extra cleaning before they had company. They agreed to evaluate their system in a month.

Money and time

When each woman in a couple has approximately the same amount of money and income there are fewer potential problems. But the couple needs to consider spending and saving patterns as well. When Dru and Anna look at their income levels they find that Anna has a higher, more consistent income. Dru makes a liveable wage, but tips fluctuate; there is also always the threat of the bar's closing. Anna spends much of her income on nice clothes and good music. Dru prefers to save most of her money, and is uncomfortable with Anna's spending habits. Again, the differences do not need to keep the couple apart but they need to be honest with each other and find a way to live together without feeling threatened by each other's decisions about money. Dru and Anna probably should not merge finances, but instead use the three-pot method described in Chapter 5 to cover their joint living expenses and allow them to use the rest of their money individually. Sharing living expenses can save money which is then available for individual use and joint projects such as a special vacation.

When a couple lives apart, how and with whom each spends her time may not be much of an issue. If Dru and Anna have the same expectations of how much time they will spend together, fine. Usually, however, the two women have different fantasies and do not tell each other. Anna is used to working overtime whenever she wants more money, is bored, or when her company calls her. Dru likes to spend lots of time with Anna—at home, at the movies, eating out, or with friends. They will need to compromise on the time schedules they kept when they lived apart. In this case, Anna can continue to work overtime, although less than before; and she can spend an agreed-upon amount of time with Dru. Dru can still see a lot of Anna, but she will need to spend some of her leisure time alone or with other friends. If Dru and Anna move in together without sharing their expectations, they may interpret each other's demands as inconsiderate. Of course, living together can potentially give them more time together in the evening, mornings, and on weekends. The time they used in commuting to each other can now be spent together.

There are no guarantees, of course, but the more two

people know about each other and their living habits before they share a common household, the more likely they are to enjoy living with each other. It can be quite wonderful to live with someone, but the success of the venture depends on being honest about thoughts and feelings, and learning how to negotiate differences. We strongly urge couples to take the time to figure out what they want in their living arrangements, to discuss these matters in advance, and identify any potential trouble spots. A couple must look closely at what each partner wants/needs and then design—and redesign—the arrangement that is most satisfactory. In Chapter 5 we talk about how couples, whether they live together or not, can design creative ways to manage work, money, and time.

Chapter 5

Work, Money, and Time

Whether partners live together or not, they have to deal with the issues of work, money, and time. How they resolve such questions as how out to be at work, whether or not to merge finances, or how much time to spend together dramatically affects the quality of their relationship.

Work

The vast majority of lesbians know that they have to work to survive; no husband is going to take care of them. Because women's salaries are typically two-thirds those of men, and because women are often shunted into low-paying jobs and kept there, it is usually a financial necessity for both partners in a lesbian couple to work. In addition, the majority of lesbians believe that both women in a couple should work. The couples interviewed for Philip Blumstein and Pepper Schwartz's book, *American Couples*, based their reasons for this on the idea of fairness and the strong desire to be independent. They also saw work as a way to avoid dependency and the low status accorded the homemaker role. However, as women, lesbians have not been trained to take on the traditional provider role. For all these reasons, we usually arrange our relationships so that no one person is the sole provider except under special circumstances, such as a partner being ill, returning to school, or bearing a child.

Given these attitudes, it is not surprising that lesbian couples usually try also to create an equitable sharing of household tasks. Indeed, these high ideals of fairness and equity associated with work can be a source of friction.

Helene had always been a hard worker and career oriented. To Beth, work had just been a necessity; she much preferred to put her energy into her relationships. For the first four years they were together, Helene worked long hours, insisting that this was essential to her career plans. During this time, Beth did more than fifty percent of the housework, and she was always available to listen and help Helene unwind from her highly stressful day. Then Beth took on a new and challenging job. For the first time in her life she was really excited about her work. However, this new development raised some problems. Beth now got home later than Helene. When she did arrive home, she just didn't feel like cooking. Beth's cooking had formerly been a hobby for her and a treat for Helene. Beth now had much less energy in general. She was less available to listen to Helene talk about her "hard day at the office." In fact, she wanted Helene to listen to the report of *her* workday—something new for Beth. What was Helene's reaction? She was grumpy and unhappy about all these changes. Beth was resentful that she was not getting her turn, and felt unsupported. She even began to wonder if Helene was threatened by the possibility that Beth might eventually make more money than she did.

Before Beth took her new job, she was the more relationship oriented partner. It is quite common for one partner to focus more energy on the relationship and the other to be more involved with work. After all, this is the traditional model for male-female relationships. Although it tends to be less extreme for lesbians, the dynamic still may be present.

Helene and Beth are facing a major transition. Beth is changing from a "job" where she worked out of need for money, to a "career," where her work is meaningful and enjoyable to her. While a job can be neutral or even unpleasant, "It's just a job," while a career can mean "getting paid to do work you love to do." It would be ideal if we could get paid more for a career than for a job, but this is not always the case. For example, a musician may decide to spend her time performing rather than working at a job that pays more. Or a lawyer may decide to continue working at that job, rather than take a pay cut in a career she would prefer.

Early in their relationship, Helene had a career and Beth a job. With Beth's change to a career, the balance in the relationship was upset. No longer was Beth directing as much energy into the relationship. This shift was hard for Helene to accept.

Helene and Beth need to renegotiate their expectations and probably their responsibilities. Helene could shift to doing more caretaking of Beth and of the relationship. Or they could both agree to be satisfied with both being more focused on work. Helene is, in fact, very supportive of Beth's new career. However, she misses the attention she used to get. She needs to share her feelings with Beth or Beth may continue in her suspicion that Helene is competitive over earnings.

How out to be at work

In the workplace, we constantly have to manage information about our lives, our lifestyle, our difference: to display or not to display; to tell or not to tell; to let on or not to let on; to lie or not to lie; and in each case, to whom, when, how, and where.

Much attention has been paid to the pressure of society's disapproval and the problem of internalized homophobia. But this continual process of deciding how out to be has not been emphasized enough. We are often self-conscious and focused on whether or not to come out. Or we are asking ourselves, "Do they know about me already?" "Can they tell?" and "How will they respond if they do know?" The strain of this recurring decision-making interferes with many, or most interactions in everyday life. It can sap energy from the couple relationship and can be a source of conflict between the partners.

Every summer Benita's company put on a huge barbeque. Every summer she and her partner Ellen had a big fight about going. Benita was out at work and proud of it. Ellen wanted to go with her, but was afraid that she would run into someone there from the school district where she worked.

Kim's partner Vera was very closeted at work. Vera's supervisor stopped by the house occasionally to drop off paperwork. Before he arrived, Vera always asked Kim if she would mind leaving the house for a while. Kim looked "too much like a dyke," and Vera did not want her supervisor to suspect anything. Kim wished that she did not feel hurt by this, but she did.

These examples illustrate the kinds of problems that can arise when partners have (or want) different degrees of outness at work. The more out partner may pressure her lover to be more public in order to validate the relationship, or to make a political statement to the larger world. She may not be sure whether her lover's closetedness is really necessary. Maybe it is an indication of shame about being a lesbian or about the relationship. The more closeted partner may see her caution as essential to her job, her work relationships, and her ambitions. Both partners may feel misunderstood and unsupported.

When one partner is more out than the other, it is important to identify the issue as being one of differing degrees of outness rather than differing levels of commitment to the relationship. "If you really loved me, you wouldn't care what your co-workers thought" or "If you really loved me, you would be more affectionate in public." In our examples, Ellen does not love Benita less because she doesn't go to the barbeque. Or she may go, but be unwilling to be openly affectionate toward Benita at the event. This also does not mean she loves her partner less. Some women are uncomfortable about being publicly affectionate, period. Their discomfort may be increased, of course, if they are afraid that someone from the workplace might see them.

It is sometimes hard for us as lesbians to tell how accurate we are in assessing the negative consequences of being openly lesbian. If Vera or Ellen did not hide their sexual orientation would they lose their jobs? Or their credibility with co-workers? Some fears may be unrealistic or based on internalized homophobia. Others may be quite realistic. Most of us grew up in an environment that promoted negative attitudes about lesbians and lesbianism, even though this is changing. Getting rid of negative attitudes about oneself is a lifelong process. As one woman said, "Just when you think that you are *done* with coming out, you meet someone new or the issue arises in yet another way."

It is no wonder that we may feel that it is hard enough to deal with homophobia in the workplace, much less having to spend energy on the issue at home. JoAnn Loulan (1986) suggested that we should all have something like a decompression chamber in the entryway of our homes. Then we could simply walk through this chamber and quickly change from the closeted or armored lesbian we may have to be at work to the sensitive, loving, and comfortable-with-her-lesbian-identity woman we want to be at home. Unfortunately, we may expect—or our partner may expect—that we instantly change when we walk through the door.

Some women decide to leave their jobs or change careers in part because of the strain that being closeted at work puts on their relationship. Others stay because they love their work or because they cannot afford to quit. When partners differ in how out they are on the job, they need to approach any problems this creates with compassion for each other's concerns and feelings. Even if a couple does not agree, each woman can try to understand and respect her partner's perspective and decisions.

When both partners are out to the same degree at work, they may have less tension over this issue. Similarly, when each woman in a couple has a comparable income, they may have fewer conflicts about money.

Money

Women who have been married or involved romantically

with men may be more likely to anticipate that their partners will be competitive over income. They have good reason. In a capitalist society money is often equated with ability, status, talent, and goodness. There is a cultural tendency to blame the victim; the poor are considered to be somehow responsible for their situation. In heterosexual relationships, money is often used by men to establish dominance and status just as it is in the work place. They may resent their wives if they make more money or even if they are successful in their work. This same dynamic can occur in lesbian relationships—though usually to a lesser degree. Couples deal with differences in earning power in a variety of ways. Some partners pool their resources completely, while others divide household expenses proportionally to their income. Still others pay equal shares regardless of income.

Marcie and Doreen are a good example of how income can affect a couple's interaction. One of the hardest issues for them was that Marcie had always made a great deal more money than Doreen. This problem surfaced in a number of ways. Marcie liked clothes but she felt guilty buying something for herself that Doreen couldn't afford to buy for herself so she didn't buy things she wanted. Doreen insisted on paying her own way whenever they went out to eat. This meant that they didn't go out as often as Marcie would have liked, and their choice of restaurants was very limited. For her part, Doreen resented that the daycare work she loved to do was so poorly paid. Even worse was that Marcie's field—computers—was very well paid and had so much status. Though they were both women in the eyes of society, Marcie did "men's" work and Doreen "women's."

Marcie had proposed pooling their money, but Doreen resisted this idea. Doreen was afraid of feeling less independent. Though she didn't like the phrase "poor but proud," that's how she felt. Like many lesbians, she did not assume she had the right to her partner's resources, even after many years together. She wondered if she should try treating Marcie's money as if it were her own, as Marcie had suggested.

Pooling resources

Even when each woman in a couple has approximately the same amount of money and income, they still have to deal with whether or how to merge their finances.

The longer a couple is together, the more likely they are to pool their money. This may happen because of the trust they have built up over the years or simply because of convenience. Merging finances raises particular issues for lesbian couples. While some of us decide to keep our money totally separate, others open a joint bank account after a few months. Because there are so few symbols to validate lesbian relationships, having two names on checks may take on this kind of symbolic meaning. Joint credit cards or co-signed loans may provide a similar sense of feeling married. However, having joint plastic, joint accounts, and co-signing loans can be risky.

As long as both partners are good money managers, communicate well, and are happy in the relationship, the chances for problems are minimal. However, if one partner is an impulse buyer, forgets to note checks written, or just has very different spending habits than the other, resentments are possible. Many lesbians are burned financially when a relationship ends.

Mary Kay ended up paying for a number of purchases that her ex-lover Barbara made on a joint credit card after they split up. She was stuck with the bills because the card was in her name.

Florence discovered one day that her partner Bea had almost emptied their joint savings account to place a bet on a horse that "couldn't lose"—but did.

We don't say no to having joint accounts and merging finances, but it is important to be clear and realistic.

There are various strategies for doing this. In their book *Second Marriage*, Richard Stuart and Barbara Jacobson talk about the one pot, two pot, and three pot arrangements. The one pot model assumes complete interdependence. Couples pool all of their resources and decide together how to spend them. In the two pot model both partners maintain control over their own resources. They may decide to share expenses either equally or proportionally, but the money is kept separately. The three pot model assumes that partners have both shared and separate monies. There are three pots: hers, hers, and theirs. Each has total control over her own pot, and the couple decides together the use of money in the common pot. There are two major variations of the three pot model:

1. Couples decide on a fixed amount of money or percentage of income for the separate pots. They then pool the rest, making sure that there is enough to cover shared expenses.

2. Couples decide on a fixed amount or a percentage of earnings for the commmon pot. The two partners keep the rest in their separate pots.

No model is necessarily better than the others; it depends on your economic situation and your personal needs and values. Lesbian couples may choose the one pot approach because their resources are very limited and they need to pool all they have just to cover expenses. Or they may decide to merge finances as a symbol of their coupleness and intention to remain in the relationship. Or they may simply value mutual support. A couple may choose the two pot approach for a variety of reasons. One of them may have children from a previous marriage and need to track expenses for legal reasons. Others make this choice to avoid conflict, to feel independent and separate, or because of a bad previous experience.

Some women choose the three pot approach out of their belief that partners should have separate as well as shared money. Variations of the three pot system allow lesbian partners to be both together and separate with regard to finances. Sharing expenses and buying things together is one way couples may try to generate "glue" to hold the relationship together in difficult times. Having her own funds allows each women to make independent choices about her own life.

One way Marcie and Doreen could ease the money tensions would be to adopt a three pot system. Each could contribute a percentage of her income to a joint account to pay for household expenses and entertainment. Then each would keep the rest of her earnings separately. This would broaden their choice of restaurants, and Marcie could still indulge her passion for clothes. Doreen could feel secure, knowing that all expenses were covered, and she could even save some of her separate funds.

Whatever decisions a couple makes about finances, it is essential to have a clear agreement. It is helpful to write it down, because our memories are often poor about what we talked about a year ago, or even a month ago. The whole purpose of having this written agreement (or contract) is to clarify the arrangements and prevent future problems. Couples who already live together, or who are planning to, need to discuss and agree about how they will share the rent and household expenses. If one partner owns the house in which they both live, is the other partner paying rent or buying in? Other questions include: How will household tasks be divided? What about items you buy together? What about things each partner owned before you moved in together? Does she expect that you will support her when she goes back to school in two years? Do you expect that she will contribute financially to the support of your children from your previous marriage?

Value differences

For some couples, value differences based on class background complicate the process of coming to agreements about work and money.

Sally grew up in a working-class family. Her mother saved everything she could earn. She even went without lunches in order to put aside money for Sally's college education. Sandy, on the other hand, was raised in an upper-middle-class family that always had plenty of everything. Both of her parents had inherited money, and Sandy's father was a senior officer in a large corporation. Sandy and Sally soon ran into conflicts over money. Whenever Sandy wanted to buy something they did not absolutely need, Sally balked, and always had some excuse for not spending the money. For Sally, spending was like throwing away a life preserver.

The two women fought over what to buy without realizing that this problem reflected their childhood values—not their current realities. When they finally talked about what was happening, they were able to take into consideration Sally's anxiety and Sandy's lack of concern about spending money. Sally figured out just what monthly amount they needed to put into a saving account in order for her to feel secure. For her part, Sandy worked out a budget showing how much they needed to pay their expenses each month. Then they allowed themselves to spend the remainder for fun and joint purchases.

As if all this weren't complicated enough, what is considered "politically correct" about money may vary. In some lesbian circles the prevailing view is that we need to live simply and to share our resources with other women. This may mean having a sliding scale or charging lower fees if you are a professional, or it may mean living in a working-class neighborhood by choice. In other circles the current belief may be that women need to claim and display their long overdue economic power: to charge fees comparable to their male colleages, to live in upscale sections of town, or to wear fashionable clothing. Whatever the local politically correct standard, lesbians are frequently pulled by opposing sides in deciding how to earn and spend their money.

To sum up, money is rarely a simple issue. It reflects a number of underlying themes. These include trust, commitment, and the question of permanence that pooling of funds raises, plus all the tension of societal roles, power, class, and self-worth. Lesbian couples have an opportunity to forge truly egalitarian—and caring—relationships, by facing these issues directly.

• • • •

Contracts

Some lesbians think it is being cold and crass to talk openly about things like money, credit cards, sharing expenses, and future expectations and obligations. On the contrary, discussions about these topics provide opportunities for growth for the partners in a relationship and for the relationship itself. There are a lot of practical details involved in sharing one's life with a partner. To act as if love is all we need is to ignore some practical realities. And it misses a wonderful opportunity to create an agreement and contract that celebrates the specialness of the relationship.

Others assume an agreement is useful only in case a couple breaks up. But it is also useful during the course of the relationship. It means that issues have been discussed, resolved, and plans made. Contracts can always be changed; evaluating a contract annually is one way to think through, appreciate, and renew a relationship commitment. Lesbian couples usually don't have marriage vows to renew. But we can use contracts to accomplish the same purpose.

Jane and Sarah drew up a contract in which they agreed on how they would share the expenses of living together. They also specified how they wanted to divide up the tasks of daily living for the next year while Sarah was in school. They included in their contract their decision to be monogamous and a number of lighter items such as:

"Jane vows to retain a sense of humor about having so many animals in return for Sara's promise to clean up any dog shit in the yard."

"Sarah promises to respect Jane's passion for her TV soaps."

"Jane promises to leave dirty dishes in the sink, not on the kitchen counter."

Thus contracts can acknowledge day to day living issues and the depth and richness in a relationship while at the same time providing guidelines for the "what ifs" every couple faces. Once done, these guidelines can contribute to the glue we've talked about as they provide a sense of structure and commitment.

Time

Many lesbian couples complain that there is not enough time: not enough time for work and for separate activities and for time together and for time with the kids and for keeping up the house or apartment, and so on.

For women particularly, the issues of time, work, and money are related. The statistics about women making sixty-three cents compared to men making a dollar, and the concepts of comparable worth and equal pay for equal work underscore this problem. A woman may work long hours and still not make enough money to live on, or to support her children. Or she may sacrifice having any free time so that she can make more money; or prioritize having free time over money and settle for a less comfortable lifestyle.

Ariel decided to take on a part-time job so that her contribution to the savings account would be equal to her partner Becky's. They were saving for a down payment on a house, and Ariel wanted her share to be a true fifty-fifty. Becky didn't like Ariel working more, because they hardly saw each other, but she understood and respected her partner's strong feelings.

Reba had figured that she and Jewelle would have more time with each other if they lived together. She had anticipated that the time they used to spend commuting would be available for couple activities. Instead, they seemed to have less time together after the move. For one thing, Jewelle spent more time with her separate friends. Reba decided that they definitely needed to talk about it. She regretted that they had not discussed their expectations more fully before moving in together.

Mary Beth and Carlotta worked different shift schedules. This meant that some weeks they barely saw each other; some weeks they could spend most of their free time together.

One way they managed to stay connected during the periods when they were on different shifts was to leave love notes for each other—on the pillow, in their lunch bags, in the refrigerator.

Sometimes the problem is not so much that there is not time, but that a couple is dissatisfied with how they are spending their time.

Aline and Veronica felt that they didn't have any quality time with each other. Their weekends were filled with chores and busyness, even though they both insisted that what they really wanted on the weekends was to relax. It just never happened that way. Once they realized that enjoyable free time required them to have clear goals and to make plans, their weekends became much more satisfying. They figured out ways to do the chores and errands during the week, and they could go camping on weekends.

Kim and Ginny were both self-employed. They each set their own work schedules and took very little time off. Their vacations were few and far between, and typically ended up being more frustrating than fun. Kim liked to plan far ahead and be packed a week in advance; Ginny left everything to the last minute. Partly as a result of this style difference, even talking about vacations usually turned into an argument. The few vacations that they did manage to take ended up being compromises that neither was really happy about.

Obviously, in order to solve this problem, Kim and Ginny need to talk to each other. They each need to clarify what they want and then to problem-solve. Their solution might mean: separate vacations; long weekend vacations with each other; regular time together on certain weekends; one of them organizing a vacation she wants them both to take, and the next time the other one's organizing a vacation of her choice—somewhat like taking each other on a date, but in this case an extended date; or yet another creative solution.

Separating work and the relationships

One case in which these themes of work, money, and time

are very intertwined is that of lesbian couples who are in business together.

Dori and Sung-Lin operated a mail order business together. They also worked regular nine-to-five jobs. Their big complaint was that the only time they had together was spent working on the business. There was never any time for fun. Finally the business generated enough income so that one of them could quit her other job and take care of the business. This left much more time for them to be together doing the recreational activities they had missed so much.

Jeanine and Dotty went into business together after being lovers for two years. They had both always dreamed of owning a restaurant. Now, three years later, they were out of the red and felt they could begin to relax a little. As they looked back, their comment was that the hardest part for them had been keeping their business relationship separate from their lover relationship. Until they figured out how to do that, they had many a fight, supposedly over how to run the restaurant, but really about their relationship—not their work. One time, for example, they had an intense disagreement over the redesign of the restaurant menu, when the real issue was Jeanine's unhappiness with their sex life. That kind of argument seldom happened anymore.

One strategy that helped them keep clear was their agreement not to talk about business matters at home, and not to talk about private matters at work. As much as possible, they leave the restaurant behind them when they come home. And they leave at home issues in their personal relationship when they go to work.

Whether couples work together or not, the relationship suffers when one or both partners is not able to leave her work behind her when she comes home. In her book, *Leaving the Office Behind*, Barbara Mackoff provides a variety of suggestions and techniques to ease the transition from work to home. These include:

- slowing down at the end of the day by saving easier tasks for that time;
- listening to relaxation tapes and/or music on the drive or bus ride home, or when you arrive home;
- arranging with your partner and children to have some time alone immediately when you come home—particularly after a bad day.

Each of these issues—work, money, and time—is complex in and of itself. And they overlap as well. As lesbians we have a unique opportunity to develop couple relationships that emphasize equality and a balance of power between partners. How we handle these issues of work, money, and time determines, in large measure, how close we come to an equitable sharing of power and responsibility in our relationships.

Chapter 6

Sex

A lesbian is usually defined as a woman who is sexually attracted to and/or who has sexual relations with other women. It is an ironic paradox that although we are defined by our sexuality, we have little information about it. Homophobia, sexism, and traditional cultural taboos on the open sharing of information about sex have all contributed to this lack of knowledge. One result is that we are often not sure which are typical—and thus normal—aspects of couple development. We may wonder which sexual behaviors, fantasies, or desires are acceptable, politically correct, or truly lesbian.

Current controversies about sadomasochism, lesbian erotica and pornography, and butch/femme roles reflect our struggles to define, understand, embrace and—in some cases—judge our sexuality and that of others. The lesbian community has been divided over some of these issues. For example, when it comes to butch/femme roles, some lesbians who came out long after the women's liberation movement of the 1960s think it is campy and fun to play with these roles. Many feminists reject them as a throwback to the oppressive fifties. And some women, who have not heard that butch/femme roles are politically "incorrect," are living them.

Margaret Nichols speculates that butch and femme may reflect interesting differences between lesbians that we have been hesitant to examine because we have been somewhat confused and disquieted about them. Perhaps butch/femme advocacy is, in part, a reaction to the boring feminist clone look of the seventies. Even those who reject the roles as oppressive can usually categorize one partner in a couple as more butch and the other as more femme, and often at least try. Nichols suggests that as long as they are not made to be rigid and confining, butch/femme roles may actually help lesbians transcend limiting heterosexually defined sex roles. In a similar vein, Amber Hollibaugh and Cherrie Moraga indicate the possibility that going through roles may be a way of getting beyond them.

For those who are interested, we have included in the bibliography a number of references on these controversies about roles and sexual behavior. For the remainder of this chapter we want to focus on three concerns commonly expressed by lesbian couples.

In our experience, lesbian couples often voice concerns and questions about sexual frequency, initiation, and desire. Because these three subjects occur so commonly, we consider each of them to reflect issues that arise in the normal development of a couple's relationship.

Eleanor woke up luxuriously savoring the familiar sounds and smells of a Sunday morning. She and Eve had been together for nine years and had had their own Sunday ritual for the last three. Eve got up early, made coffee and read the paper. By the time Eleanor woke up, Eve had everything ready for a delightful breakfast in bed. Eleanor loved this comfort, but she wondered what had happened to the lovemaking that had been their Sunday morning fare the first years of their relationship. She remembered how they would make love, take a bath together, and then go out to breakfast. Eleanor frequently wanted sex, but now Eve usually wanted to make love only every month or so. Eleanor masturbated a lot and was content most of the time. But today she found herself wondering if anything was wrong.

Eleanor and Eve illustrate all three of the frequently encountered concerns: frequency, initiation, and desire. Their sexual contact has decreased over the course of their relationship. Eleanor wants sex more often than Eve and she wants

Eve to initiate it. We will look at each of these concerns in turn.

Frequency

To return for a moment to the impact of definitions, the most common term used to refer to a same sex partner is *lover*. The word implies, assumes, and requires sexual contact. If a lesbian couple is not being sexual, are they still lovers? While a heterosexual couple would be likely to continue to see themselves as married if they went through a period of reduced or no sexual contact, a lesbian partner may interpret this same situation as signalling the end of the relationship. At the very least she may wonder, like Eleanor, if something is wrong. Not having the security of marriage vows, lesbian couples frequently attach powerful meanings to sexual contact—and to sexual satisfaction.

Historically, women's sexuality has been defined by men, and satisfaction has been linked to frequency rather than to the nature and the quality of the sexual experience. We do not really know what a woman-defined standard of sexual frequency would be. In this void of information, we are often unclear about what we personally want sexually, our right to have or do what we want, how often, and what meaning to attach to it.

Almost all couples have less sexual contact the older they get and the longer they have lived together. Philip Blumstein and Pepper Schwartz report that lesbian couples, like Eve and Eleanor, explain this reduced frequency as due to lack of time, lack of physical energy, or just to being used to each other. While the lesbian couples in their study report having sex less often than other types of couples at every stage of their relationship, sexual frequency for all couples varies depending on what stage of the relationship the couple is in.

In her book, *Lesbian Sex*, JoAnn Loulan notes that sexual frequency for lesbian couples begins to drop off after about the first six months. If a couple knows that redued sexual frequency is common after the romance stage, they are less likely to panic. If they don't know that this is to be expected, one or both may be threatened or frightened. This in turn could lead to problems such as each sexual contact being intepreted as proof of love or of commitment to the relationship.

Reduced sexual frequency is also common during the conflict stage of relationships. For one thing, many do not want to be sexual when they are angry with their partner. Also, not being sexual can sometimes achieve the distance that one or both partners desires at this stage in order to feel separate. Yet another situation arises when a couple tries to avoid the conflict of this stage by avoiding sex entirely.

Randy and Stella both hated to fight. When Randy got angry with Stella about how busy she was and how she was always too tired to have sex, Randy kept her feelings to herself. She didn't want to fight about it. Eventually Randy just lost interest in being sexual.

Whatever they do about their sex life, Randy and Stella need to learn how to deal with their conflicts more openly and constructively. Couples who develop skills to resolve conflicts can more easily talk about and work on sexual wants and needs in the same way as any other area of concern or difference.

Enhancement

Lesbians like Eleanor and Eve, who are in the later stability, commitment, and collaboration stages, talk about boredom with lovemaking routines and a lack of passion. If these couples want to enhance the sexual part of their relationship, they must give it priority. This means talking about sex, dealing with differences and/or conflicts, and making sex a focus in terms of time and energy. The following list of ideas to increase passion was generated by women in couples' enhancement groups facilitated by one of the authors.

- Go away to a motel for the weekend.

- Go to the hot tubs.
- Make a "pass."
- Give each other a massage.
- Tell your partner she is the most special person in your life.
- Go on a "date."
- Have flowers delivered.
- Long kisses.
- Take a risk together, e.g. sky-diving, roller coaster, and so on.
- Romantic movies/videos.
- Try out some new lovemaking techniques.
- Read to each other from lesbian novels.
- Have dinner in front of the fire.
- Meet some place and pretend you are strangers.
- Take time away from your partner so you miss her.
- Cultivate some sexual fantasies.
- Tell stories or fantasies to your partner while you are touching her.
- Just take the risk that whatever you try may not work out perfectly but try anyway.
- Try some of the exercises in books such as *Lesbian Sex* and *Lesbian Passion* by JoAnn Loulan, and *For Yourself* and *For Each Other* by Lonnie Barbach.

It is interesting to note that many, if not most, of these suggestions have a romantic element. Margaret Nichols suggests that lesbians are the last of the modern day romantics. This has disadvantages as well as advantages. As women, we often do not recognize our own sexual arousal and we are less likely to initiate or press for sexual contact. As lesbians, we also have to deal with the effects of internalized homophobia, negative experiences with men, and the potential disadvantages of fusion or merging in intimate relationships. If a high degree of difference between partners is important to maintain sexual tension, increased intimacy which may lessen difference, may lessen sexual interest as well.

Perhaps romance is not the only way to increase passion in a relationship that is in, for example, the commitment stage. Nichols suggests that we may need to introduce barriers/tension/differences in order to enhance sexuality. We could try experimenting with new sexual techniques, using sex toys, playing with costumes, and other strategies to accentuate differences between partners and thus heighten passion. However, we caution lesbian couples to determine whether they or their partners are in any of the at risk groups for Acquired Immune Deficiency Syndrome (AIDS). (See Chapter 7.)

Sometimes the terms which we use to describe our sexual contact may be crucial. Laura Brown (1985) points out that for many lesbian couples, sex equals genital contact and orgasm. Passionate kissing, cuddling, necking and petting are not considered to be sex. They are therefore not added into the frequency count.

A different but related situation arises when partners actually avoid these supposedly nonsexual activities, because they are afraid they will be pressured to allow these erotic, sensual contacts to lead to genital sex and orgasm.

Initiation

Another legacy of sexism relates to initiation of sex. Men have traditionally been the initiators and women have been encouraged to wait to be approached. Thus lesbians, many of whom were previously heterosexual, are often not comfortable in the role of sexual initiator. And, even if one partner is more skilled and comfortable with initiating, she may resent always being responsible for taking the lead.

This describes Eve exactly. Because Eve is more comfortable with initiating, Eleanor relies on her to be the initiator. Eve resents having what feels like all the responsibility in their sexual relationship. She wishes that Eleanor would take a more active role. But she knows that this is hard for Eleanor, who is most comfortable when sex "just happens." The problem is that for most couples, after the romance stage, sex does not just happen. So it is important that Eve and Eleanor talk about their wants and feelings as they work on ways to address Eve's concern about unbalanced initiation. Perhaps they need to clarify exactly what is and what is not initiating. Sometimes Eve may be looking for particular words or behaviors, and not recognizing things that Eleanor says or does as being initiation. Also, there may be ways that Eve can encourage and support Eleanor to initiate more often. And Eleanor may need to be more aware of what interferes with her initiating, and what she might do to overcome these hurdles.

Desire

According to JoAnn Loulan (1984) it is not necessary to wait for sexual desire in order to initiate or to respond to sexual contact. What is required is the willingness to be sexual. She points out that sexual desire can be intellectual, emotional, or physical. We don't have to have physical sensations to be sexual. We can have a mental desire to be sexual and act on it. We may feel very close to our partner and want to have sex because of that emotion. Or we may indeed have physical sensations that lead us to want to be sexual.

In her description of the sexual response cycle, Loulan emphasizes that "pleasure is the goal of the sexual experience. And pleasure can be experienced without any other stage except willingness."

Sexual Response Cycle:

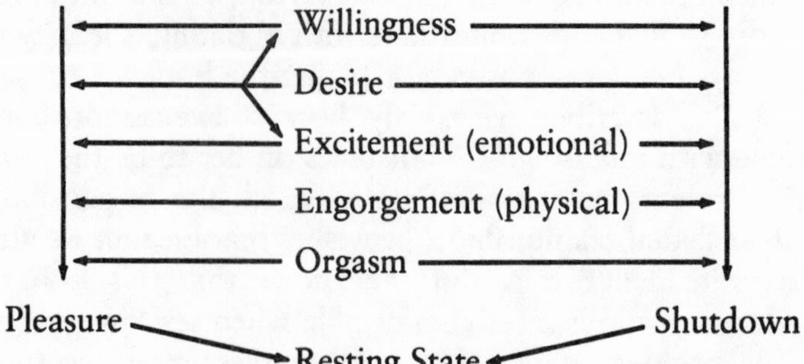

In her model, each of the five stages can lead to pleasure, to shutdown, or to another stage. Willingness, for example, can be pleasurable in itself, or it can lead to desire, or directly to excitement, or to shutdown and the resting state. Her point is that willingness, not desire, is the prerequisite for initiating sexual contact.

There are many factors that influence desire and willingness to be sexual. One of these of great importance to lesbians is internalized homophobia. A lesbian may avoid being sexual to avoid feeling the anxiety, guilt, or shame that she has about being a lesbian. Or she may feel compelled to be a perfect lover to prove how content she is with her lesbian identity.

Linda felt so guilty and anxious every time she was sexual with another woman that she decided to give up sex entirely. It was just too hard.

It took Justine years to realize that sex was more a performance to her than a pleasure. She had been so intent on being a good lover/good lesbian that she didn't relax and enjoy herself.

Neither Justine nor Linda feels good about being a lesbian, although they show this in different ways. Working on their internalized homophobia could help them become more comfortable sexually.

Other factors that may influence our sexuality on a deep level are trauma and early abuse. Being two women in a relationship doubles the chances that one will be from among the estimated 38% of women who are sexually abused in childhood (Diana Russell). Or one or both partners may have been assaulted sexually as an adult. These experiences have profound effects on the survivors—particularly on trust and self-esteem. Survivors may also suffer flashbacks of the abuse during sex (or at other times) and may carry a burden of shame from their experience.

After she was sexually harrassed by a man at work, Claudia did not want to be sexual with her partner Trish. Trish wanted to be supportive to Claudia, but she also felt hurt and rejected.

Lenore had been sexually abused by both of her parents as a child. Sometimes she had flashbacks to those experiences when she and her partner Esther made love. This happened less and less as she began to talk about it and to trust Esther more.

Physical and emotional conditions and states also affect our sexual desire and willingness. Some of these are transitory, while others may last for a long time. Some examples of more short-term states and conditions are the following:

Lee Ann and Sandi had a fight on the way out of the house in the morning. That night Lee Ann was still furious, and making love was the last thing she wanted to do. (Anger with partner.)

Malka blamed her lack of interest in sex on the fact that she was under so much pressure to meet production deadlines at work. (Situational stress.)

Tina had gained some weight over the holidays and was very self-conscious about her body. She was less willing to be sexual than usual. (Anxiety about sexual attractiveness.)

After her skiing accident, Mona was in a lot of pain. Between the effects of the medication and her fear of aggravating her condition, Mona's interest in sex was minimal. (Medications; physical injury.)

Other situations which may last for a longer time include recovery from chemical dependency, more chronic physical conditions, and emotional illness.

Kirsten was so concerned about infecting her partner, that every time she had an outbreak of herpes she slept in the spare room. Sex was out of the question.

After so many years of being together, Ruby knew that when Nadine had one of her bouts with depression, she would not want to be sexual—maybe for months.

Val and Georgie had not realized how much their sex life had been dependent on alcohol and drugs. Now they sometimes felt that they were starting over. Clean and sober, they had to learn how to be sexual again.

Whether the issues are about frequency, initiation, or desire, two things are most important in a couple's sexual relationship. The first is that each woman explore and honor her own personal sexual wants and needs, rather than imposing someone else's standard on herself. Second, these wants and needs must be shared with partners so that both can be involved in the ongoing process of achieving mutual sexual satisfaction.

Chapter 7

Monogamy or Nonmonogamy

While many distinguish between having "just sex" outside the primary relationship and having "a meaningful affair," women in general seem to be less comfortable than men with the idea of casual, recreational sex. However, in some ways, being a lesbian may encourage nonmonogamy. For one thing, there is no legal contract, like marriage, to automatically forbid sex outside the relationship. There may be no contract or agreement at all. Another factor that is conducive to nonmonogamy is that women often do not separate love and sex; close friendships may become eroticized and we then may become sexually involved with our "friend." For women, emotional rather than sexual attraction may transform a friendship into an affair. However, most lesbians say they prefer to be monogamous in their committed relationships. In this chapter we look at some of the advantages and disadvantages of monogamy and nonmonogamy; affairs and their consequences; jealousy; bisexuality; and lesbians who are married to men.

Advantages and disadvantages

The first thing that must be taken into account when a couple is deciding whether to be monogamous or nonmonogamous is what each woman's preference is. It does not matter how many advantages to any system there are if one or both women does not feel good about it. Regardless of the choice they make, the couple should set up an evaluation of that decision after a set amount of time and agree to modify whatever is not working.

Monogamy

An advantage to monogamy is that it helps the couple feel more secure and less vulnerable to a breakup due to an outside attraction. A monogamous couple has only one sexual relationship to organize. This saves time which can be put into other interests. They may also feel more relaxed knowing that they do not have to worry about whether their partner will find someone else more sexually exciting or whether the partner will decide to go out with someone else this weekend. A monogamous couple who do not live together can focus all of their sexual energy on each other without the drain of daily living that can blunt sexual attraction. Another advantage to monogamy is that it invites the women to keep their attention within their relationship so that the creativity generated from that focused attention enhances that relationship. While there are no guarantees, monogamy also offers a context in which couples may deepen their intimacy as a result of confronting difficulties in a direct way; the women do not have the ready option of using an affair as a distraction from a threatening situation with their partners.

Monogamy has disadvantages as well. One of the main ones is that it makes it more difficult for the two women to act on changing sexual attractions and interests. This can set up a dynamic in which one of the partners becomes attracted to someone else, wants to have sex with her, and does not because of her agreement to be monogamous. If this happens at a time when her attraction to her lover is at a low ebb, she may find herself moving away from her lover and towards the forbidden attraction. Many relationships have ended because one woman wanted to have sex with someone else and saw ending the relationship as the only way to accomplish this end. Monogamy requires that time be taken to nurture the sexual component of the relationship. Long-term couples often report sharp drops in romance and genital sex. If two women want a long-term relationship that includes sex, they have to spend quality time working on keeping sex alive and well. When they do not spend this time, the couple is more vulnerable to one of the women's leaving for another, more romantic, sexual relationship.

Sometimes monogamy serves as a cover for one or both partners' terror of being abandoned by her lover. Partners may also feel that monogamy gives them permission to monitor and criticize each other's activities. In this situation the issue is not monogamy itself, it is fear of being left, or of being out of control. But anxious partners may use monogamy to protect themselves from experiencing their fears.

Nonmonogamy

Nonmonogamy allows for changing sexual attractions and may leave the primary relationship more flexible and able to cope with outside attractions. Most women in nonmonogamous couples say that the quality of sex in their primary relationships is enhanced by their being nonmonogamous. They believe that they feel more sexual towards their partner for a longer period of time than they would if they were in a monogamous relationship. The couple does not carry the burden of having to maintain romance and deepen intimacy at the same time—a difficult feat. A healthy nonmonogamous relationship can give each partner the opportunity to follow up on her sexual attractions in an agreed-upon way. This can strengthen the relationship by bringing renewed energy back into the couple relationship. Successful nonmonogamy almost always requires structure and guidelines to protect the primary relationship. Usually the couple agrees to a flow between being monogamous and nonmonogamous, depending on how the women feel at any given time. So, if one partner is not feeling secure, she may ask that they be monogamous for the next few months. When she feels stronger they open the relationship again. It is useful to limit who it is all right to have sex with and under what conditions. It is also a good idea to avoid having sex with women in the couple's friendship circles. Sometimes the couple says it is fine to have sex with someone else only if it happens with someone one of them meets while out of town. Others are open to outside sex, but only when there is no emotional involvement with the sex partner. A couple who lives together may want to agree that neither of them brings another lover to their home. When nonmonogamous couples do not live together it can be easier to coordinate their affairs with other women without disturbing the balance of the primary relationship. These guidelines are designed to provide enough structure so that both women feel secure in their relationship and still have the freedom to have affairs that do not threaten the primary relationship.

Nonmonogamy has its drawbacks as well. The women may not be adequately prepared for sharing their partner and find it hard or impossible to work through the discomfort. Even when a couple has agreed to have sex without emotional involvements, it is very common for lesbians to fall in love with their casual sex partner and to leave the primary relationship anyway. Margaret Nichols observes that for women, romance and sex are linked, and that when romance goes, so does sex. Thus, when one partner in a long-term relationship has an affair with someone else, the romance in that affair may entice her away from the primary relationship.

Nonmonogamy takes more time to coordinate, both for the couple and the individual(s); there are more people, events, and feelings to keep on top of. Nonmonogamy can be a cover for someone who is afraid of being too intimate; by having other lovers she can dilute the primary relationship enough to make it safe for her. Again, nonmonogamy is not the problem here; the fear of being hurt or abandoned is.

Nonmonogamous couples need to be particularly aware of sexually transmitted diseases, especially Acquired Immune Deficiency Syndrome (AIDS). AIDS is not transmissable by casual contact, but lesbians are at risk for being exposed if we have shared needles while using I.V. drugs or had sex with someone who did; or we have had a blood transfusion in the United States between 1978 and 1985 or have had sex with someone who did. If we use sperm for insemination from anyone whose history places him at risk or whose history we do not know, or we have sex with anyone in any of the high-risk groups, we are at risk. Lesbians who have been in long-term, monogamous couples for more than fifteen years are in the lowest risk category.

Unsafe sex refers to any sexual activity that involves contact with a partner's bodily fluids, the most risky being semen and blood, including menstrual blood. The risk of blood exchange increases with any kind of sexual activity that cuts or bruises the body. This includes but is not limited to vaginal or rectal penetration with anything that could break the skin, fist fucking, and any other activity that draws blood, such as some sadomasochistic activities. Rimming (putting your tongue on someone's anus) and sharing sex toys that have been in contact with someone else's body fluids are also unsafe. Safe sex includes masturbation, rubbing each other's bodies, hugging, dry kissing, fantasy, and anything else that does not involve exchange of bodily fluids. Possibly safe sexual activities include french kissing (only when we do not have bleeding or cut gums), oral sex with a barrier such as a rubber dam (this is a piece of latex that you can get from dentists or dental supply houses), and hand to genital contact. The latter is made safer by using a latex glove or finger cot. (Adapted from JoAnn Loulan's book, *Lesbian Passion.*) We urge lesbians to find out about potential lovers' sexual histories and if there is any doubt to use safe sex techniques.

We know few long-term nonmonogamous couples. Most often the relationship ends because one of the women falls in love with someone else. This may mean that monogamy is more conducive to long-term relationships, if that is what a couple wants. Or it may mean that lesbian couples have not spent enough time developing guidelines for having healthy, nonmonogamous partnerships.

Affairs

Partners in lesbian couples have outside sexual relationships for all kinds of reasons. These reasons may be clear at the time or may only be clear later in time, or may never really be clear. Some of the more common motivations are:

1. *To end a relationship*

Marnie knew that Jeanine would never really believe that she was serious about ending their relationship unless she got involved with another woman. So she did.

Tracy fell in love with Starr while she was still in a relationship with Nancy. The more involved she got with Starr, the more fully she realized that her relationship with Nancy was over—and had been over for a while. It was as if it took getting into a new relationship to become aware that the old relationship was over and needed to be ended.

2. *To provide a distraction or an ego boost*

Lucy was devastated when she discovered that Tori, her partner of five years, had cancer. Looking back now she says that her affair with Rene provided a distraction from the stress and worry she was going through over Tori's illness.

Laura insisted that she had no idea why it happened. Most of her friends figured that she slept with Shannon to boost her ego. Laura had been feeling pretty low ever since she got laid off. And to top it off, her partner Lee had just gotten a raise. When Shannon paid so much attention to her, Laura found it hard to resist.

3. *To feel separate*

Since one hazard for lesbian couples is too much togetherness, some partners respond to this tendency to fuse or merge by having sexual affairs to establish their sense of separateness and independence.

When Dana started to feel closed in by her primary relationship, she typically ended up having a sexual relationship with someone else.

The woman who has an outside sexual relationship may have feelings ranging from irritation at being discovered to guilt about her behavior. Her partner's feelings may include hurt, anger, relief, betrayal, and fear. Both may be unsure about what the affair means for the future of their relationship. Can the partner who did not have the affair ever trust her lover again? Can the other woman be sure that she will not continue to have outside relationships? Can either or both of them restructure their relationship to include outside involvements?

When a woman in a relationship that has been explicitly defined as monogamous has a secret affair, her partner is likely to learn about it sooner or later. How each woman interprets the meaning of such an event may vary.

Lil and Juanita had been together for seven years when Lil had a brief affair with a woman she met in a nearby city. Juanita was very upset when Lil told her about her fling, as Lil called it. Juanita felt hurt, angry, and confused. One day she wanted to pack up and leave and the next day she felt scared and followed Lil around the house like a puppy dog. For her part, Lil sometimes felt guilty and sometimes defiant. She felt bad that Juanita was upset but she also knew that she really loved Juanita and that this fling was not a threat to their relationship. She refused to believe that what she had done was so terrible. But she was also afraid of losing Juanita. So she kept negotiating, and courting Juanita until they were a couple again.

Clearly, Lil's affair created a crisis in her relationship with Juanita. As they talked and fought and cried together, some things about their relationship came to light. Although they cared deeply for each other and were committed to the partnership, there was some work they needed to do. In some ways they had been taking each other for granted. They used this crisis to clarify what they wanted in their relationship and to reevaluate how they could have more of that with each other.

A couple may break up over an outside affair. Or they may reevaluate their relationship and recommit to it. In any event, being sexual outside the couple, whether agreed upon in advance or not, usually shakes up the relationship to some degree. Good communication and clear agreements as well as ongoing dialogue are helpful to provide or restore trust between the partners and a sense of security in the relationship.

Dealing with jealousy

Whether we think it is politically correct or not, most of us experience feeling jealous. Many, if not most, of us would feel jealous if our partner was sexually involved with someone else; this is true when we are monogamous and when we are nonmonogamous. We need to acknowledge our feelings and then we can move on to dealing with them.

From the beginning Marcia and Sonja defined their relationship as nonmonogamous. After two years together they had talked about how they had been so enamoured of each other that they had not even wanted other women. Sonja, who had not even wanted to live together, laughed at how much she enjoyed their shared house. Marcia, however, had begun to notice that she was attracted to a woman at work. She told Sonja about this and was very clear that this attraction did not pose a threat to their relationship. But she did want to have sex with this woman. Sonja was surprised at the strength of her reaction. She was torn by the news. On the one hand she really believed in nonmonogamy but on the other she was scared and jealous. She hoped Marcia would decide not to have sex with this other woman.

Objectively, sex outside the couple relationship is potentially disruptive. It triggers insecurities and fears. Even though she tries not to, Sonja wonders what this other woman is like, is she more attractive than Sonja is? Will she be a better lover than Sonja? What if Marcia decides she would rather be with her?

It is possible for Sonja to use her feelings to justify getting out of the relationship with Marcia. She can say that Marcia is at fault and insensitive. Or she can use her feelings to work on deepening the intimacy between them. This is hard to do because jealousy is usually a closet emotion. We talk about being jealous but we rarely directly ask the questions that inflame the jealousy. One big issue for lesbian couples is whether the other woman is a better lover. Since our lesbian identity is frequently grounded in our sexual behavior, how good we are at it directly affects our sense of being lesbian. So, if *she* is a better lover then something is wrong with me! If sex in the primary relationship has lost its exciting edge or if the couple is having trouble with other areas in their life then sex in the affair usually does feel better. We are not likely to ask if she is a better lover in those circumstances. But we do need to ask if something is not right in our primary relationship. Has our technique gotten boring? Are we angry and not talking about it? Immediately we are confronting our jealousy instead of letting it fester.

The other part of this is that it does hurt when our lover has an affair and we may be jealous of the energy and sex she is putting into the other relationship. We need to nurture ourselves when we are in pain and use our friends to support us. At these times our lover, who may be our best friend, may not be the best person to ask for a hug when we need one. We may need to tell a friend or two what is happening in our relationship so that we have someone who will understand why we feel so bruised. We may need to do this even if the lover who is having the affair wants it kept quiet. Whether we are in a nonmonogamous or monogamous relationship we can still feel pain when the other has sex outside the couple.

When jealousy lingers for a long time it may be that the woman is unable or unwilling to give up a feeling that can create or maintain distance in the relationship. We need to talk to our partners about our feelings and sometimes seek counseling if the feelings will not go away after working on them with friends and lover.

Bisexuality, or when the other woman is a man

Sometimes one or both of the women in a lesbian couple is bisexual. When one of these women has an affair it can be with either a woman or a man. This adds other dimensions.

When the couple is nonmonogamous the bisexual woman may have short affairs or she may have ongoing relationships with men. In one situation we know, a lesbian couple had been together for four years and one partner's relationship with a man was three years old. Clearly, the bisexual woman enjoyed sex with both of her lovers and liked having intimate relationships with them as well. In this case all three people involved felt good about the two relationships and valued the stability both relationships gave to each other.

When a bisexual woman is in a monogamous relationship and she has an affair with a man her lover may feel particularly threatened. The affair may signal the end of the bisexual woman's lesbian attraction and a move towards heterosexual attraction. As we said above, the affair may be an end to the relationship, a distraction, or an ego boost, or a way to feel separate. Or the woman may be saying she wants an open relationship that can meet both sides of her bisexual nature. If both women are bisexual they may decide to open the relationship to allow for relationships with men.

Usually, however, lesbians do not like it when their partners become sexually involved with men. The main fear is that the bisexual partner will decide she prefers living a heterosexual lifestyle and will give up her primary, lesbian relationship. Some lesbians and bisexuals do leave their lesbian lovers and have relationships with men. We think this is often due to society's homophobia and heterosexism in general and to the specific woman's internalized homophobia in particular. Realistically, there is pressure to be heterosexual and give up our lifestyles as lesbians. Families usually rejoice when their lesbian daughters return to the heterosexual fold or leave what they think is the lesbian "phase." Most of us at least occasionally wish for acceptance and support; and sometimes a heterosexual relationship looks like it will take care of those needs. While some bisexual women are truly happy with either a male or female partner, the move to a heterosexual lifestyle does not solve a lesbian's longing for acceptance. We are better off working with a therapist on our internalized homphobia and our anger at society .

Another worry is the question of who is better in bed, the female or male lover. Many lesbians most fear their partners' involvement with men because they cannot compete with male-female sex. Others feel better with her partner's having a male lover, because the sex is just different, not real competition at all.

Another dynamic is created when a lesbian couple uses one of their male lovers as the sperm donor for a baby. All three of them could share parenting or he could agree to stay out of the parenting all together. There is a high risk in this situation for the nonbiological mother if she is not the man's lover. If the bisexual woman decides to live heterosexually with the man and "their" baby the lesbian partner has no legal recourse. She will probably lose her parenting status.

As with all couple issues, the more the women talk about their bisexuality the better prepared they will be if one of them has sex with a man. If one woman knows she is attracted to men and wants to leave open the option of having sex with them, she needs to tell her partner. Some lesbians do not want relationships with bisexual women and others are relieved to find out that a potential partner feels the same way she does.

Lesbians married to men

Another kind of nonmonogamous relationship is where one or both of the women are married to men and consider themselves lesbians. Married lesbians live two lives. While they appear to have straight lives, usually in long-term heterosexual marriages, they in fact consider themselves lesbians and may have been in a lesbian couple for years. Of course, there are also heterosexually married women who have been in long term relationships with other women and do not consider themselves lesbians.

Married lesbians are often in their 40's or older and when they first married there was even less support than now to pursue a career, which often left them vulnerable to poverty and/or dehumanizing jobs. Even though these women may now be able to be financially independent and have support from other lesbians, they stay in their marriages for a number of reasons: children, economics, comfort, habit, fear, loyalty or religion. Race and class differences also affect how women view the options of marriage and coming out as lesbians.

When their relationships are long term it may be due, in part, to what several women have labeled as "balance." They are able to maintain a dynamic tension between their Mrs. role within the heterosexual world and lover role in the lesbian world. They report getting "the best of both worlds." They can focus intense energy on each other when they are together and still maintain their separateness because they have to go home. The trade-offs required to maintain this balance are complex. Coming out into the lesbian community or changing perspectives about their marriages may drastically alter the balance that has supported their lesbian relationships.

Married lesbians are typically very isolated. They rely on each other and sometimes a very small resource pool of other people who are usually women and often are very closeted lesbians. Married lesbians, further, are sometimes criticized by the lesbian community for holding on to their "heterosexual privilege." This pushes the still married lesbian away from a potential support group and coming out.

It is interesting to note that while lesbian couples report that the mystery and romance typically fade within the first six months to a year, married lesbians, on the other hand, seem to have an abundance of intrigue and romance. Indeed, they sometimes see that as an advantage to their choice. Thus, another trade-off seems to be that in exchange for giving up time together, a potentially larger support group, and a more congruent lifestyle, they have a relationship that retains much of the early stage romance and sexual excitement.

Such a delicate balance of trade-offs can be costly unless the two women address the issue of their growth as individuals. As with all couples, when one woman changes, the relationship must change or it is likely to end. Married lesbians in couples have two areas of possible change. The first is individual growth that all women have, such as becoming more assertive, and the second is attitudes towards lesbianism and men. Married lesbians have found a way to live intimately with a man, to do without contact with the broader lesbian community and to do with only intermittant in-person contact with their woman lover(s). If one woman in the couple begins to change her thinking about any of these issues, the entire relationship may be at risk because the balance is threatened.

Marjory and Nancy had been lovers for eight years when Nancy decided to leave her husband and move into her own place. Until that time they had seen each other four times a week but usually in public places such as in restaurants and movies.

With this move, Marjory immediately lost one of the protective devices that kept Nancy's and her time together regulated. Even though both may want the increased time together, they will feel the effects of such a shift. Both women need to evaluate how much time they want to spend together and to communicate openly about their wishes. Nancy may assume that they will spend a lot of time at her new house. In fact, Marjory may prefer to spend their time together going out and may assume that their relationship will continue on unchanged. Nancy may even assume that Marjory will want to leave her husband as well. It is not unusual for a married lesbian to end her relationships with husband and lesbian lover at roughly the same time. It is as if the lesbian relationship was dependent on the marriage for its survival and vice versa.

The relationship is threatened for another reason when one woman in a couple wants more contact with other lesbians. This may happen because something has changed in the woman's life, such as her children leaving home or it may be due to a change in attitude. Since married lesbians are quite closeted, the choice of one of them to have more lesbian contact is usually very threatening to the one who wants to remain closeted.

Adele and Harriet had been lovers for eleven years. Adele had made a promise to herself that when her husband died she would start going to gay pride marches and women's events. He had been dead for a year and she had been having a wonderful time being out. Harriet, however, was absolutely terrified that Adele would become one of *those* kinds of lesbians.

New or increased visibility within the lesbian community also exposes the couple to other women who are potential lovers. Adele might meet a woman who likes being more out than Harriet and who is interested in Adele. Previously they had only each other and a few select, respectful friends. Being more out may also expose the woman to more social pressure to end her living arrangement with her husband. Thus, contact with the broader lesbian community may be a mixed blessing in that it offers affirmation and support for their lesbianism but may threaten the couple's balance, and hence, existence.

The married lesbians we know who have left their husbands and come out report that they are happier now. They say that remaining in their marriage was a way to stay safe in their known world. They were also afraid that their lesbian relationship could not sustain them through all the changes coming out means. While we cannot know what makes people happy, it does seem that when married lesbians are free to be out as lesbians they feel better that they can now live a lifestyle that matches their inner experience and definition of themselves. They are relieved and glad to have their lesbian relationship be the only one.

When a couple chooses monogamy or nonmonogamy, they need to identify what each of them needs to feel good about the relationship and then to set up a structure that allows both of them to get their needs met. This is true for lesbians, bisexual women, and lesbians married to men. It is important for couples to have ways to discuss their concerns and to evaluate which ever system they choose. Even if one or both of the women violates the agreed upon structure, the couple does not necessarily have to break up; there may be room for further negotiation which can enhance their intimacy in the long run. The crucial variable is communication and a willingness to redesign and refine what makes the couple happy.

Chapter 8

Friends, Family, and Sense of Community

In this chapter we examine what friends, family, and a sense of community mean for lesbian couples. What we find is that each of these can be a source of support for the couple relationship, or a strain on it.

Friends

In contrast to lesbian couples, heterosexual couples more often keep romance separate from each partner's leisure activities. Men spend leisure time with their men friends and women with their women friends. While lesbians may also spend time with separate friends, they tend to share leisure interests with their partner. Thus, they focus romance, friendship, and camraderie in one person. Because they often concentrate so much energy on the relationship, lesbian couples may have few outside friends.

Terry and Simone had been best friends for three years before they became lovers. They worked in the some office, ate lunch together every day, and even took most of their coffee breaks at the same time. On weekends they liked to go hiking or skiing. Sometimes they went with another couple or a friend, but mostly they did everything with each other, or alone when one of them was unavailable.

Neither Terry nor Simone had separate friends, because they were so focused on their relationship and on each other. There are other reasons that a couple may have few friends.

Many couples lead very busy lives. They are so involved with working, going to school, keeping up a household, raising children, and maintaining their relationship that they never seem to find time to spend with friends. Some couples are geographically isolated; others are closeted. In addition to these factors, one or both women may be unsure about how to have friends without weakening the couple relationship.

Having friends can be difficult when partners have different expectations and different patterns of relating to friends. Some women describe themselves as loners. Others prefer to have one best friend or a very small circle of close friends. Still others have a wide circle of friends and even more acquaintances. The fact that partners have different styles of making and maintaining friendships may not be clear early in the relationship. In the romance stage many women neglect their friends entirely as they focus on the new lover. When the couple emerges from this stage, the women may discover that they have different wants and styles regarding friends. One woman in the couple may want to spend most of her spare time with her partner, who is also her one best friend. The partner, on the other hand may be insistent about having a lot of time with her separate friends.

If our partner is our best friend, who needs other friends? We believe that it is a good idea for couples to have a balance between individual time alone, couple time, and time with separate and mutual friends. Even though it is hard to do this, it is important not to neglect any of these elements for too long.

Friendship networks

Friends support us. They tap and stimulate interests and perspectives which we may not get in our primary relationship. On a practical note, separate friends are folks we can eat pizza with when our partner is on a diet, go skiing with when our partner hates the cold, complain to when our lover "does it again," talk about old times with when our partner is new, and help us feel good about ourselves because we know they love us.

It would be ideal for each of us to have as many as seven

people who would drop everything and come running if we called for help. At any particular time one may be out of town, another sick, a third out sailing, and so on. So having a number of people in this category keeps us from putting all our eggs in one basket. We increase the probability of getting our needs met.

In their book, *Brief Encounters*, Emily Coleman and Betty Edwards strongly advocate that each of us have a supportive network of three friendship circles. They visualize each of these circles as surrounding the person who is in the center. The friendship circle that is closest to the center (and closest to the individual) is called the Tender Circle. These are the people we spoke of earlier who would drop everything and come running if we needed them. Whether our connections with the people in our Tender Circle are blood connections, or legal ones, or historical ones—they are strong and deep. Whether they are straight, or gay, or lesbian, these people are dependable, available and in frequent contact with us. They like us and love us the way we are.

The second circle is bigger and a little further out from the individual in the center. This group of Congenial Comrades is composed of fifteen to twenty people who are important to us in some way. These friends provide companionship and we see them regularly but not necessarily frequently.

The third circle is called the Outer Rim. This circle is made up of thirty to fifty people. Contact is not frequent, but these people may provide stimulation and serve as resource people on whom we can call for specific needs, such as getting a recommendation for an electrician or advice about a project.

These authors maintain that couple relationships are enhanced, not harmed, by the presence of supportive friendship networks. We agree.

As we mentioned earlier, partners likely have different patterns of relating to friends. Not everyone has, or even wants to have, each of these three friendship circles filled up. The important thing is to have a friendship network which provides the caring and the stimulation that we need.

It can be useful for each partner to inventory her network periodically. Does either partner have shortages in any of the circles? When good friends move away, or become involved in new jobs or new relationships, it can leave a large empty space in the network, for example. And many women believe they are not good at meeting people or at making friends.

A traditional place for lesbians to meet each other has been at bars. However, many women are not comfortable in this atmosphere, or don't care for the people they meet there. Bars are one place, but certainly not the only place, to meet people. A number of resources exist (see bibliography) to help with overcoming shyness and developing skills and strategies for making friends. Ginny NiCarthy, in her book, *Getting Free*, has a number of suggestions for reaching out. If you already have acquaintances, she suggests starting there. Make a list of these people and see which ones you might like to spend more time with. These are possible friends. She points out that while we can make friends anywhere, some of the best places to meet people are classes, volunteer organizations, social groups, and work. Joining a hiking club, or a political group, or volunteering some time to a lesbian/gay organization are ways to meet new people who share your interests.

Jealousy

It is not always easy even to find friends, much less maintain the balance between time alone, couple time, and time with separate and mutual friends. Jealousy may become an issue. One partner may be jealous simply of the time her lover spends with separate friends. She wants more time together.

Sometimes this jealousy about time is complicated by the fact that the separate friend is a former lover. Often a lesbian's closest friends are previous partners. We think there are at least three reasons for this. First, the lesbian community is usually relatively small in size. Second, many lesbians have been involved in a number of relationships over time. And third, the women value these relationships and try to keep them from ending completely. Lesbians often work very hard to make the transition from lover to friend. For all these reasons, former lovers may be very much a part of a lesbian's life.

Understandably, a new lover may be jealous of the ex-partner's closeness, threatened by the friends' shared history, or suspicious of their discussions about her. On the other hand, the former partner may also be jealous. She may get concerned about being neglected or displaced somehow. These dynamics can result in difficult situations and hurt feelings.

Sarah felt left out when she and her partner Jael spent time with Jael's best friend/ex-lover, Marge. Marge and Jael seemed to talk endlessly about old times, old friends, and old in-jokes.

Gloria was furious about the birthday present her partner Consuela received from her previous partner. The gift in question was what Gloria described as a "sexy negligee." Consuela thought that Gloria was making a big deal out of nothing.

Sue was hurt when her old partner and best friend Nadine started spending time with Judy. Nadine became almost totally unavailable because she was always with Judy. The situation was complicated by the fact that Sue and Judy had barely spoken to each other in years because of an unresolved dispute about money.

In these situations, and in the many others which can arise with former and new lovers, open communication is the key. Another factor is time.

It is not too much to hope that new lovers (and ex-lovers) can recognize their feelings of jealousy, hurt, or threat. Ideally they will express these feelings to their partner (or friend). For a while, the new lover and the ex-lover may communicate mostly through the woman who is their common link. The woman who is trying to manage a new lover relationship and a friendship with her ex-lover may be in the middle. If she is honest with each of the other two, being in the middle can be more tolerable, and eventually she can remove herself and let her new lover and her ex-lover work things out between them. If these women have direct contact with each other, they often become more human and less of a threat to each other.

With time, jealousy usually fades as the new partner and the old friend are reassured about their respective positions and importance. When this does not happen, the woman in the middle needs to look long and hard at her role in the situation. Is she helping to reduce tensions or is she contributing to them? Is there some payoff to her in keeping the rivalry going? For example, does she enjoy being the center of attention? Or is she avoiding making a commitment to the new partnership and so holding on to the ex-partner in an unhealthy way? Lack of clarity fuels jealousy. The woman in the middle needs to be clear with each of the other two. And her actions need to match her words. If she wants her former partner to believe that the friendship is important, she needs to put energy into maintaining it. If she wants her new partner to believe that the couple relationship comes first, she needs to make sure that she makes it a priority.

Each woman in this triangle—new partner, ex-lover, and woman-in-the-middle—needs to examine her own feelings, motivations and behavior honestly. Then she will be in a better position to communicate more openly and honestly with the others.

Sometimes it is not an old relationship, but rather a new one that needs clarification.

Jena and Bobbi were each in long-term relationships when they met at a union training session in Chicago. They liked each other right off, and were excited to learn that they were both moving to Boston within a year. As their friendship grew, Jena became aware that she was attracted to Bobbi. She wasn't sure how Bobbi felt. When she finally raised the subject, she discovered that Bobbi was attracted to her as well. Neither of them wanted to risk hurting their long-term relationships, and yet they wanted to maintain their friendship. They decided to acknowledge the feelings of attraction but not act on them. Both women felt fortunate that their decision was mutual.

For many lesbians, emotional attachment precedes sexual attraction. So, in many lesbian friendships, one or both women may find that they are sexually attracted to their friend. Sometimes a woman will become aware of these feelings only after her partner confronts her with the fact that she is flirting with her friend. The partner may feel jealous about the flirting and want clarification about whether or not the friends will be sexual with each other. Sometimes the friends talk about it openly and make a joint decision, like Jena and Bobbi. For other friends, the decision is made without discussion—the intense feelings of attraction pass. Whatever the friends decide, they need to keep the communication lines open and the trust quotient high with their partners, if they are in a couple relationship.

Couple friends

Not only do we encourage partners to have separate friends, but also to have couples as friends. In fact, many couples find that they gradually spend more time with other couples and less with single friends. It is important to have both.

Just as individual friends validate our individual identity, so couple friends validate our identity as a couple. Some of the ways they do this are by treating us as a couple, by assuming that we will continue to be together, and by comparing notes with us about relationship issues.

Couple friends can broaden our experiences and expand our models of couple relationships. Hearing about how another couple divides up household tasks may give us new options. When we are fighting a lot, the discovery that other couples have had periods of intense conflict can reassure us that our relationship has a chance of surviving. Talking with couple friends can normalize our experience. What we are feeling, or thinking or going through becomes more "normal." Other people have had similar experiences. So we don't have to feel crazy or weird, and we may even get some positive suggestions for how to handle our situation.

Some couples hesitate to talk about having any problems in their relationship. They believe that friends, particularly couple friends, do not want to hear about difficulties. In some cases this may be true. Other couples may be so hungry for confirmation that a lesbian couple relationship can work that they do not want to hear about problems. Long-term partners may feel the pressure to be a "perfect couple" most acutely. However, if we are unwilling to hear about the inevitable difficulties that our couple friends face, we cut them off from using us as a resource. And couple friends can be an extremely valuable resource for each other. But like any other friendships, these relationships require open and honest communication to provide effective support. Friends cannot help us when they do not know what is going on.

Couple friends can also help create an atmosphere of safety and support in the broader world. Not only is it hard to be a lesbian in a homophobic culture, it is hard to be a lesbian couple. Couple friends, just because they are also a couple, validate our relationship. In addition, they may be fun to be with, to say nothing of providing good advice and supportive hugs.

For example, some women have couple friends who are vacation buddies. They have more fun because they feel safer and more comfortable being a lesbian couple when they are with other couples. This can be true for a number of forays into the predominantly heterosexual world. Everything from going to a fancy restaurant to attending a PTA meeting can be more comfortable with a group.

Of course, this does not mean that friendships with other couples are always easy. Monogamous and committed couples say it is hard to meet other committed couples to socialize with. Finding couples in which all four women are compatible can be a challenge. Sometimes two friends get together with their respective partners only to discover that the partners do not enjoy each other's company. The friendship then remains a separate one, rather than developing into a couple friendship as well. Or a couple friendship may end because a partner in one couple has a falling-out with one of the women in the other couple. Or there may be competition. Sometimes one woman feels that their couple friends like her partner better than they like her. This situation can happen, for example, when one partner is more outgoing than the other.

A special complication in lesbian couple friendships has to do with the threat of sexual attraction developing, and what the women decide to do if that happens. There are more possible romantic combinations with lesbian couple friends than with traditional heterosexual couples, because each of the women in one couple could be attracted to one or both of the partners in the other couple. The problems and strategies discussed in the previous section on jealousy apply to situations with couple friends, too. Good communication and listening skills, and clear agreements between partners in a couple go a long way to prevent, as well as resolve, these situations. Sometimes couples find it useful to discuss openly their feelings with the other couple, as well as with their respective partners.

Family

The term family can have various meanings for a lesbian couple. Family may mean the birth/biological or adoptive family of each partner. Or family may refer to the couple-with-children unit. For many lesbians, the term family means chosen family rather than birth or adoptive family. It is primarily because of homophobia that a lesbian may have a chosen family. Many lesbians have been rejected by their biological/adoptive families. Others are not out to all or any of their relatives, for fear of rejection.

Birth/biological/adoptive family

Partners often differ in their degree of outness to their respective families. This can cause strain in the couple relationship.

Pat dreaded the Christmas season. Every year for the last four years, her partner Sandy had gone to visit her parents in another state for most of the holidays. Pat wanted to spend this Christmas with her and with her family. She did not want to pressure Sandy to come out to her own folks, but she was tired of never spending holidays together.

In this situation, Pat and Sandy have very different relationships with their families. Pat's parents treat Sandy like a daughter-in-law. They have not responded that way to all of Pat's partners. They were very cold to Pat's first lover when Pat came out to them. They blamed her partner Trish for "leading Pat into this deviant lifestyle." Pat had always been close to her parents, and their rejection of Judy was very painful for her. In fact, she now thinks that her parents' attitudes were a big factor in the breakup of that relationship.

Eventually Pat's parents began to accept the fact that her lifestyle was not a passing phase. Now they have adjusted and seem comfortable with it most of the time. They are very fond of Sandy, and supportive of the relationship.

On the other hand, Sandy has never been particularly close to her parents, but feels obligated to spend Christmas with them. There is a traditional family reunion over the holidays, and she knows it is important to them that she be there. Sandy feels torn between her loyalty to her parents and her love for Pat. Since her parents are in their late seventies, she cannot see the point of coming out, and upsetting them, at this stage. She resents what she interprets as Pat's pressuring her about it.

Clearly, Pat and Sandy illustrate two very different patterns and ways of relating to parents about coming out. These differences affect the couple relationship. Coming out is an individual process and a personal decision. However, if partners spend traditional family holidays separately, one or both partners may feel that the other is not taking the relationship seriously. Their togetherness is not being made a priority, and this seems to diminish the relationship.

For some lesbians, the biological family was and is a protection against an oppressive and hostile mainstream society. This is particularly true for many ethnic women and women of color. Coming out to family means risking the loss of this support and sense of identity and community. Many of these women decide that it is better to keep their lesbian couple relationship in the closet, rather than risk such an enormous loss. Unless their partners are in similar situations, it is not always easy for them to appreciate what is at stake.

Even if both partners are out to their parents and relatives, all problems do not magically disappear. Obviously, the family may reject the partner. Or they may be more subtle in their exclusion. Refusing to recognize clearly and acknowledge a lesbian partner as part of the family is also exclusion.

Sometimes it is hard for a couple to tell just why parents do not accept the relationship. This can be particularly true for couples of different races, or from different class backgrounds. Are they being rejected or excluded because they are black, or white, or working class, or Jewish, or lesbian or what?

Chosen family

For couples who are not out, or are not close to their blood-related families, the chosen family may have special significance in supporting their lesbian identity and couple relationship. Parents, siblings, children, and other relatives may, of course, be part of a chosen family. The point is that family membership is by selection, not by birth or legal status alone.

Partners, ex-lovers, and friends are all prime candidates for inclusion. Many couples do not think of their partners and friends as a chosen or extended family. This may be the case even when they have clear arrangements and agreements about spending holidays together, co-parenting and god-parenting responsibilities, or communal living. We believe that for lesbians and lesbian couples, this network of friends, children, and relatives constitutes a chosen family. These people validate and support our couple relationships. They are there to share the joys and the hard times. They may not always agree with us but we know they respect, accept, and love us for who we are. These chosen families illustrate the building of a community on a personal scale.

Couple with children families

The chosen family of a couple may include children. As we discuss in depth in Chapter 9, some children come into the couple relationship through a decision by the couple to add children to their family. Children in these families are very much chosen. Other children come to the couple from a previous marriage(s). How much these children are a part of the chosen family of the couple depends on a number of factors. One of the main ones can be whether or not the couple is out to them.

Many lesbians are afraid of custody battles with ex-husbands or of rejection by their children. So they remain closeted. When a mother is not clearly out to her children, they may sense that something is going on, but be confused about what it is. Lesbianism becomes a family secret. Sometimes mothers feel forced to come out to children because the kids are being teased at school about having a "lezzie mother."

Coming out to children raises many issues. When children have this information about a parent, they have to manage the information just as their mother does. They have to decide who to tell, or if to tell. They may have to deal with oppression from peers, as well as with their own values and attitudes about sexual orientation. They may even come out *for* the couple, by telling friends or teachers—a surprise for many couples.

Younger children often take the news in stride, while adolescents may have more difficulty. In the middle of coping with their own emerging sexuality, dealing with their mother's lesbianism is an unwanted burden. Lesbianism is no more acceptable to the adolescent peer culture than it is to the adult world. Probably less.

Difficulties can be increased if a youngster is unhappy about the parents' divorce. The child may blame the lesbian partner and try to break up the couple or punish the partner, and so on. All the problems of divorce and blended families can apply, but with the addition of lesbianism.

The partner of a lesbian mother does not have an automatically defined role with the children. She is neither a stepmother nor a stepfather. The child (or children) may wonder, "Just who is she anyway?" "Who is she to us?" and "What does her living with me and Mom mean?" In addition, the legal mother may have mixed feelings about how much of a parental involvement she wants her partner to have with the children. This role confusion can be increased if the lesbian relationship is a secret. The partner may feel confused about her role, may feel like a third wheel and hold back from connecting with the child as much as she would like. The pros and cons of coming out to children to improve the family dynamics versus the possibility of a custody battle need to be weighed carefully. And it would be unfair of us to imply that a lesbian partner cannot have a good relationship with her partner's children unless the couple is open about their relationship with each other.

We do believe that the most full and mutually satisfying chosen family experience happens when a lesbian couple is open and honest about their relationship. However, this may not seem possible for some couples. And the family can still be a loving and supportive one.

A sense of community

The term "community" means very different things to different lesbian couples. In smaller towns, all the lesbians—all ten of them—probably know each other. In midsize population centers, the women may have at least "heard the name" or recognize other lesbians by sight.

In larger cities, there are any number of communities. Many of these communities are really friendship circles with no overlap or connection with each other at all. We've heard women say, "I've lived in Seattle for nearly ten years and I think I know a lot of lesbians. Then I go to a concert and there are hundreds of women, most of whom I've never seen before. Where do they all come from?"

Many of the smaller "communities" of lesbians are isolated from each other. Groups of women who have been friends for years are one example. These women may be in long-term relationships. They find a strong support network for themselves and their relationships in their friendship circle. Social life may be focused around gathering at each other's homes. This may be particularly true for lesbians who came out prior to the late 1960s. They had to survive in an even more hostile environment than now exists, and have maintained these friendship circles in part for the protection they offer. Others maintain these social patterns because of the difficulties involved when a couple opens itself to the larger lesbian community.

For example, respecting "couple boundaries" is sometimes a problem in the lesbian community. Because lesbian couples rarely "marry," their relationship rules are not always clear. People outside the relationship may wonder, "Are they monogamous? Do they intend this to be a long-term relationship? Is it okay to spend time with them separately or only as a couple?"

Even when the couple's agreements are clear, sometimes friends are not supportive or respectful of the relationship. The prevailing attitude may be that "couples are short-lived, so if you are interested in a woman who is in a relationship already, you just have to wait a bit, because she soon will be available." This attitude is certainly not supportive of the current relationship. Indeed, the greeting from people a lesbian has not seen for some time may be, "Are you and ____ still together?" The expectation is clear that you won't be. If the answer is, "Yes, we are," the questioner may be surprised.

Social support for relationships

Most of us who are in committed relationships want social approval and what gay minister Larry Ulrig, in his book *The Two of Us*, calls affirmation of the bonding. We want the people who are significant in our lives to affirm our relationship with our partner. In this culture, this affirmation process typically involves arranging for our partner to be introduced to our friends, co-workers, parents, and relatives. We want these important others to accept our partner, approve our choice, and provide support and encouragement as the relationship develops. Lesbian couples are likely to experience barriers at every stage of getting this social affirmation. Until the clergy of the Metropolitan Community Church (MCC) began to conduct Rites of Blessing and Holy Unions, the formal affirmation of marriage or celebration of commitment was not available to gays and lesbians from organized religion. Now, some of the clergy of various other Christian denominations (e.g., United Methodist, Unitarian, Episcopal) as well as Reform and Reconstructionist Jewish rabbis and Friends Meetings (Quaker) have performed these services for gay and lesbian couples. Now that some of the established churches are recognizing lesbian couple relationships, those couples who wish to celebrate their commitment in their own religious tradition, with the support of their community, have more options to do so. And where this is not the case, the MCC provides an alternative.

Many lesbian couples have designed and conducted their own rituals out of a desire to affirm, celebrate, and symbolize their relationships. Some of these rituals are private; others are public and include family and friends.

Mary and Eva wrote up their own vows expressing their love and commitment to each other. One weekend when they were at the ocean, they read the vows aloud and exchanged rings.

Deirdre and Kim designed their commitment ceremony for their fifth anniversary celebration party. They included the tradition of "jumping the broom" in their ceremony. It was important to Kim, as a Black woman, to include this tradition. It goes back to the time of slavery in the United States, when slaves were not allowed to marry legally. They were married in the eyes of the community through this ritual, literally jumping over a broom together.

While some lesbian couples, like Dierdre and Kim, feel a part of the lesbian community, other couples are isolated from the lesbian community and identify themselves as belonging to other communities.

Elizabeth and Mary were both in their late fifties. They had lived together for thirty-two years. Elizabeth was a teacher at an elementary school, and Mary was the secretary at the Methodist church downtown. They had several close friends, all of whom were lesbian couples in similar situations. Elizabeth was sure she would never come out, for two reasons. One was that she loved teaching and would do nothing to risk her job, and the other was that she had read about the lesbian lifestyle and was sure she wanted nothing to do with it.

These women are voluntarily isolated from the larger lesbian community. However, they both felt a strong bond with the Methodist fellowship and got a lot of their social needs met through church activities. They were on committees together, and in many ways the other members of the congregation treated them as a couple.

Carrie and Marilyn lived on Carrie's farm in southern Minnesota for almost all of their fourteen years together. These women felt accepted and supported by the other members of their small farming community. However, once in a while they went to Minneapolis to a bar or a restaurant just to see "others like us," as Marilyn put it.

Each of these couples is isolated from the lesbian community, the first by apprehension and disinclination, and the second by geography. However, each couple has found other communities to identify with, belong to, and get support from. Without some form of community, isolation can force a couple in on itself so much that the partners get absolutely sick of each other. They may then end a relationship that might have stayed healthy had they been less isolated. Lesbians are already an isolated group. Regardless of how much we consider ourselves a part of a lesbian or other community, we are separate from the mainstream heterosexual society. When we are isolated from a sense of community, we do not have role models for our choices, or friends to balance us in our relationships. This can cripple a couple. Ideally, lesbian couples should be able to meet other lesbians freely, play and work with them, and grow from these interactions in the same way that heterosexual couples can. Until that time comes, we need to understand the extra pressures on our relationships and take care of ourselves the best way we can. This may mean evaluating how necessary it is to isolate ourselves from other lesbians. If it is crucial, then we need to find ways to nurture ourselves as individuals and as couples through involvements with other communities of people. If it is not necessary, we can direct energy toward building a community for ourselves which includes other lesbians and lesbian couples. The heterosexual world is not going to build a community for us. We need to do it for ourselves.

Chapter 9

Lesbian Couples with Children

There are three kinds of families headed by lesbian couples: *nuclear*, with children who are born to or adopted by the couple; *blended*, where children are included who came originally from their mother's prior relationship (usually with a man); and *extra-blended*, where children come from both sources.

In addition to discussing each of these three types of situations, we group the major issues for families into three categories. The first section, titled "Coming Out/Being Out," encompasses homophobia and custody issues, as well as coming out problems. The next section, on " Types of Families," includes each of the three family situations and particularly how both the family and society view the role of the nonbiological or nonadoptive mother. Finally, we consider "Interrelationships between the Family and the Broader Society." This last section includes both coming out and the role of the nonbiological partner, as we look at the legal relationships between lesbians, their children and society, and the practical problems of everyday living. Throughout, we pay particular attention to how the language we use to describe these families both creates and restricts our view of them.

Coming out/being out

Coming out refers to the different degrees of recognizing, acting on, and accepting a lesbian identity. One of the decisions that lesbian mothers, partners, and coparents face is whether or not to come out to the children, when and how to do so, and how much to be out as a family to the rest of the world. In her book, *Gay Parenting*, Joy Schulenburg reports that of the eighty percent of the parents who had come out to their children, many had taken years before saying anything, and even then had only mentioned their gayness rather than discussing it in any depth.

Among the main factors that affect decisions about coming out are the fear of upsetting the children, or being rejected by them, and the threat or possibility of a custody battle.

The emotional pain and stress of a marriage's ending most often do not bring out the best in people. In this atmosphere, many women fear that their husbands will struggle with them for sole custody of the children if their lesbianism becomes known. And this fear may continue long after the divorce is final.

Donna and Irene both had been recently divorced. They had four children between them. When they decided to move in together, they explained their combining households to the kids as a plan to cut expenses. Irene had wanted to come out to the children and work on being a family, but did not do so out of respect for Donna's situation: Donna knew that her ex-husband would be likely to sue for custody of the children if he found out about her relationship with Irene.

After four years, it was hard for Lori to pretend that she was just a friend to Becky, rather than her lover. Becky had refused to allow any lesbian literature or material in the house and was very careful that she and Lori were never affectionate in front of her three children. Since the children visited their father regularly, Becky didn't want to risk their saying anything to him that could lead to custody problems.

Even when losing the children is not at stake, many women fear that their children will reject them, or be upset or harmed by the knowledge that their mother is a lesbian.

When Dee and Janice first became lovers, Dee had been clear that she did not want to parent Janice's ten-year-old son, Erik. In addition, Janice had wanted to wait until Erik had his own sexual identity established before she came out to him. She was afraid of somehow influencing him. Partly for these reasons, Janice and Dee did not live together. Time marched on. Erik turned fifteen and they had not yet discussed their relationship with him.

After her husband died, Audrey acted for the first time on her feelings for women. She was fifty-eight years old. Her five children were all grown by that time and three of them had families of their own. She decided not to say anything to them about her lesbian relationship because she was afraid that they would be negative and unaccepting of her partner if they knew. As it was, her children included her partner Mattie as part of the family. Both she and Mattie doted on the grandchildren, and the possibility that they would not be able to have contact with them was another reason not to come out.

Three years ago, Ramona had been convinced that her two young daughters would have totally rejected her if they knew about her lifestyle. At four and nine, they had been upset enough about the divorce. So she had decided it would be best if they lived with their father—and he had agreed. But she had always planned to have them live with her eventually. Now that she was settled, she was ready for them to be with her. However, she still had not come out to them. She couldn't imagine their living with her and her partner and not knowing; but she was afraid they wouldn't want to move in if they did know.

As parents, these women face a double dose of the coming out dilemma. They have to deal with society's homophobic attitudes—which have influenced their children—and they also have to fight their own anti-lesbian conditioning. Audrey faces the possible homphobia of two generations—her adult children and her grandchildren. Between them, Janice and Ramona confront children of different ages, sexes, and in different living situations. Janice's reluctance to come out to her son Erik and thus present homosexuality as a viable option, suggests that she may not feel secure and confident in her own lesbian identity.

. . . .

How do children react?

What do we know about how kids react to having a gay or lesbian parent? According to Joy Schulenburg, children are amazingly flexible, and most of those she interviewed responded positively. Most children are more concerned about their own relationships with their parents than about their parents' sexual orientation. "Just so she's still my mom, I don't care about that other stuff" is a very common reaction.

Of course, the childrens' reactions are affected by their ages and by the timing and approach of their mother in coming out. Most children and parents seem to think it is better to tell a child when he or she is young. This avoids the risk that the youngster will find out from someone else or in an undesirable way.

"The kids at school are teasing me. They say you are a lezzie. Is that true?"

"Dad says that you and Jane are queer. What is he talking about?"

Another advantage of talking to the children early is that they are less likely to have adopted society's negative attitudes toward homosexuality. Schulenburg suggests that this negative conditioning is pretty well established by age eleven or twelve, and that boys seem to be more susceptible than girls. In addition, children's feelings about a mother's lesbianism may change over time. Just because a child is uncomfortable or accepting at one age, or at one point in time, does not mean that she/he will remain that way. Continuing to talk is important.

The following are some guidelines for coming out to children (adapted from Schulenburg):

- *Sort out your own feelings about being a lesbian first.*

  If you are confused or ashamed or panicked, your children are less likely to react with calm and acceptance. The most positive coming out experiences are reported by parents who were comfortable with themselves as people. When parents accept and affirm their own sexuality and identity, their children are more able to do so as well. The children have a positive model.

- *Reassure your children that your sexual partnership does not change your relationship with them or your feelings for them.*

  This is particularly important for younger children. Make sure that they understand that you are still the same person and that you love them just as much as ever.

- *Be prepared to answer questions.*

  Some children are young enough to have little curiosity and no questions—yet. Older children may want to know why you can't just find a man to fall in love with and marry, or why people don't like lesbians.

- *Be prepared for your child to withdraw for a while.*

  This is more common for preadolescent and adolescent children. They may not want any additional information and may resist talking about their feelings. Give them time and check in periodically. You need to recognize that their main concern is likely to be for themselves—how will this affect them. The assurance that you will be sensitive to their feelings and will not embarrass them in front of their friends may be helpful.

- *Stay calm.*

  Even children who have a negative initial reaction often come around. Just as it often takes time for a parent to accept having a gay son or a lesbian daughter, so it can take time for a child to accept having a lesbian mother.

Adolescent children may be afraid that having a lesbian mother means that they will be gay or lesbian. Clear and informed communication between parent and child is the best antidote to this fear. It is useful to talk to your child about how sexuality is developed; it is a complicated process that depends on biological, emotional, and environmental factors.

Most lesbians and gay men have heterosexual parents; the sexual orientation of a parent does not cause the sexual orientation of a child. But the parent's attitudes can influence a child's feelings about sexual orientation.

Make your explanations simple and straightforward, and gear them to the age and level of understanding of your child. It is also important to leave the door open for further discussion. Children adapt better when there is ongoing dialogue about these issues. Sometimes friends or partners or other resources can be helpful in talking with children about their questions.

Coming out to children does mean taking a calculated risk. The risks—such as temporary or longer term rejection by the children, custody problems, or overt hostility towards the mother's partner by the kids—need to be taken seriously. On the other hand, there are some clear advantages for a lesbian couple in coming out and being out with their children. Secrets and avoidance interfere with intimacy—between the adults, between the children and the adults, and between the children. If the couple is out, the women are more able to be themselves and to nurture their relationship than if they are closeted, especially if the children live with them. And everyone can then work on defining and clarifying a definition of family that suits their particular wants and situation. Being out with the children has advantages for the youngsters as well. They do not learn homophobia from their mother's secret-keeping and may learn how to recognize and deal with it in other people. The children also grow up with a parent who is modelling positive self-esteem instead of self-effacing behavior.

Types of families

We have used the terms *blended, nuclear*, and *extra-blended* to describe the three kinds of families headed by lesbian couples.

• • • •

Blended families

When one or both women bring children into their lesbian relationship, it creates a family structure much like blended heterosexual families. One of the main differences, however, is that there is no legal status that describes how people are connected to each other. The mother's lover is not a stepmother, nor are the children her stepchildren. If the couple is not out to the children, the other woman may be "just a friend" or "my mom's roommate." Even if they are out, there may not be better language. There is no commonly accepted word. Some children call the partner "my mom's lover" or "my mom's partner," but this is only half the truth, since it ignores the possible relationship between the partner and the child.

Role of the partner

While language is a large barrier to incorporating blended families into society, the actual role played by the biological mother's lover also needs to be clarified. Since there are no accepted role models for this kind of family, each family can figure out what works best for them.

Madelaine had a five-year-old son, Tony, from her marriage of ten years. When she became involved with Sonja, they decided that they wanted to live together but not have Sonja take an active parenting role. Everyone liked this arrangement, especially Tony, who found that he had gained a good friend.

Mamie had four children and two uninvolved ex-husbands before she met Tamara. Mamie wanted her partner to be another parent. Initially the children resented Tamara, but eventually they were glad to have someone else in their lives whom they could count on besides Mamie.

Toby and Marsha met at a preschool parents' meeting, and after a brief courtship, became lovers. Even though they did not live together, Toby and Marsha became extended family to each other's children, and were able to give each other time off from mothering every now and then.

It does not matter much what arrangement a couple comes up with; what is important is that it takes into account what the women and children want. Since the mother and her child(ren) were a unit before the addition of a partner, it is very common for the new adult to function as an additional caring adult without assuming a parental role. The children's ages play a large part in this. Younger children are more likely to want and receive more parenting, while older children may resent even their biological or adoptive parent's parenting—let alone a newcomer's.

If the mother's lover does become involved with the children and takes on a parenting role, the family needs to be clear about what that means. Does it mean that both women have equal authority in the home and spend equal amounts of time with the children? Does it mean that in the event of the biological mother's death, her partner would get visitation rights or even custody of the children? Lesbian "stepmothers" have no legal status in the eyes of the courts. It is most common for nonbiological mothers to lose the children to one of the children's blood relations. If it is the lesbian couple's intent to have the nonbiological mother get custody or even visitation rights, the biological mother needs to word her will and power of attorney specifically to that end. This has no binding legal effect. The biological or adoptive father will always have precedence unless he has been declared unfit or waives his parental rights. Or the court may place the child wherever it chooses.

Some lesbian couples have children as a part of their lives but not living with them all the time. When one or both women have children but do not have custody, the children are still part of the family, especially for the biological mother. Her partner may not feel the same way.

Nancy and Brenda dated for three weeks before Nancy found out that Brenda had three children living in another town. Brenda saw her children one weekend a month and for three weeks in the summer; it had been like that for two years. Brenda missed her children tremendously, and the pain she felt about being separated from them spilled over into her relationship with Nancy. Nancy didn't know Brenda's children, and obviously could not relate to them as a family.

On the other hand, living together as a family does not guarantee a feeling of togetherness, either.

Judy's lover, Candy, had three children who in Judy's eyes were demanding, ungrateful, and rude. Judy also realized that she was not just a little jealous of the time Candy gave to the children. Candy went to school plays and sports events, helped with homework, drove the kids where they wanted to go, and generally was a mother first—and a lover second.

In this case, Judy did not feel much a part of the household. She was jealous of how much time Candy spent with the youngsters, and she didn't really like the children much anyway. No matter what kind of relationship the different family members have with each other, they will all need to adapt to the addition of someone new. Women who are considering getting involved with a woman with children need to ask and observe how much time and energy the mother spends on her children. The couple needs to negotiate the limits of "mother" time and of "lover" time. If either of the women is uncomfortable, they need to consider the long-term implications of being involved in a relationship where there is ongoing stress about priorities. If the women do become a couple they need to discuss general parenting philosophy and how they want to translate that into effective parenting that also allows for enough quality couple time.

Generally, we think couples need to nurture themselves with time together, time with friends, time with the children, and time alone. This may mean teaching the children how to enjoy time away from their mother—or doing it even if they do not always enjoy it. The mother also needs to be very clear with her children that she, too, wants time alone with her lover and that the lover is not the "bad one." It is easy for the lover to become the limit-setter and the mother to be the "good mommy." One way to avoid this is to have both women set limits, take the children's side sometimes, and be clear with each other about what they want to communicate to the children. In the story above, Judy could have saved Candy some time if she had been willing to transport Candy's children occasionally. Candy could have helped if she had set aside specific time for her and Judy to spend alone, and had made it clear to the children that they were expected to take care of themselves on that day or evening.

Nuclear families

When a lesbian couple adopts or arranges for the conception of a child together, it is common for both women to parent the child. Even though only one of the women is biologically related to the child or only one may be the legally adoptive parent, the two women usually consider themselves equal parents. Some couples, however, add a child or children to their family with the intention of only one woman being the parent, or with the intention of having other women or men be primary parents (coparents) with the biological mother. As with blended families, it is crucial for the couple to figure out how they want the nonbiological/nonadoptive/ parent(s) involved.

Unfortunately, regardless of how partners themselves define their family roles, the world outside their family will most likely apply traditional definitions to fit its concept of how families ought to be. Usually institutions will call the biological mother a single parent who has a friend, lover, roommate, partner, or whatever their language allows. If it is the intention of both women to parent equally, they will have to spend time and energy to be recognized as such.

In the case of bearing a child, this begins with finding nonhomophobic prenatal care for the biological mother-to-be. Ideally, the midwife or physician should look upon the childbearing woman's partner (or whoever is so indicated) as the child-to-be's other parent. This means including her in any health care visits, birthing classes, hospital tours, and discussions of how to take care of the baby and the mother after the birth. This kind of health care is more likely to be available in urban areas than in rural ones. If the couple is not out to the healthcare provider, it is highly likely that the nonbiological mother will be seen as a very supportive friend who plans to help out.

As the due date gets closer, the partners, whether in or out of the closet, need to have powers of attorney and wills that specifically cover potential problems during labor. The nonbiological mother should be able to authorize emergency care for both her partner and their baby should the need arise.

Couples also need to decide how they will present themselves to the world as the child grows up. Birth is only the beginning! Will the nonbiological mother go to teacher conferences, school plays, soccer games, and so on, or will she stay in the background when the family is outside the home? It is obviously not necessary to answer all of these questions before the baby arrives, but we recommend discussing your philosophies of child-rearing, and, at least in theory, how you want to share your decisions with the world. One question that couples do need to discuss in advance is the role of the nonbiological mother in the insemination, pregnancy, and birthing process.

Adopting parents

Couples who adopt face, for the most part, the same issues as bearing parents; however, they also need to decide how they plan to apply for adoption. Will they apply together as a couple? Or will one woman apply alone—with or without the adoption agency's knowledge of her couple status? Most adoption agencies will not consider a lesbian couple. But if they do, the partners may find themselves at the bottom of the priority list for healthy infants, if that is what they want. They are more likely to be offered older/disabled/troubled children who have prior histories that make them difficult to place. The same is true when one of the partners applies to adopt as a single woman. If one partner is the legally adoptive parent, the nonadopting partner is subject to the same issues as the nonbiological mothers discussed previously. As with all adopting parents, even when their application is approved, the couple have to wait an undetermined length of time for the child. This waiting can be extremely stressful.

When a couple breaks up

The courts are not prepared to acknowledge, let alone honor, nontraditional family structures. Therefore, difficult as it may sound, it is particularly important for lesbian couples to discuss custody and visitation arrangements in the event that the relationship dissolves. The nonbiological or nonadoptive mother would face an uphill court battle, for example, should her partner decide to take their child away. Generally, both parents want the other to continue to be involved, even after a break up, but it is far better to have thought out the arrangements beforehand, under happier conditions. While they will not be legally binding, they will show prior intent and can give the women a starting point if they agree to negotiate. We recommend that a couple use a therapist or a mediator, when possible, to negotiate a visitation or custody agreement. In that way, the family may be able to stay out of potentially hostile court arenas.

Extra-blended families

When a lesbian already has a child and brings him/her into a new family and then the couple adds another child by birth or adoption, they have created one of the most unusual family structures in our society. This type of family is becoming more common in the heterosexual community as well, and is challenging mainstream institutions to adapt their services to meet this new family model. However, extra-blended, lesbian-headed families are usually not acknowledged—much less accommodated.

One potential problem is that the new child is being reared in a positive lesbian environment while the older child or children may have been reared originally in a heterosexist and homophobic household. Thus, situations that seem normal for one child may be embarrassing or ludicrous or seem immoral to another child in the same family. The child from the previous relationship may have other parents and grandparents to visit and from whom he/she receives attention, presents, and money. The younger child may feel left out. The older child could be jealous of the new one. The children may view the two lesbians differently. One may be a parent and the other just another adult to the older youngsters, while to the youngest child, both are "mama."

Georgette and Sam had been lovers for six years. They lived in an old farmhouse with Georgette's son, Tyree, and Sam's daughter, Theresa. Sam had just given birth to a loud little boy, James. The two older children, who normally fought constantly, were amazed to find themselves united—against the new arrival. He cried too much, got more than his share of attention, and was the darling of the lesbian community in the area. Tyree had not talked to his mother about it. Georgette was so tired from getting up at night that Tyree figured that she wouldn't listen much anyway. "At least he's a boy," Tyree had thought, "Now I'm not the only one."

The issues can be complicated and tangled. Talking among the family, asking friends to bring gifts for the older children if they are bringing things for a baby, spending time with other lesbian-headed families, and family counseling can be particularly useful for these families. It is also important to confront homophobia, both when it comes up, and at other times by educating the children about lesbians and gay men.

In other families, everyone is excited about the new arrival and the family blossoms.

Marge and Toni had adopted a two-year-old deaf girl. Toni's ten-year-old son Mark was very excited. The family had been studying sign language, and Mark was clearly very talented; he was a better signer than either of the women. Until all this happened, Mark had been belligerent towards Marge and angry about the impending arrival of the little girl. Since the arrival of his sister, as Mark called her, something had shifted. He delighted in helping his sister and was even initiating contact with Marge. Toni thought this was due to Marge's praising him so much as they learned American Sign Language (ASL) together. The two women felt that their family was finally going "to happen."

Mothers in extra-blended families have to be very careful about their wills and powers of attorney. The relationships are different within the family, and so are not consistent from one child to another. The partners need to be clear with each other about how they want to present themselves to the rest of the world. Are both of them parents of all the children? Do they parent only their own biological/adopted children? Who takes the children in case of one or both women's death? Can both women authorize emergency health care regardless of who is the legal parent? When the couple is clear, they are more likely to be able to use societal legal processes and institutions to meet their needs more effectively.

Relationships between the family and society

Lesbian couples with children exist within a broader context than their own families. At times, the interaction between a lesbian family and broader society involves legal relationships such as wills, but for the most part, we want to discuss here the situations that arise in everyday life.

Lesbian community

Doreen was finally pregnant! The odd thing of it was—some of her friends were just not excited. They had actually become more distant and less available in the last two months.

Maya hung up the phone. She had just spent two hours talking to her best friend, Susan, who was worried that Maya would no longer have time for her, would become totally baby-focused, and probably wouldn't want to go to the bars to dance anymore. Maya wasn't sure either. She had felt out of sync the last few months, and really was nervous that she was changing into a mother instead of a dyke. And she didn't know that many lesbian mothers in Cleveland with whom she could talk about her feelings.

Janice had just moved in with her partner, Beth, and Beth's two teenaged girls. Janice, Beth, and the girls got along well; the problem was with Janice and Beth's friends. Some of them didn't seem to want to have much to do with the four of them as a family. Other friends, though, especially other mothers, were very excited to have another lesbian-headed family in town. Janice wondered if her friendship circle would change drastically.

While the lesbian community may be supportive in general about lesbians having children, sometimes the translation of that theory is ragged. Some women, who do not want children of their own, like children, but have little idea of how to incorporate them into their world. Others are so afraid of the changes that come with children that they avoid their friends who are pregnant or who have children. Some lesbians have chosen not to have children and prefer not to have them in their lives. Parents need to respect these differing feelings and make time to be with their friends in the various ways that are nurturing to individual people. The friends, on the other hand, need to realize that mothers have less free time than nonparents, and to have patience when they get less time than they would like with friends who are mothers. The issue really isn't whether there will be changes, because there will be; the issue is how we can adjust to the changes, and have friends and children in our lives.

The lesbian community in general is not as child-oriented as the heterosexual community. We have fewer children living with us, and know fewer couples adopting and giving birth. We need to figure out ways to respond to couples who do have children, and the couples need to figure out what kind of help they want from us.

Doreen and Tammy had a party for their friends, and

asked everyone to talk about what they were most upset and most excited about in regard to the baby.

Maya asked her good friend Susan to be present at the birth.

Janice and Beth made a point of spending time alone with some close friends who really did not want to be with the teenaged girls.

Couples can ask for concrete things like company during the day, help cleaning the house, babysitting, or being a check-in person for the teenager. They can also ask for more abstract things, like sharing feelings, the way Doreen and Tammy did, to help in the transition. Lesbians need to ask if childcare is needed when there are mothers coming to events, and in general need to be sensitive to the double role that lesbian mothers play.

Families of origin

Generally speaking, however, it is more tricky for lesbian-headed families to relate to the broader world than it is for them to relate to the lesbian community. One of the most important parts of the broader world is the parents' families of origin.

Kit's parents were dumbstruck when she told them she was pregnant. They hung up the phone and stared at each other. What would they tell their friends?

Tomiko's family didn't take her parenthood seriously when they found out that her partner was pregnant. They assumed that Tomiko would be "like an aunt or something." It wasn't until they saw her with her son, Kim, that they realized she was really a mother.

Our families are almost always surprised when we tell them we want to have, will have, or have children in our lesbian families. They want to know, "How? Won't it hurt the children?" and "How does it affect us?"

Our families can have a devastating effect on us, or they can add to our happiness immeasurably. We need to remember that they may not move as quickly as we would like, or embrace our concept of family as unquestioningly as we want them to. It does not mean that they won't get there, in the end. It does mean that we need patience, and often it means we have to educate them. On the other hand, it can be harmful to maintain contact with a family that is openly hostile, or likely to stage a custody battle. It is not necessary to put up with abuse. We need to take care of ourselves and our children. Sorting out the balance of where to draw the line is the hard part. Some lesbians have told their parents that they will not make visits to them unless the whole family can come. Others have ended phone conversations or visits when parents have begun to say hurtful or abusive things. We think it is a good idea to tell family members of our intention to take care of ourselves and our children this way and then to do it if necessary.

The rest of the world

Children bring us into contact with other worlds we might never touch otherwise. Lesbian parents need to be very clear about how they want the world to see and treat them; otherwise the partner who is a nonbiological or adoptive mother may never be acknowledged, let alone listened to.

Martha went to pick up her daughter Sarah at her father's house for their regular weekend visit. Martha took Kevin with her. He was her three-year-old son from her lesbian relationship with Monica. Sarah's stepmother knew that Monica was Kevin's biological mother. When they knocked on the door, she asked him, "Where's your mother?" He looked at her as if she was stupid. She said again, "Where's your mother?" Finally, Kevin said disdainfully, "Right here," and pointed at Martha. Martha said, "He considers both of us his mothers." "Oh," said the woman, "Kevin, where is your other mother?" He replied, "She's at work."

Kevin did the educating here and the other woman corrected her assumption. We usually have to push harder than other parents for recognition and be prepared to cope with uncomprehending stares.

Barclay was white, as was his biological mother, Sheila. His other mother, Gladys, was black. When Gladys went to get Barclay after baseball practice and he said, "Gotta go, my Mom's here," the coach stared, shook his head and muttered his incomprehension.

When Tanya got into trouble at school, her principal asked for a parent conference. Tanya's biological mother, Faith, wanted her lover, Estelle, to go with her. Estelle was a professor of education at a local community college. Faith figured she could use the support, and besides, Estelle was very knowledgable about children, and about Tanya in particular. The teacher could not figure out which woman to talk to—the "mother" or the "expert."

Roberta and Sally were adopting an East Indian infant. The agency they went through knew that they were a lesbian couple, and had cleared them for adoption partly because of the strength of their relationship. But the court would let only one of them adopt legally. It was important to both women that the world treat them as equal parents; so they didn't tell anyone which one of them was the legal mother.

As a couple gets ready to include children in their lives, they need to decide what roles they want to play—in their families and in their contacts with the outside world. By roles, we mean who will parent, who will talk to school officials, go to PTA meetings, coach Little League, and so on. A particular challenge is how to include the nonbiological or adoptive parent, when most institutions simply do not acknowledge her. At first, the thinking is abstract; then as the child ages, more and more of the child's world becomes a part of the couple's world, and the decisions become increasingly concrete. As we have said earlier, the more advance planning you do, the easier this contact with the broader world will be. This is especially true with legalities such as adoptions, wills, and powers-of-attorney in case of emergencies. How out the couple is will also affect how they portray themselves and their family to the world. A completely closeted couple is not likely to risk exposure by having a nonlegal mother be the main school contact. A more out couple may decide to talk to everyone ahead of time to minimize the shock when contact is necessary—such as with physicians when the children get sick.

Often we have little control over our children's contacts with the world. Our children simply do what is natural for them, as they become their own people. Sometimes these contacts with the world outside the family are hard and painful; often they are wonderful and heartening.

Janet was chewing her nails again. Today, her daughter Heather was bringing home a friend from school. No big deal, except that this friend knew nothing about Heather's two mothers—Janet and Mabel. All of Heather's friends up until now were children of her mothers' friends and were supportive of the lesbian mothers. Some of the children even had two mothers themselves. But now—in five minutes—Heather was bringing home a little girl she had met in the first grade when school started a month ago. Janet wondered what Heather would say, what her friend would say, and what the friend's parents would do. All of a sudden, Heather and her new friend walked in and said hello. Janet held her breath as they walked past her to Heather's room. As the two girls disappeared around the corner, Janet heard Heather's new friend, Janie, say, "How lucky to have two moms. Do you get more cookies ?"

It is difficult in this culture to be part of an alternative family. We need all the services other parents need, but we need to screen them carefully to receive as nonhomophobic treatment as possible. The extra work is draining and can exhaust a couple who are already tired from work and childrearing. Fortunately, the effort is worth it. Lesbians and the children we have so carefully thought about and worked to have and keep can be happy, loving families. The networks we create to survive in a hostile world are, once established, a source of love and support that many other families never know exist.

Chapter 10

How Racism Affects Couples

There is no way to grow up in the United States or in many other countries without learning about racism. It is a pervasive and persistent social poison which affects us all.

We realize that it is difficult at best to discuss racial, cultural, ethnic, class, and religious traditions separately. Even using phrases such as "women of color" and "white women" runs the risk of reducing people to their pigmentation and failing to acknowledge their diversity. We also realize that we are only able to highlight some areas of a very complex topic. Racism affects self-esteem, job opportunities, and an individual's personal comfort and actual safety in walking around in the world, to name a few areas. And racism affects all lesbian couples, whether partners are both white, or both women of color, or are of different races. Just because some women have worked on their racism does not mean it disappears from couple relationships. In order to understand how racism affects lesbian couples, we need to look at what racism involves and how it impacts the individual women in the couple as well as the dynamics between them. Because the women in interracial relationships in particular challenge and confront racism in themselves and with each other, we have focused this chapter on these couples.

Defining language

Prejudice refers to preconceived ideas and attitudes which

This chapter is based on a manuscript by Vickie L. Sears.

are based on a person's being of a particular race or ethnic background or religion, or having a particular occupation or other group membership. We exercise prejudice when we make judgments about others in a generalized way without sufficient reason. Most of us learn prejudices in the growing-up process of accepting the values of our own group. However, we don't always act out our prejudices as discrimination. To discriminate is to act in a way which has a differential and usually harmful effect on members of another group.

Racism involves prejudice toward people of a different race combined with the power to impose and societally reinforce discrimination. The discriminatory actions can be open or covert and can be done on a one-to-one basis or on an institutional scale. Deborah's father, for instance, worked at a company which had no people of color in management positions and had never questioned their absence. The company's practice and the employee's acceptance of it represent institutionalized racism. Deborah's mother and father could not hide their surprise when they found out that Deborah's new Korean-American partner had an MBA and was a highly paid management consultant. Their reaction represents individualized racism.

It is important to acknowledge that people of color may exercise prejudice toward whites or toward people of races other than their own. However, this is not racism, because people of color in this society do not have the institutional/economic power to enforce discrimination

No matter how well we may understand how discrimination happens, to act in a discriminatory way diminishes both the giver and the receiver of discriminatory treatment.

Societal structure

Which groups are affected by racism and how drastic the effects are depends on the social and economic power structure of the society.

Unfortunately, in most countries the dominant culture

has created a hierarchy based on race. This produces both a ranking system of social acceptability and competition between racial groups for access to limited resources, such as jobs and educational opportunities.

The lower a group is in the hierarchy, the more severe the discrimination and the more negative the stereotypes about that group are likely to be. This fact contributes to factionalism within racial groups as well. For example, historically, in white-dominated cultures, lighter is better. If a women of color has internalized this belief, she may put herself down for being dark, may discriminate against her darker-skinned sisters, or may try to associate with lighter-skinned women. Internalized racism is complex. In some ways it is like internalized homophobia; the oppressed individual believes the myths of the dominant culture.

There are other pressures for people of color in a racist society. They have to deal with being seen as the vessels of some special knowledge and experience which is wanted by others and yet not always respected. They always have the potential of becoming tokens when some group or other needs to have racial representation. Many people of color feel a tremendous pressure to be accepted, since they are not seen just as individuals but as representatives of their group. Many report having to perform ten times better than whites just so that they will be seen as being as competent.

Dealing with racism

Sharon and Greta had been walking peacefully down the street, when a small group of white teenaged boys started following them and making racist remarks about "black lezzies" and "nigger lovers." Greta instinctively crossed the street to get away from them, then realized that Sharon wasn't with her. She crossed back and began shouting at the boys, thinking herself very brave. The boys eventually retreated. Meanwhile, Sharon had just kept walking. When Greta caught up with her and asked why she hadn't either run away or fought back, Sharon just shrugged. "Life's too short to spend worrying about a bunch of white boys."

According to Vickie Sears (1987a), a phenomenon which occurs over the years as people of color experience racism and witness its effects on family, friends, and community is the development of what might be called armoring. This means that a woman of color builds a shell around herself as protection from the onslaughts of racism. A woman of color does not have the "protection" and relatively greater freedom to move about in the world that white women take for granted. So she evolves her armor. She learns to watch every new situation and person for potential racist comments or dangers. She learns how to pace her responses to them.

On the other hand, a white woman does not usually have to evolve armor to deal with racism. A white partner of a woman of color is likely to be less prepared to deal with racial incidents, including some of the comments people have been known to make to interracial couples: "It must have been a blow to your family" "Couldn't you find a sister?" "How in the world did you meet?"

Many women of color encounter and anticipate such things as slow service in public places or the condescending use of first names by service providers. White partners typically do not. They may not notice the discourtesies or not understand that the reason for them is racism. They may try to explain the situation away with something like, "The waitress is probably just busy, that's why it is taking her so long to serve us," thus reinforcing the racism. Or they may be totally thrown by the situation.

Sue had always thought of her family as accepting and liberal. They had never made a fuss about her choice of lesbianism or her deep political involvement in Central American issues. Sue was unprepared, therefore, when she brought home her new lover, Dolores, a Salvadoran refugee and activist. Her parents and brothers said all the wrong things, from confusing El Salvador with Nicaragua to telling Dolores that the United States wasn't a racist country and that they had a Black friend.

Sue could hardly wait to get Dolores home to apologize for her family. She was amazed when Dolores told her flat out that Sue had acted as bad as any of them. Sue had put Dolores in a very awkward position by trying to defend her and promote her instead of just letting her be herself.

It took a lot of angry words and tears before Dolores and Sue were able to set up some ground rules for how they would deal with the next racist situation in which they found themselves in. For Dolores it was an unpleasant fact of life in North America; for Sue it was the beginning of learning not to think her good intentions automatically put her in the right.

Dealing with racial incidents typically requires the white partner in an interracial couple to become more aware of the privileges of her skin color. She also needs to develop coping strategies and even armor, but it is because she is partners with a woman of color. No matter how much anger, pain, and fear a white partner feels, it is her partner who is the target of the racism.

The partner of color will have to work through her resentment both of white privilege and of having to teach her partner how to deal with racism. Because the woman of color partner is more experienced, her knowledge and skills can help the couple figure out how to handle these situations. One way to do that is to replay each incident verbally and explore how each partner felt. Ultimately, both will feel less vulnerable.

Couples other than interracial ones can also use this replaying strategy to deal with racism. For example, it is a racial incident when racist remarks are made in an all-white group. White lesbian couples need to address and confront racism as they encounter it.

Work and money

Because of racism, people of color do not have equal access to educational and/or training opportunities and to well-paying jobs. Some interracial couples have to deal with the effects of this inequality.

Carol had a good job as a computer programmer at an insurance company where she met Olivia. Olivia had gone to business school to learn to be a word processor, but had not been able to afford to go further. As a Puertorriqueña she also felt pressure to help her family financially. In the tradition of the white middle class, Carol's family did not expect for her to contribute to the family. Because she earned almost twice as much as Olivia, Carol wanted to pay two-thirds of the household bills. They finally agreed to a fifty/fifty split, since Olivia felt she would be in a hopelessly imbalanced situation otherwise. Olivia continued to provide help for her family, and money was tight for her. After struggling along for two years, Olivia negotiated a loan, with Carol as a co-signer, so that she could go to school for further training.

Not all couples are able to work things out as well as Carol and Olivia. The point is that when there are economic power differences between partners, they need to be negotiated (see Chapter 5) so that both can live amicably with differences in such areas as job prestige and earning power.

Of course, the white partner is not always the one with more education and/or a higher income. For example, Marietta had a degree from Columbia and worked as a lawyer; her income was much higher than that of her partner, Teresa, who was an artist. However, Marietta always felt awkward going to art gallery openings in the small Northwest city where she and Theresa lived. Frequently, Marietta was the only Black person there, and she felt torn. She had grown up going to the Museum of Modern Art and the Metropolitan Museum of Art, and had a strong appreciation for art. On the other hand, she felt extremely visible and not completely comfortable in this particular art gallery scene.

It was only after some painful discussions that Marietta and Teresa were able to acknowledge that some of their assumptions, fears, and expectations about each other were based on their being of different races. They decided that it would help both their careers and their personal lives to move to a larger city which had a more racially mixed community. They knew that the move wouldn't solve all of the problems. However, they realized that a different city could offer them more opportunities to experience and to create racially integrated environments.

Group member adaptations

There are several other situations which require good communication between partners. One of these is related to the fact that many women of color have learned from an early age to be adaptive in their lifestyle. They have had to learn to behave according to white values and expectations when that was needed, and to be themselves within their own group. They constantly shift between two different behavioral expectations. It takes skill and courage to be able to do this. Frequently a white woman does not notice it when her partner adapts her behavior among whites. But, she may notice a great deal and feel uncomfortable when her partner behaves according to, say, Black values and norms when she is with her Black friends. When partners are of different races, one may feel left out if she does not speak the other's language or understand her style of humor. She may feel threatened by, rather than appreciative of, her lover's cultural adaptability.

Ruthie had been clamoring for years to meet some of Denise's relatives in Tokyo. But when they finally got there, Denise was sorry she'd brought Ruthie along. There was a lot of family history Denise wanted to learn and she didn't feel comfortable talking Japanese around her lover. Outside America, Ruthie's manners seemed brusque and her voice loud and abrasive. Until they had a long, frank discussion about it, Denise had been increasingly embarrassed for her lover and had found herself pretending that they weren't lovers, only very distant friends. Eventually, they decided that Ruthie would travel around the country on her own for a while and take responsibility for learning something about Japanese culture, while Denise stayed with her relatives. When they met again in a week Ruthie had more understanding of the culture and was content to enjoy her visit without trying to make everyone like her. Denise realized that she needed to talk more about her feelings instead of distancing herself from Ruthie. Afterwards, they both agreed the trip had been demanding but that they had learned from it.

In addition to pressures from the outside, a woman of color may face pressure from her family or peers to find a lover within her own group. A woman of color who chooses a partner of a different race may be seen as disloyal. She may be rejected by members of her own group as well as her partner's group. She may feel anger and shame for even having feelings for someone of another race. Added to this can be the effects of internalized racism. For example, a woman of color involved with a white partner may be asking, "What's wrong with me that I can't find one of my own kind?" as well as "What's wrong with her?" Paradoxically, her white partner may be asked these questions, too, by her family or friends. Either partner can also grow lonely and become defensive if she is separated from members of her own group.

Unless she has a strong cultural/ethnic identity herself, a white partner may find it hard to understand that her partner wants to spend time alone with a group of her people. It is important that women of color get the validation, support, and comfort that can come from being with other women of color. White partners will need to deal with feelings of exclusion and loss. It is understandable for the excluded partner to have these feelings and to express them. However, it does not mean that the woman of color has to stop meeting her own needs because her white lover feels left out. An appreciation of each other's needs and feelings and open communication are important.

Community expectations

In growing up, many women of color see themselves as a

part of a group where interdependency and cooperative effort promote individual growth within the community. In this situation, the group norms and expectations are very important. White children, however, typically are taught or take for granted an ethic of "rugged individualism." They do not grow up as much with the idea that they are part of a group. This varies, of course, depending on class and ethnic group, but, overall, whites tend to have a more individualistic attitude. When a woman of color comes from an extended family system where everyone is interwoven and interdependent, it often means that problems are handled inside that system. There may be no precedence for talking and problem solving outside the family structure. To lose that family system can be devastating, whether the loss is due to having a partner of another race (prejudice) or of the same sex (homophobia). It means the loss of a crucial support network. Thus, the coming out experience can be very difficult for a woman of color who is strongly identified with her group. Many decide to remain closeted. A white partner, in particular, may not fully understand the risks involved. She may misinterpret her lover's decision to mean that she does not love her enough to come out.

It is important for partners in interracial couples to know the enormity of the pressures their lovers may feel. Those pressures are not necessarily daily, but can be restimulated in different situations.

An additional pressure on many lesbians of color is to continue their group by having children. Issues of genocide, high infant mortality rates, a high early death rate, and racism can all lurk in their minds. In the Native American world, for example, children are seen as being the future. Having children and raising them to be healthy, responsible community members is very important. In this situation, for a woman to choose not to produce children means that there may be heavy community pressure. And most people assume lesbians do not have children (Sears, 1987a). In addition, there are pressures against being very different and against calling attention to the racial minority group; being a lesbian of color may do both. Because of differences in the expectations flowing from the communities or families of origin of women of color, issues of coming out may vary significantly from those of white women. In interracial relationships, it is critical to be aware and respectful of these differences.

Falling into the traps

Another issue for interracial couples is dealing with their stereotypes and expectations based on race. Some whites may wonder if women of color want to be with them in order to enhance their status in the world and gain access to the benefits that come from white privilege. This is a good illustration of a racist belief. In fact, being with a white woman may not enhance her partner's status at all. In the Black community, for example, it would depend on such factors as class background and education.

Women of color may worry about a phenomenon described as "the ethnic chaser." Ethnic chasers are white people who are always eager to be lovers of or partners with a person of color. They may actively seek out being with women of color because they feel guilty about being white at some very deep level, or they seek to acquire color by proximity, thereby proving how liberal they are. A woman of color may experience wariness and even fear about a white woman who has expressed an interest in her. Given the history of cultural appropriation, a woman of color may also be wondering what she has about her, culturally, that attracts the other and could be stolen from her. No one chooses to have these thoughts rumbling through her when she finds herself attracted to another woman, but they may be there.

After a passionate, long evening of lovemaking, Joan said to Aki, "I always heard that Asian women were quiet and passive, but you asked for everything you wanted." The pain that admission caused Aki led to a series of discussions about what stereotypes each woman had about the other's group.

These issues can destroy a relationship; working them through can bring a couple closer. Even if they surface immediately, it may take months before they are discussed. However, the cost of ignoring them is a loss in understanding, trust, and intimacy.

Rhonda, a white woman, and Clarice, a Native American, had only been lovers for seven months. They were both students. They had been talking about the manifest destiny movement, with Clarice giving her perspective on history from a Native American's viewpoint. She suddenly asked Rhonda if she were going to "steal ponies" (this means to take something special without honoring or acknowledging the debt) and use Clarice's ideas in a paper Rhonda was writing. Rhonda got very hurt and angry. It took Clarice a while before she understood that she had treated Rhonda in a prejudiced way, because she had accused her of doing what "white people do"; that is, they always steal from people of color. In the end they were able to sort it through, and laugh, because both of them had thought that the first conflict about racial differences would be initiated by Rhonda.

All relationships challenge partners to engage in an often difficult struggle to confront assumptions, beliefs, and values that can lead to misunderstandings, hurt, and anger. Some women may decide that to enter an interracial relationship is too fraught with perils. Perhaps they've already tried it and decided it was too much work. Perhaps the pressure from their group is too great. Sometimes, no matter how much the women want their relationship to work, they are not able to resolve the racial issues at that point in their lives.

When partners are of different races, there's a lot of learning about new things, and this can cement a relationship and stimulate the partners to grow. As is the case when any lesbians decide to share their lives, there are hazards and joys. Don't let difference keep you from falling in love. Rather, embrace difference for the gifts it can bring to the relationship.

As we said at the beginning of this chapter, racial, cultural, ethnic, and religious traditions are often inseparable.

Values and attitudes about such matters as family obligations, child rearing, ancestors, food, spiritual practices, and homosexuality vary from one group to another. Couples need to become aware of these differences, to acknowledge their importance to the individual partner, and to negotiate incorporating them into the couple's life. For instance, when a couple has a child, it is crucial to give the child positive role models from both parents' groups and traditions. In the next chapter we discuss in more detail how couples can deal with differences such as those based on culture, spirituality, and class.

Chapter 11

Differences

Novelists, poets, and songwriters do not agree on how intimate relationships get started. Some believe in love at first sight; others, that love follows after getting to know a person. Social scientists are just as blind as lovers are supposed to be when it comes to being able to say why two particular individuals love each other. One psychological theory of attraction is that opposites attract. Another is that similarities do. Perhaps we require enough similarity with our partners to provide some common ground, and enough difference to provide interest and challenge.

In the previous chapter we discussed some of the issues that can arise when partners are of different races. Even when they are of the same race, partners may differ in important ways. What is the effect on a relationship when the partners come from different class backgrounds, are of significantly different ages, or have different politics, or values, or spiritual paths? What if they define their sexual orientation differently? Each of these differences affects how a person looks at the world. This has practical implications for day-to-day living.

Class

In the United States, many people deny that class exists. We emphasize individuality and individual responsibility so much that we largely ignore the influence of class attitudes and values on a person's behavior. Each of us is influenced by the class we came from as well as by the one we identify with.

And we are also affected by the class our parents came from and the one they identified with.

Class not only refers to income and education but to a world view—whether you believe you have power in the world and in your life. Being middle or upper class is often associated with a sense of entitlement, a belief in one's rights, and an optimism about future possibilities. This perspective influences attitudes about work and money, about taking risks, and about setting goals. The upper class often makes money without working, while for many middle-class people, work is something that, even if it is not lucrative, should be emotionally fulfilling. From a working-class perspective, work is for survival. If you like it, or if it is creative or expressive, or is what you really want to do, you aren't really working. Historically, for working-class people, the availability of work and working conditions have been under someone else's control.

Josie and her partner Wa-chang realized finally that some of their worst fights happened because they were from different class backgrounds. Josie's family had been the "poorest family in the parish." Wa-chang came from an upper-middle-class background; she could not really remember wanting for anything.

One of their ongoing battles had been about Josie's job at the hospital. Wa-chang wanted her to quit and start her own business. Wa-Chang believed in Josie's talents as a clothes designer and had faith that people would beat a path to her door, once they found out how good she was. Josie was not convinced. She thought Wa-chang was naive about making a business work, and certainly did not understand Josie's feelings. When they began to understand their class background differences, they came to appreciate some of the causes of their conflict. Josie was not just been being stubborn, difficult, and ungrateful for Wa-chang's support. And Wa-chang was not just a naive, foolhardy risk-taker. Each had been approaching the issue from her own class perspective and failing to appreciate her partner's.

Wa-chang grew up believing that the future was bright, and that she deserved having things turn out well. It is relatively easy for her to take risks. For Josie, planning for the future, not to mention taking risks, is somehow asking for trouble. The same risk is a bigger risk for someone who does not have that class confidence. "Going for it" is much easier when you are confident that things will turn out well.

Because many working-class families are poor, this affects later attitudes toward money and security. As adults, some people become very frugal, as Josie did. Others figure they might as well have some fun and spend what they have before it is wiped out by the inevitable future disaster. The very idea of choosing to be poor may be regarded as pretentious and stupid by those from working-class backgrounds. Trying to get along with one car for environmental reasons, or keeping the heat down and walking around with layers of sweaters when you can afford to keep the house warm, or buying clothes at Goodwill when you don't have to are all examples of choices that may appear ridiculous from a working-class perspective.

Possessions had never meant much to Billie. All through her twenties, she prided herself on the fact that she could put everything she owned in a foot locker; and there was no problem getting it shut, either. Not having a lot of stuff made her feel free. She hated the way advertising duped people into buying things they didn't need. She refused to have any credit cards and thought those who did were asking for trouble. She preferred to keep her living style simple and even spare. "Less is beautiful," she was fond of saying.

Her partner, Vera, had grown up poor and hated it. She finally had a good job and wanted to indulge her longing for comfort and convenience. She liked having a dishwasher in her apartment; and if she had to arrange time payments to afford the couch she wanted, so be it. These two had many a heated discussion about how Vera spent money. What always got to Vera was when Billie started lecturing her about materialism and consumerism. Vera figured that she was entitled to a little comfort, and wished that her partner would "get off her high horse."

While Billie and Vera may never agree about "things," they can come to understand each other and to problem-solve specific issues.

For some couples, the issues relate more to growing up *with* money rather than without it.

Diana could have lived comfortably on the income from a trust fund left by her grandmother. She desperately wanted to spend her time writing poetry, but felt guilty about making that choice. She questioned why she should be able to write fulltime when other women in her writers' support group could not afford to. Diana's partner, Estelle, was understanding, up to a point. But sometimes Estelle got tired of hearing about it. Estelle was very practical and could not see the point of Diana's working at a job she hated when she didn't have to. For Estelle it was a simple as that.

Probably the main problems in mixed-class relationships arise when the partners assume that they know what each other thinks or means. Since class differences may not be obvious, partners may fail to understand that their individual perspectives and behavior are outgrowths of class differences. Or they may think that a family feels discomfort with a partner because she is a lesbian, when at least as much of the discomfort is because she is from a different class background.

In general, when there are relationship issues or conflicts in the areas of work, money, taking risks, and making future plans, it is worthwhile to check out how class background differences between the two of you may be influencing the situation.

Age

Sometimes couple differences are due to the fact that the women are of significantly different ages. Of course, it is impossible to say just how much of a difference is "significant." However, an age difference of ten years or more often feels significant to the partners.

As with other couple differences, age differences can have advantages as well as disadvantages. Some areas that age can affect are goals and aspirations, perspective, energy level, and shared cultural history.

Some partners enjoy hearing their older lover tell stories and reminisce about the "old days." Others feel left out, and may even feel discounted because they don't recognize the songs or the names which are so familiar to their partners. Sometimes the older partner may miss the understanding that she experiences when she is with friends of the same age. They have lived through the same cultural times together and have a comfortable sense of shared experience that is missing with a younger lover. In this situation, both women may need separate friends to validate their different experiences.

Many older women have as much or more energy than their younger partners. Where this is not the case, both women may have regrets about not being able to share activities or interests. Sometimes the younger woman worries about her partner's health and possible dependency later. Her partner may be concerned about being a burden or being abandoned. These issues are not limited to partnerships where there is an age difference, of course. Such concerns and feelings need to be aired and discussed. There may not be any definite solution, but at least the partners can work toward resolving them as much as possible.

An older partner inevitably has a perspective which reflects having more experience of life than her lover. Many couples use this to great advantage. The younger woman benefits from her partner's experience and life-knowledge and the older woman has an opportunity to be helpful. Partners need to retain a balance here, however. Having less experience does not invalidate the younger woman's ideas and perspective. Both women need to feel competent and repected.

Cynthia and Marie were not very concerned about their age difference when they first got together. For the most part, the fifteen-year span between them was an advantage. With her schooling far behind her, Cynthia had enjoyed watching

Marie's progress through her graduate training program. She was pleased to offer tips, and knew that their relationship would have had more rough spots if she had not understood, more than Marie, what the pressures of graduate school would be. For her part, Marie loved the feeling of being settled and stable that living with Cynthia provided.

After Marie graduated, she took a "fast track" job with a consulting firm. She was required to work long hours and travel a good deal. At the same time, Cynthia was moving in an entirely different career direction. She had accomplished most of what she had set out to do in her field. She was ready to work less and spend more time relaxing and pursuing other interests. She would have liked Marie to be more available.

Cynthia and Marie realize that their work goals and aspirations reflect, at least in part, their age difference. They are at different stages in their work lives. Their plan is to make sure they listen to each other and discuss how they can satisfy their separate needs as well as nurture their relationship.

Politics

Gina and Bernice met each other at an organizational meeting for a Women Take Back the Night March. Gina was a little intimidated by Bernice at first, because she seemed so sure of herself and so at home with the intense debates over issues like the march route and speakers for the rally. Gina was a newcomer to political action and a little afraid of personal confrontation. Somehow they ended up on the same subcommittee, and have been together ever since. But the relationship has not always been smooth. And much of their conflict has been about politics.

Gina came from a small midwestern farm town. The members of her family prided themselves on being broad-minded and liberal. And they were, but only if you compared them to other people in their town. So Gina's background was pretty conservative, particularly compared to her partner's. Bernice was proud to be a "red diaper baby," so called because her parents were communists. Both of her parents made an intense commitment of time and energy to political activities. Although she did not define herself as a communist and was nowhere nearly as active as they were, she did carry on the family tradition of political involvement.

Gina held back saying anything about Bernice's political views or activities for far too long. She was afraid that Bernice would accuse her of being politically naive, or just plain wrong. She was all too aware that Bernice read more about politics than she did. And Bernice was so articulate that she could dance rings around Gina with her words. So when Gina did express herself, she tended to come on very strong and be somewhat defensive.

Over the years, these two women have fought about a number of issues. Some of their landmark battles have been about food. Bernice hit the roof when Gina brought home items that Bernice wanted to boycott. Once it was a Nestle's product. Then it was head lettuce, and most recently bananas. But these issues were nothing compared to their struggle over Bernice's trip to Nicaragua. Gina was desperately afraid that something would happen to her partner; that she would be hurt or even killed. That was Gina's overriding concern. And she did not hear a convincing argument for why Bernice should go. As far as Gina could see, the trip would not do any good. But Bernice was determined. She believed with all her heart that United States citizens must stand up for peace and self-determination in Central America. Her way of doing that was to go there. She felt that Gina's lack of understanding minimized the importance of the trip.

Although Gina never did completely support the decision, Bernice eventually did go. They discussed it enough so that, although they did not agree, at least each felt that the other had heard her concerns. Both partners wondered sometimes how they managed to stay together when they looked at the world so differently. Often they chalked it up to the things they did have in common; increasingly they credited their good communication. And frequently they acknowledged that their differences brought a richness to their relationship that more than balanced out the conflicts.

Values

Not all couples have to deal with differences that are as sharp as those of Bernice and Gina. But most couples find out sooner or later that their values are somewhat different. Some areas of possible differences are child-rearing, family loyalty, and spending money. Let's look at some examples of these value differences and then address how couples can work with them.

Different values about how to raise children can arise in any kind of family. Blended families, in which one woman is the legal mother and the partner comes along later, seem particularly vulnerable. Such was the case for Doreen and Masie. Doreen moved in with Masie and her three children after they had been in a relationship for two years. Doreen had always thought that Masie was too lenient with the children, although she tried to keep out of it. She liked the children and seemed to get along fine with them until the move. When she was actually living in the same house, she found that some of their behavior was intolerable. Doreen wanted Masie to "shape the kids up" about keeping things neat. She hated that they paid little attention to her when she tried to get them to "clean up after themselves." Masie wanted Doreen to be happy, but she did not want to nag the kids about things she did not think were important. She felt torn.

This kind of situation is difficult because it can get complicated very quickly. And strong feelings are involved when there are children. It can help if the partners get clear that their differences have to do with their values about raising children, not about what is "right" and what is "wrong." They can talk more with each other about how they themselves were reared. This often clarifies where the values come from and puts the current situation in a broader context. In every blended family, the role of the parent's partner must be worked out with everyone—adults and children. And it takes time for the "old" family to incorporate a new member.

Chris resented the hold that her partner Angela's family had on her. If Angela got a letter from home, she would drop whatever she was doing to write back. She called her mother every few weeks, whether they could afford it or not. The final straw came when Angela's father got sick. Chris came home from work to find her partner on the phone making airline reservations for the next day. Angela did not seem to care that she was still on her probationary period at her new job and might lose it. Not to mention that they had been planning for a summer vacation and this trip would eliminate that possibility. Even if Angela did not lose her job, she would use up all her vacation time. Chris was furious. And she was hurt that Angela cared so little about her and about their relationship.

Part of the difficulty for Chris and Angela stems from their different experience and definitions of family. Chris comes from a polite, but not very close family. They see each other once in a while, and call or write every now and then. To Chris, a family is something you come from, and she left home a long time ago. Angela, on the other hand, has very different values about family. From a close knit Puerto Rican family, she has strong ties based on her cultural tradition. Family obligations come first. Not to be with her family in a time of crisis would be unthinkable. It is not that she doesn't love Chris, or that their summer plans are unimportant. It is just that she cannot and will not ignore her obligations to her family. To do so would be to deny who she is. She is very saddened by her partner's inability to understand this.

One of the reasons that value differences are hard is that our values are very important to each of us. And we truly believe that our values are best; maybe even "right." If we thought that other values were better, we would change the ones we have. So it is hard to accept that someone we love and respect actually has values that differ from ours. How can she be so misguided? Or stubborn? Or just plain wrong? When our values are challenged because our partner is different and does not agree, we may forget that our differences are part of what attracted us to each other in the first place. We need to understand each other's values, their history and their meaning. And we need to believe that we can be different from each other, and both be okay.

Spiritual paths

Some couples find that they have differences stemming from their spiritual traditions or from their current spiritual paths.

Corrine grew up in a southern Baptist Black church and sang in the choir. Her church activities were crucial as a part of her support network in her extended family. Sashiko was a Buddist and committed to its spiritual disciplines. They each attended spiritual functions alone and with each other.

From an Orthodox Jewish family, Leah disliked the "Christmas season" intensely. Her partner Sue grew up a practicing Roman Catholic. They were able to compromise some. They exchanged presents with each other on the solstice and Chanukah, and Sue usually spent Christmas Eve or part of Christmas Day with friends who celebrated them.

When Van and Jesse began their relationship, neither of them was involved with a church or with anything they would have described as spiritual. In the last few years, Van had gone to various workshops sponsored by New Age religious groups. Jess was very skeptical but kept her attitudes to herself until Van started getting involved in channeling. That was just too weird for Jesse. She didn't trust the woman Van was consulting; and she didn't really understand it when Van described her relationship with her own personal guides. Jesse started to feel as if Van's guides were running their relationship. Van paid more attention to what "they" said than to what Jesse said. Jesse was afraid that if Van had to choose between her guides' advice and Jesse's, it would be no contest. The guides would win.

Jesse and Van illustrate a situation where partners start off with similar (or at least not different) values, and then one partner changes. The question then is, can the relationship accomodate the changes when one partner moves in a different direction? There is no hard-and-fast rule. It depends on a lot of factors. How good is the communication between the partners ? How much history do they have together that provides a foundation when these changes are happening? How critical are the differences to their everyday life together? How much room do they give each other to be separate? Partners need to be able to be different and to feel comfortable about it. Each of us has to answer for ourselves how different we can be from our partner, and the degree of change in her that we can handle. But these answers cannot usually be predicted ahead of time. It may be that we once thought we could never live with someone who meditates, but when our lover of fifteen years begins the practice, we realize that she is still the person with whom we want to live.

Definition of sexual orientation

Not all women in couple relationships with other women define themselves as lesbians. Some women cannot bring themselves to use the "L" word. Others define themselves as bisexual or refuse to adopt any "label." There are couples for whom the relationship is an extention of friendship. They see it as a unique relationship, in which the gender of the other person is not important. "It is the person I love, not whether they are male or female." If either partner in such a couple begins to identify herself to others as a lesbian, it could result in the end of the relationship, should her partner not be able to accept this change.

Another situation is that of partners who have, from the beginning of their relationship, differed in the way they define themselves. As a child, Gretchen knew she was different; later, she learned that the word for her difference was "lesbian." She had been involved for two years with her partner, Kay. Kay had been married for twelve years and began to relate to women romantically after her divorce. Unlike Gretchen, Kay had always been attracted to men. When Gretchen pushed her on it, she described herself as bisexual, but she disliked using any term which she felt gave her a limiting label.

These two women define their identity very differently. One of the consequences has been that Gretchen is afraid that Kay is not really committed to the relationship. She is sometimes upset by the fact that Kay is attracted to men. She doesn't like to admit it, even to herself, but she feels threatened when Kay mentions that a particular man is attractive.

It is important to remember that the same label has different meanings for different people. One women who calls herself bisexual may mean that she used to be attracted to men but is no longer interested in relating sexually to them. Another woman may mean that she wants to relate to both men and women. The same descriptive label may also serve different purposes at different times for the same person. For example, Kay may describe herself as bisexual as she explores a lesbian identity—leaving her options open. Later she may decide to define herself as a lesbian. At another period in her life she may return to defining herself as bisexual in order to include her attraction to a particular man. What is important about labels in terms of lesbian relationships is that each woman is as clear as she can be about which identity she wants to adopt and what the implications of the identity are for the relationship. For example, if a women defines herself as bisexual, does this mean that she wants to relate to men while she is in a relationship with a lesbian partner ?

In summary, couples can be strengthened and enriched by the differences which partners bring to a relationship, as well as by those which reflect individual growth and change while they are together. When dealing with differences, it is important to remember that stress can play a crucial role. Often partners can tolerate great differences when they are rested, have good emotional and social support individually as well as for the couple relationship, and are enjoying their lives. Differences can seem overwhelming when partners are stressed. Then it is common for them to focus on their differences as *the* problem and ignore other sources of stress. Once again, awareness, and good communication skills can help in sorting the situation out and in working toward regaining balance and clarity.

Chapter 12

Understanding Each Other

We communicate whether we intend to or not. We can't *not* behave, so we can't *not* communicate. Good communication is complex. It includes not only the spoken words but also the music and dance—our voice tones, eye contact, body posture, and gestures. And our actions, or lack of actions, are even more powerful than our words.

Jo insisted that she really did want to spend time with her partner Hortensia's family. But whenever the family invited them over for a visit, Jo was always too busy to go. Hortensia believed what Jo did, not what she said. She concluded that Jo didn't like her family, and wondered if it was because her father tended to drink too much on family occasions.

Gloria got very frustrated when she asked her partner Kit what was wrong, and Kit responded, "Oh, nothing," with a big sigh in her voice. Gloria didn't believe the words when the music didn't fit. Kit's slumped posture and her tone of voice suggested that she was upset about something.

There are many purposes for communication. We communicate to ask for help, to pass the time, to negotiate getting something we want, and, especially in intimate relationships, to get approval from our partners. Often we are not aware that part of the reason for our communicating is to get approval—until we don't get it. Then we feel unappreciated and hurt.

Lucille told her lover Sandra, "I bought some towels today at the January white sale at Sears." When Sandra responded with "Do you think we really need them?" Lucille felt criticized and unappreciated.

On the surface, Lucille was simply conveying information to Sandra about the towel purchase. But beyond conveying information, she also wanted approval and recognition. She wanted Sandra to acknowledge her for being clever and thinking ahead, for being thrifty by buying on sale, and for being considerate because Sandra mentioned months ago that it would be nice to have some new towels.

Self-esteem was a major part of this discussion of towels. This is often the case. We talk about towels, or household tasks, or how we were raised, but self-esteem is the real topic. And when we don't get the approval and recognition or agreement we want, we may feel slighted or rejected. We may get very upset and respond as if our core identity is "on the line" over what seems to be only a trivial matter.

Blocks to communication

Particularly if we are stressed or when the topic is a sensitive one, we may listen poorly and interpret incorrectly.

Tina had moved into Francine's house because neither of them wanted to uproot Francine's children from their familiar school and neighborhood. But Tina had never quite felt it was her home. For one thing, she was used to living in the city, and Francine's house was in middle-class suburbia. Tina had put most of her furniture in storage, except for her desk and her comfortable old reading chair. One day Francine asked Tina if she had ever thought about redoing the upholstery on the chair.

Thinking she heard disapproval and irritation in Francine's voice, Tina blew up. She felt angry and defensive that Francine should criticize and want to change the one thing that had helped Tina feel she belonged in the house.

Out of necessity, we all filter information. It is not possible for us to attend to everything that is going on at any one time. For example, if we are absorbed in reading a book, we filter out the traffic noise and may not even hear someone calling us. In addition to filtering, we also classify our impressions into familiar categories and then fill in the details. We pay attention long enough to decide if the present experience is similar to one we have had in the past. While it is the source of many problems, this classification is also necessary. Unfortunately, as soon as we classify the experience (or person or situation) as *similar* to a previous one, we often act as if they actually *are* the same—whether they really are or not. This, then, becomes one way we help the past to repeat itself.

Clare grew up in an alcoholic family where parties always ended up being drunken brawls. On many occasions she left parties early and insisted that her partner, Melissa, come home with her. If any party got noisy at all, Clare couldn't stand it.

Hilda's last lover left her very suddenly to be with another woman. When her new partner, Lucia, commented that a new co-worker at her office was very attractive, Hilda felt panicked. She was afraid to ask Lucia any more about the woman.

When we filter out some details and fill in others without checking them out, we operate on incomplete and biased information. Sometimes this may work to our advantage, but often it can lead to misunderstanding and hurt or angry feelings.

Another block to good communication is making assumptions. This can take many forms. We may assume that we know what the other person means, or that anything that can be described in words is a fact. We say, "Tammy is untrustworthy," or "Sheila has a great sense of humor," as if these are objective facts rather than opinions. We tend to treat opinions as facts because life moves at a fast pace and there isn't time to gather and carefully evaluate all the information we receive. So we take short cuts. We get a little information, infer the rest, and come to our conclusions. Then we let this all solidify, and from then on we act as if we know the Truth.

• • • •

Different perspectives

We need to learn that other people really do see things differently than we do, and that their view is as true for them as ours is for us. One way to help realize this is to understand the difference between what Richard Stuart and Barbara Jacobsen call "hard" and "soft" meanings. "Hard" meanings apply to concrete items that can be measured objectively like a "table" or a "tree," or to very clear concepts like "grandmother" or "student." "Soft" meanings are much more difficult to define, because they involve personal, subjective judgements. Words like "trust," "respect," and "control" may mean different things to different people, depending on their values, attitudes, and experiences.

Barb agreed to go to her former partner's third Alcoholics Anonymous birthday celebration. In doing this Barb saw herself as "mature" and "unselfish," because she was setting aside her old pain and resentments to recognize her former partner's growth. She assumed that her new lover, Martha, would see it the same way. Not so. Martha felt that Barb was being "inconsiderate" of her feelings and "disloyal" to their own relationship.

Both Barb and Martha believe that their perceptions are accurate. However, it is not an objective *fact* that Barb is being either "mature" or "inconsiderate." These are words with "soft" meanings that involve opinions and value judgements. If this couple confuses fact and opinion, it will be impossible for them to understand each other's point of view. Just as they could argue endlessly without understanding each other in this situation, so a couple can argue about what somebody *really* said.

This is because in any communication there are two real messages. There is what the speaker thinks she said, and what the listener thinks she heard. Whether the interpretations of these are the same depends a lot on the context of the communication. The message always occurs in a context that includes the history of the relationship, the current emotional states of the people, nonverbal behavior, and the overall situation.

Tess and Roberta discussed taking a vacation:

Tess: "I wish we could go to Hawaii this winter."

Roberta: "Hawaii's too expensive and besides I can't take time off work."

Tess: "Well, Ginny and Doris manage to go."

Roberta: "Well, maybe you'd better find yourself a partner who makes more money than I do."

Tess: "Well, maybe I should."

This conversation led to a major fight that left both Tess and Roberta feeling hurt, rejected, and angry.

What happened?

To understand what happened we need to know something about the context of this discussion.

Background

Roberta thought that Tess disapproved of her work at the childcare center because of the low pay and long hours. On her part, Tess felt unhappy that Roberta never seemed to want to have time with just the two of them.

Current Situation

They had just seen Tess's former lover, Ginny, and her partner, Doris, who were leaving for Hawaii in two weeks.

Tess thinks: "Maybe if we went on a vacation together we'd feel closer."

She says: "I wish we could go to Hawaii this winter."

Roberta thinks: "Why is she always suggesting things we can't afford? Next she'll be on my case about getting a different job."

She says: "Hawaii's too expensive, and besides I can't take time off work."

Tess thinks: "There she goes with that work stuff again. I

know she thinks I'm lazy and she has always resented that my grandmother left me that money."

She says: "Well, Ginny and Doris manage to go."

Roberta thinks: "Now she's comparing me to Ginny again. Can I help it if I'm not rich? She has no respect for me."

She says: "Well, maybe you'd better find yourself a partner who makes more money than I do."

Tess thinks:"She doesn't really care if I stay or go."

She says: "Well, maybe I should."

We notice how the topic moves quickly from vacation to finding a new partner. The discussion was really about the relationship all along, but neither woman knew that until they were both too angry to talk about it.

To reduce miscommunication, we need to recognize that, while good communication is complicated, we *can* improve our skills, just as we can learn other kinds of skills. We can learn a set of specific techniques that are particularly helpful in making it more likely that the messages we send are the messages received.

Communication skills

The good speaker tries to be clear and precise. She states exactly what she is thinking, feeling, or wanting. She assumes neither that her listener is a mind reader nor that her listener will not understand. The good listener tries to understand what the speaker intends. She does not fill in the gaps with assumptions and guesses. Good communication means having the impact you intended to have. When this is achieved, the speaker's intent equals the impact upon the listener.

The following skills can help both the listener and the speaker.

Listening Skills

Sometimes we confuse listening with hearing. Our partner asks, "Were you listening to me?" and we pull ourselves away from cooking dinner or watching television long enough to say, "Sure, I heard every word." Maybe we *can* even remember some or all of the words we heard. But we aren't really listening when our attention is divided. Good listening can be described as a commitment and a compliment. When we truly listen to our partner, we make a commitment to try to understand how she feels and how she sees things. As much as possible, we put aside our own judgements, assumptions, attitudes, and feelings (our filters) while we try to look at things from her perspective. Listening is a compliment because we are saying to our partner, "You are important to me. I care about your feelings and your experiences."

Good listening is active, not passive. We have to resist the tendencies to mind read, to judge without asking for more information, or to concentrate on our own response rather than on understanding what our partner has said. *The only way to find out if we understood what our partner meant is to ask*. This means that to be a good listener we have to ask questions and give feedback. We gather information by asking questions about what our partner is saying. Then we need to check out our interpretations by giving feedback to see if what we thought we heard is what she intended to communicate. In this give-and-take of the communication process, we get a fuller appreciation of what is being said.

Let's look at what happens when *neither* partner is using good listening skills:

Caren: "What a day I've had."

Wande: "It couldn't have been worse than mine. First the truck kept stalling so I was late getting to that new painting job. And then the woman was so bossy, she stood over my shoulder all day and complained about everything."

Caren: "The truck always does that. It's no big deal. The profs are piling on so much work that I don't know how much more I can stand. And then I got back my English paper and I got a C."

Wande: "I was ready to blow up at this woman and quit the job, but I didn't want to lose the money."

Caren: "You can bet I'm worried about money, too. Those loans are just piling up, and if I flunk out I'll have to start paying them back and won't even have a degree to show for it."

Wande: "Can't you think about anything besides school? Don't you care anything about me?"

Caren: "That's just great! My profs think I'm a lousy student and you think I'm a rotten partner. I might as well give up."

In this example, Caren and Wande were so caught up in their own situations that they didn't listen to each other. They were competing to be heard, and the conversation quickly deteriorated. Both ended up feeling mistreated.

Good listening techniques by either Caren or Wande could have averted this disaster. Here is one way that Wande might have responded differently:

Caren:"What a day I've had!"

Wande: "I figured something was up when you looked so exhausted. What happened?"

Caren: "The profs are piling it on. And I got a C on that English paper I worked so hard on."

Wande: "You sound really discouraged."

Caren: "I am. I'm not even caught up yet and they just keep adding more tests and assignments. I'm afraid of what might happen."

Wande: "Are you afraid you'll fail?"

Caren: "Yes, sometimes I am. And then I'll end up with all these loans and nothing to show for it."

In this situation, Wande set aside her own upset feelings while she listened to Caren. She asked questions ("What happened? Are you afraid you'll fail?"). By doing this, she got more information about how Caren was feeling, and why.

She also did some feedback of feelings ("You sound really discouraged"). This feedback allowed Wande to check out whether her perception of Caren's feelings was correct. And it was. By asking questions and giving feedback, Wande developed a fairly good understanding of Caren's concerns. And Caren felt understood. After Caren had a chance to be listened to, it was then Wande's turn to talk about her day, and Caren's turn to listen actively.

The initial conversation could just as easily have been changed by Caren as by Wande. Here is how Caren could have used good listening skills:

Caren: "What a day I've had!"

Wande: "You think you had a bad day! I had problems with the truck and that painting job was horrible."

Caren: "It sounds like we'll have a lot to talk about tonight. Why don't you start by telling me about your day?"

Wande: "Well, first the truck kept stalling out so I was late getting to the job. And then the woman kept following me around all day, complaining about everything."

Caren: "That sounds awful. What exactly did she do?"

Wande: "She decided she didn't really like the trim color she had picked out, so she had me change it. Then she kept telling me how to paint. And the final straw was when she blamed me for paint spatters on her sidewalk that I never made."

Caren: "It sounds like you couldn't do anything right."

Wande: "Exactly."

Here Caren took the role of asking questions ("Why don't you start by telling me about your day?" "What exactly did she do?") and giving feedback. ("That sounds awful. It sounds like you couldn't do anything right.") Her questions and feedback helped her be sure that the message Wande sent —the intent—is the message received—the impact.

In each of these examples, both partners asked two questions near the beginning of the conversation. Richard Stuart and Barbara Jacobsen recommend the "two-question rule." According to this rule, the answer to the first question is followed by a second question based on that answer. The two-question rule helps us to stay focused on the other person rather than slipping back into our own concerns. When we show our partners that we care about their thoughts and feelings because we truly listen, they are likely to do the same for us.

Often the situations where it's hardest to use good listening skills are those where we need them the most. One of these situations occurs when we are being criticized or when our partner is upset with us.

Lindarae and Reba had just come home from a party. Lindarae did not feel well before they went. At the party she felt hurt and angry because Reba spent so much time talking and dancing with others and so little time with her. In addition, she had wanted to leave much earlier than they did.

Lindarae: "I never want to go to a party with you again."

Reba: "I didn't realize you were so upset. What's going on?

Lindarae: "You just ignored me all night while you danced with every woman there. And then I couldn't get you to come home. You can be so insensitive!"

Reba: "So, when I danced so much and wanted to stay, you felt bad?"

Lindarae: "Who wouldn't?"

Reba: "It's true that I was having fun dancing, and that I wanted to stay longer than you did. Was the party really awful for you?"

Lindarae: "Well, I really didn't feel good even though I tried not to show it. And then I didn't know as many people as you did. I hoped that you would spend more time hanging out with me. It seemed like you didn't even care how I was doing."

Reba: "I can understand why you felt bad. If I saw it that way, I would have been upset too. I'm sure I could have paid more attention to how you were doing. Maybe we need to work out some signals or have some plans for checking in with each other at parties."

Lindarae: "That sounds like a good idea."

In this situation, Reba did not assume she knew why Lindarae was upset. She asked, "What's going on?" When she got some information from Lindarae, she gave her feedback to make sure she understood ("So . . . you felt bad?") Rather than getting defensive and counterattacking, Reba acknowledged that her partner was correct about some things (Reba had enjoyed dancing and had wanted to stay at the party longer). Then she followed the two question rule and asked for even more information from Lindarae ("Was the party really awful for you?"). When Reba understood more clearly what was going on for her partner, she appreciated Lindarae's feelings, and said so. This gave Lindarae support and reassurance. Then they could both move to learning from this experience and to problem-solving for the future.

In this example, Reba demonstrated good listening skills. She also used other skills that helped make sure that her intent equalled the impact on Lindarae. These other skills are those involved in expressing ourselves.

Expressing skills

Expressing ourselves clearly and precisely requires us to be aware, to disclose ourselves to some degree, and to make sure our body language is consistent with our messages.

Matthew McKay et al. describe four kinds of expression. We express our observations, our thoughts, our feelings, and our needs.

1. *Observations*:

When we express our observations we are reporting "just the facts"—no inferences, no opinions, and no conclusions. We stick to what we have seen, heard, or personally experienced.

I did the laundry this morning.

It was so hot at work in the summer of '83 that they sent us home early five days in a row.

I heard that Bonnie is moving to Toledo.

2. *Thoughts*:

Our thoughts depart from the facts and involve coming to conclusions: developing opinions, beliefs, and theories.

Liana is a wonderful movie. (Opinion)

You were right to quit that job. (Value judgement)

Sex at least once a week is necessary for a good relationship. (Belief)

She must be mad at me because she hasn't called in weeks. (Theory)

We frequently express these thoughts as if they were facts, rather than our opinions or our theories. It is important to remember that our thoughts are our thoughts—not the absolute Truth.

3. *Feelings*:

For many of us, expressing our feelings is difficult. The first part of the difficulty is in even knowing what we feel. This takes practice. It involves getting to know ourselves, becoming aware of our physical responses, since they signal us that we are having a reaction, and becoming aware of the thoughts that go along with specific feelings.

One way to get more clear about feelings is to use the chart below (adapted from John Gottman et al.). When you want to know what you feel, check the chart to choose the best descriptive word. If you are feeling put down for example, where do you feel that in your body? Is your jaw tense? Is your stomach in knots? Is it hard to talk? Or is it hard to keep quiet? Are your teeth clenched? Are your eyes stinging? And what are you thinking? It may help to keep notes or a Feelings Journal to help clarify what different feelings are like for you.

Feeling Chart:

secure	relaxed	busy	close
safe	turned on	happy	warm
loving	confident	strong	overwhelmed
peaceful	enthusiastic	content	sorry
attractive	sad	depressed	
tired	grumpy	hurt	
trapped	confused	guilty	
rebellious	apathetic	ashamed	
stupid	bored	foolish	
anxious	shy	vulnerable	

Once we know what we feel, the next difficulty may be to express it. We may be afraid that our partner won't want to hear about our anger, or will think we are dumb because we feel scared. But shared feelings are the building blocks of intimacy. Sharing feelings about past events is often easier than sharing feelings that we are actually experiencing at the time. It may be easier to start with past ones and then work toward expressing feelings closer in time to when we feel them.

I felt very relieved when you started going to Gambler's Anonymous last year. (Past)

I was crushed when my first lover told me she wanted to break up. (Past)

I feel anxious right now about talking with you because I'm afraid you'll be critical of my plans. (Present)

I am so happy to see you. I feel like I am going to burst with joy. (Present)

When we express feelings, we are not making observations or judgements or giving opinions. "I feel" is different than "I think." Sometimes we can confuse these two.

For example, "I feel attacked" is a feeling. "I feel that you are attacking me" is *not* a feeling. It is an opinion and a judgement about the other person's behavior, not a statement about our own feeling. "I feel hurt" is a feeling but "I feel that you are trying to hurt me" is not. There is a simple way to tell whether a statement clearly expresses a feeling or expresses a thought or a judgement. Look at the word(s) which come after "I feel." "Hurt" and "attacked" each describe a feeling. But "that you are attacking me" is not a feeling and "that you are trying to hurt me" is also not a feeling. They describe the speaker's thoughts, not her feelings. To clearly identify these as thoughts (not feelings) the statement should be, "I think that you are attacking me" or "I think that you are trying to hurt me." Since we may have feelings as well as thoughts, the complete message might be something like this: "I think you are attacking me and I feel very hurt" or "I think you are trying to hurt me and I feel angry about it."

4. *Needs*:

As we have discussed in earlier chapters, it is often hard for women to ask for what we need. Despite the fact that we are the only experts on what we want and need, and despite the fact that no one can read our minds, we may still resist being clear about our needs. We may want our partner to figure out what we need so we don't have to get clear ourselves and ask directly for what we want. If we are afraid to ask, or we believe we shouldn't ask or shouldn't have to ask, we are likely to express our needs in an angry way.

When we try to have an intimate relationship without expressing our needs, it is like driving a car without having a steering wheel. We can go fast but we can't change directions or steer around potholes in the road. Relationships can best grow and change when partners can express what they need in a clear way.

Can you pick up my shoes at the repair shop?

I'm really tired tonight. I'd just like to snuggle on the couch by the fire.

I need for us to set a time to talk about our vacation plans.

Would you hold me for a while?

I need some time to myself this weekend. Can we spend time together Friday night instead of Sunday afternoon?

In expressing our needs, we are not blaming or finding fault. We are simply describing what would help or please us, and are making a request of our partner. It is important to distinguish between *announcing* our needs, and *expressing* our needs. When we announce, we merely make an announcement and leave out making a specific request of our partner. For example, we may say "I'm cold," hoping that she gets the message that we want her to cuddle. However, she may respond to this announcement by turning up the thermostat or by throwing us a blanket or by suggesting that we put on a sweater. And then we may feel hurt that she didn't get the hint. Our chances of getting what we want are better if we add the request to the announcement. In this case, "I'm cold. Would you cuddle with me for awhile?"

Not every situation requires using all of the four types of expression—observation, thoughts, feelings, needs. But if we leave out something or if we mix up the different kinds of expression, our intent probably will not equal the impact on our listener.

Carrie was hurt. She thought her partner Allison was making plans to visit her family and hadn't even asked Carrie if she wanted to be included. What Carrie did was to accuse Allison of excluding her on purpose. Allison had no idea what was going on and got defensive.

Carrie left out a lot in her accusation of Allison. If she had included all parts of the message, it might have looked something like this: "I heard you talking on the phone with the airlines about flights to DC. [Observation] I figure you're going to visit your family for the holidays and don't want me to go because I'm Jewish. [Theory] I feel very hurt, [Feeling] and I need for us to talk about this." [Need]

Our partners deserve to have complete messages. They are then better able to understand us and to change their behavior to meet our needs.

Deanna and Gweneth were just about ready to sit down to a gourmet dinner that Deanna had prepared when Gweneth got a phone call. She was on the phone for some time. When she returned, Deanna said, "Our dinner got cold while you were on the phone."

On the surface, Deanna was making an observation. But she delivered this message with disappointment and anger in the tone of her voice and in her body language. She left out expressing her feelings and her judgement that Gweneth cared more about whoever was on the phone than about her.

When we leave out parts of our message, or when the words and music don't match, our partners are likely to become confused and/or defensive.

Guidelines for expressing

1. *Be aware*

When we decide to express something, we first need to be clear within ourselves about the content of our message and about our intent in delivering it. Sometimes this requires preparation, maybe even rehearsal. Then, we need to be aware and consider what kind of state our partner is in. If she has just come home after a difficult mediation session with her ex-husband about child support, she may not be ready to listen to our complaints about dog hair on the rug. Being aware of the other person also means paying attention to her while we are speaking. Is she paying attention? Avoiding eye contact? Asking questions? Sitting like a lump on the couch?

It is also important to be aware of the context. Is the environment quiet and private, or noisy and full of interruptions? The dinner table with two children under six is not a place to try to have an important discussion. And while a crowded restaurant may be fine for talking about some things, it is not a place to talk about sex.

2. *Be clear and straightforward*

Clear and straightforward messages can feel risky. We

may be afraid of being criticized, hurting our partner's feelings, or not getting what we ask for. However, indirect or unclear messages usually produce the very upset and anger that we are trying to avoid. In addition, we can't get the understanding and intimacy we want unless we are honest about our feelings and thoughts.

Some suggestions for clear and direct communication are:

- *Don't ask questions when you want to make a statement.* Don't ask, "Do you really think we should spend the money?" if what you really mean is, "I'm worried about money and I don't think we can afford a VCR right now."
- *Use "I" messages when expressing your thoughts, feelings, and needs.* "I think you spend too much time with your ex." is clearer and more direct than "All our friends think you spend too much time with your ex." In another example, "I want a hug" is better than "Everybody needs some affection now and then," and "I don't like it when you leave dirty dishes on the counter" is better than "People should clean up after themselves" or "You are a slob."
- *Focus on one thing at a time.* This means staying with one topic rather than bringing in other issues. Don't start complaining about your partner's eating habits in the middle of a discussion about who is going to take the car to work. If you start to get confused because she (or you) introduced a new topic, you can say something like "I'm getting confused. I would like to talk about the car first and get that clear before we move on to another topic."

3. *Be honest—albeit with tact and consideration*

Don't say you are anxious about meeting your partner's ex when you are in fact angry about being pushed into the three of you having dinner together; don't fish for compliments or reassurance by putting yourself down.

In being honest, it is also important to be considerate and tactful. If partners convey too many *trivial* negative thoughts and feelings, the relationship is likely to suffer. So, how do we decide whether something is too trivial to mention? Just stopping to think may make this clear. If not, in evaluating whether or not to express something, we can ask ourselves whether we would want our partner to do so if the situation were reversed. Richard Stuart and Barbara Jacobsen suggest that this helps us to keep the same standards of honesty for ourselves that we require of our partner.

4. *Be supportive*

Name-calling, sarcasm, threats, and unwillingness to listen or consider our partner's opinions are all ways of communicating disrespect.

We are supportive when we respect our partner's opinions whether we agree with her or not. Another way to be supportive is to acknowledge our partner's feelings, whether her reactions make sense to us or not.

Charlene never fully understood why her partner, Kerry, couldn't stand to throw anything away. Even when Kerry explained, Charlene didn't quite get it. But she knew that Kerry had strong feelings about this and she was agreeable to setting aside storage space in the basement for Kerry's stuff.

Eve knew that Nikki disagreed with her about how to handle her boss. Nikki was clear that she would handle the situation differently than Eva. But Eva appreciated that Nikki listened to her and respected her decision—even though she disagreed with it.

All of these listening and expressing skills are keys to good communication. By working at improving our skills, we can increase our understanding of each other. And clearer understanding builds more satisfying, secure, and intimate relationships. Those who have made this difficult journey find it well worth the effort.

Chapter 13

Resolving Conflict

For various reasons, including female cultural conditioning, conflict has negative associations for many of us. It suggests a struggle in which someone wins and someone loses. Even at best, there is an unpleasant clash. Conflicts are painful, or uncomfortable, and are therefore to be avoided. Quarrels are a symptom of a relationship in trouble, of mismatched partners, or somehow of failure.

In fact, to the contrary, differences and conflict are a normal part of life. Partners *need* to deal with conflict in order to establish ground rules and communication patterns for resolving differences and defining goals for the relationship. George Bach and Peter Wyden, in *The Intimate Enemy: How to Fight Fair in Love and Marriage,* refer to the skills which are required to resolve conflict constructively as "fair fighting" skills. Lesbian couples often lack these verbal skills for confronting each other and requesting changes in clear, assertive, and information-producing ways. Much of this is due to being women in a society that trains women to be peacemakers rather than training us to deal with conflict in ways other than giving in.

Elaine and Jean had been partners for three years, and had always spent most of their free time together. Their friends kidded them about being the Bobbsey twins. Jean was very devoted to Elaine; she tried to guess what Elaine wanted and then did it before she even asked. She was a good mind reader most of the time. If Elaine felt good, Jean felt good. If Elaine was in a bad mood, Jean soon felt down. Jean could not stand for Elaine to be disappointed or upset with her. She was very uncomfortable if they disagreed about anything. The idea of a verbal fight scared Jean to death. It was unthinkable.

Jean has a hard time knowing what *she* wants. She is very focused on their relationship and on what Elaine wants. Since she can't stand for Elaine to be upset with her, she avoids knowing or asking for what she herself wants, in case what she wants is not what Elaine wants. She accommodates and sometimes even placates Elaine, at least on the surface. At the same time, Jean sometimes builds resentments. Or she may resist doing what Elaine wants, but in an indirect way. For example, when Jean doesn't want to do things, she often gets a headache. She frequently gets headaches when she and Elaine have planned to go dancing. The only place to go dancing in their area is a local men's bar. Jean hates that bar, but she has never said this to Elaine. So she gets headaches. She doesn't do this on purpose, it just happens.

Asking for what we want

One way to look at conflict between Jean and Elaine, and in other lesbian couple relationships, is that conflict is built on "wanting." Women are taught early in life that wanting is not acceptable. Wanting is greedy, selfish, demanding, and not nice. Good little girls wait until something is offered, share what they have, and should not ask directly for what they want. Getting something means that someone else will be deprived. Since other people's needs are more important, we learn to put their needs first. Jean is a good example of that training. She only wants Elaine to be happy. Then she will be happy. Deep down, Jean is afraid that if she asks for what she wants, she won't get it; furthermore, no one will love her. So she resorts to indirect and even manipulative tactics to try to get at least some of what she wants. At other times Jean convinces herself that she doesn't really want anything, or she gets confused about what she wants, or she makes what she thinks Elaine wants into what she wants. It is hard for most women to believe that we have the right to *have* wants and needs. It is a further step to become aware of what these wants are and to ask clearly and directly for what will satisfy us.

What does Jean do when she doesn't get what she wants? Though she may not be clear in her own mind as to what she wants, and does not ask clearly for what she wants, she does react when she is not happy with what she is getting. She may feel any or all of the following: disappointed, hurt, deprived, angry, betrayed, or cheated. These feelings provide the motivation for conflict. They fuel the struggle for Jean to try to get what she wants from Elaine, or to punish Elaine for not giving her what she wants, or to resist Elaine's pressure to do what Elaine wants. Jean gets headaches when Elaine wants to go to the bar. Then they spend the evening at home, which is what Jean wanted all along but did not ask for directly. Each time that Elaine suggests they go to the bar, they go through this ritual.

This kind of underground struggle happens because women are often fearful of open conflict. There are many reasons for this. Some of us hold to the belief that truly happy couples never fight. Conflict means the relationship is (or soon could be) in trouble. Trained to be peacemakers and soothers, many of us are as uncomfortable with our own anger as we are with our partner's. Anger may have been very controlled and unexpressed in our families. Or we may have grown up with family violence. In either event, many of us may have learned to ignore or swallow our own angry feelings. We give in to our partner and try to smooth over any difficulties.

Whether parents follow the motto of "Never disagree in front of the children" like Jean's parents, or they engage in brawls, their children do not learn how to deal effectively with conflict. The message they learn is that in intimate relationships there are either no disagreements, or that disagreements lead to violence.

Jean models herself after her mother, who was totally attentive to her father. Her mother never questioned her father's judgement (at least in public), never said a harsh word about anyone, and devoted herself to meeting the needs of her husband and children. There was more than a hint of the martyr. Jean remembers her mother sighing a lot and often having a pained expression on her face.

Where conflicts are not dealt with openly and directly, more devious power plays and indirect attacks are likely. Such strategies as "forgetting" something that is important to the partner, "just not being interested" in sex, apathy toward the partner and exaggerated interest in work and other people by comparison, may be signs of smouldering resentments that are not being addressed. Jean's indirect approaches included her headaches. She is also sometimes just too tired to do what Elaine wants. Elaine labels some of Jean's behavior as pouting, but Jean would never admit to that.

Recognizing and expressing wants is linked to self-esteem and a healthy sense of being separate. Jean needs to believe, "It's okay to want; I deserve to have my needs met; I have a right to ask directly for what I want." She also needs to learn that wanting and getting are different. Just because Jean asks does not mean that she will have her request granted. Since she so rarely asks for anything, but waits until it is all-important that she gets it, she is devastated if things don't go her way. Then she convinces herself that there is no point in asking for anything ever again. "I don't get what I want anyway, so why stick my neck out? I'll just be disappointed."

Conflict can change from being a "dirty word" for Jean and Elaine. If Jean gets clearer with herself about what she wants, if she expresses these desires to Elaine, and if Elaine and Jean negotiate about meeting them, Jean's indirect method—developing headaches—will not be necessary.

Fighting styles

Generally, there are three styles of fighting that couples

use to try to get what they want and to resolve differences: withdraw-withdraw, withdraw-engage, and engage-engage. Individual women may usually withdraw or usually engage in conflict, and a couple may fit into one of the styles more often than the others. However, a woman may also adopt a different fighting style in different relationships, or at different times in the same relationship, or about different issues. These pattern descriptions refer to a woman's behaviors, not to some unchangeable personality characteristic.

Where do Jean and Elaine fit in this description of fighting styles? Jean seldom asks directly for what she wants, and avoids conflict. Her fighting style is typically to withdraw. Elaine, on the other hand, is more likely to ask for what she wants and will engage with other people when there are differences. However, when faced with Jean's withdrawal, Elaine tends to withdraw, too.

A more obvious example of the withdraw-withdraw style is Sue and Jackie. They both disliked conflict intensely. When they disagreed, they dropped the subject causing disagreement and avoided each other for a while. They had agreed not to disagree. However, eventually they didn't talk to each other about much at all. Many topics were off limits because they had differed about them before. There were so many hot topics that there was little room for communication, and their sense of closeness was eroded.

Lois and Rene illustrate a different style. Lois tended to withdraw, and Rene preferred to engage. This pattern might also be called the "nailer and the nailee": one woman, armed with a hammer and nails, chases the other around trying to pin her down. For instance, Rene wanted to buy a new couch and Lois wanted to save the money for a winter vacation. The issue came to a head at the furniture store where Rene had insisted on going. Once there, she tried out sitting on all the couches and got very excited about the red velour one. The more excited Rene got, the colder Lois became. Lois hadn't wanted to go into the store in the first place and was certainly not planning to buy a couch. She felt pressured and resentful.

She had been looking forward to going to Florida the following winter and was hurt and angry that Rene was so insensitive to her wishes. Putting her on the spot in the store was just an example of Rene's insensitivity. Finally, Rene asked Lois what was wrong. Lois replied with her usual, "Oh, nothing," which always infuriated Rene. Rene blew up and began to make what Lois would call a "scene" in the store. She demanded that Lois quit sulking and tell her what was wrong. Embarrassed and angry, Lois stormed out of the store.

The third pattern is the engage-engage fighting style. Here both partners are willing to deal directly with the conflict. Depending on their skill, this pattern can lead couples to good resolution or horrible fights. If a couple has good communication and problem-solving skills, direct negotiation works well. If they do not have these skills, they may frustrate each other and, because their anger escalates, they do not resolve the conflict at all.

A model for resolving conflicts

Of those couples who do openly clash, some use conflict to make contact—to feel intensely connected. In a conflict, partners have each other's full attention. The contact is emotionally intense, and for this type of couple, making up is warm and intimate. So some couples quarrel to feel close. Other couples, who struggle with the lack of feeling separate, quarrel to get distance. They may feel enmeshed to the point of not feeling separate at all, and engage in conflicts to establish separateness, boundaries, and independence. In both cases, the approach to being either close or separate is indirect. The fight is often about something else entirely than the real issues. These "magic fights" never get resolved because they don't address the issues. They become rituals. Couples may have almost the same fight about the same thing over and over again without resolving anything. It gets to be a habit. However, if a couple wants to establish more separateness or to get closer, there are better ways to accomplish this than by engaging in "magic fights."

More frequently, however, it is not a "magic fight." Partners actually do have disagreements, differences, or dissatisfactions. As we mentioned previously, a major problem for lesbian couples often is that we have not developed good fair-fighting skills. To help remedy this, couples can use the following format to work on resolving the conflict.

The most effective way to deal with conflicts involves each partner's getting clear about what she wants and feels, expressing these, really listening to each other, and then problem-solving to resolve the issue. Obviously this requires self-awareness on the part of each partner. It also requires goodwill and a genuine commitment to work on resolving the problem. We have found that a "how to" model, which structures the process into steps, has been useful for couples. The following eight-step model has been adapted from *Self Care* by Jetta Bernhard and from *Parent Effectiveness Training* by Thomas Gordon.

Step 1: Warmup

This is a solo part, where you need to ask yourself the following kinds of questions. Am I really angry, or only mildly irritated? What do I want my partner to do or not do that is different from what she is doing or not doing now? What specifically do I dislike, or do I want? Do I really want this change or do I want to hurt my partner? Is this fight really important to me? Are my feelings in proportion to the issue?

Step 2: Set the time

Get your partner to agree on a definite time to resolve the conflict. You may have to be persistent to get some time set aside for this purpose. If you encounter some resistance, be persistent—tell her that the issue is important to you and that it hasn't and won't go away until you talk it over. Try to set the time for as soon as possible, but also respect your partner's wants here. You may wish to set a maximum amount of time, as well, since you can always decide to continue the discussion later. Sometimes it is easier to get agreement on meeting for fifteen minutes or a half hour, rather than leaving the amount of time open. If you do not finish in the time you agreed upon, arrange to continue for another set time period, or arrange to continue at a specific later time.

Step 3: State the problem

Clearly describe what your partner does or does not do that you don't like. Keep it to the point, simple, direct, and short. It is very important to stick to the *facts*, without blaming and without adding your feelings about the behavior. If you have a hard time being clear or keeping your feelings out of it, you may need to practice this step in advance—i.e., rehearse what you are going to say, your tone of voice, and so on.

Step 4: State feelings

Use "I" messages to describe how you feel—"I feel angry, hurt, disappointed, confused." Avoid the blaming quality of "you" messages, such as "You make me feel so mad when you just sit there like a lump." Instead, take responsibility for your reactions and feelings and say "I feel mad." Also include the other feelings you may have underneath, or secondary to the anger, such as "I'm scared about feeling so angry and about talking with you about it. I'm really nervous right now." It is essential to resist the temptation to blame your partner for your feelings and to end up with " . . . and it's all your fault that I feel the way I do." Blaming will likely lead to your partner's getting defensive (after all, she has been attacked and blamed), and then the fight is harder to keep on a constructive tack.

Step 5: Make a specific request

Ask specifically for what you want. Make your request simple, clear, and direct. You want your partner not to do, or to do, what? Avoid asking for changes in "attitudes" because these are not specific. For example, "I want you to be more considerate" is not specific enough. Exactly what is it that you want her to do or not to do that would show you consideration? Asking her to "clean up her dishes" is also not specific enough. It it showing the consideration you want if she brings them from the living room into the kitchen? Or do you want her to pile them in the sink? Or wash them and leave them in the rack? Or dry them and put them away?

Step 6: Respond and negotiate

This is where the partner who has been on the listening end gets to talk. In the best of cases, she will really have been able to listen without getting defensive and will have checked already, or will check at this point, that she clearly understands the problem, your feelings, and the specific request you have made. She can make this check by summarizing; for example, "Let me make sure I understand. When I don't call and let you know that I will be late, you worry about what may have happened to me. You want me to call if I will be late, so that you won't worry."

The partner then responds to the proposed change—not to your feelings about the problem or to the questions of whether or not it is a real problem. Telling you that you should not feel the way you do, or that the problem is not a real one are not acceptable responses. Appropriate responses to specific requests usually take one of the following forms:

- Yes, I'll do it.
- Yes, I agree, with the following conditions. (The conditions must relate directly to the proposal and not involve some other issue as a trade—the reason being that this introduces another whole issue, and may take the negotiations off track.)
- No, I won't do it. (This may indicate some hostility or some previously unshared strong feelings/wants.)
- No, I don't want to do that, but I would be willing to do this. (Makes a counter proposal.)
- How about a time out? Let me think about this until (a specific time in the future.)

Step 7: Reach resolution

If you have come to an agreement on dealing with the request for change, then the conflict is resolved. Set a trial period for the new behavior. At the end of the trial period, you can meet again to modify or continue the agreement. Agreements for changes can be renegotiated whenever they stop serving the needs of either partner.

If you have not been able to reach agreement in the time allotted, make an appointment for another session and declare this one over.

Step 8: Clarify the agreement

Repeat the agreement aloud, in turn, making sure you both have exactly the same understanding about it. It's a good idea to write the agreement down on paper, because our memories are often imperfect.

A variation on the theme of this format applies when one or both partners has identified a problem behavior or a problem issue, but does not have a specific request directed toward resolving the situation. The model that applies here might be the following.

The first four steps are the same:

Step 1: Warm up

Get clear about what the behavior or issue is. Ask yourself the questions listed above.

Step 2: Set the time

As before.

Step 3: State the problem

This involves both partners' giving their perspective on the issues, not in a defensive way, but rather stating all the *information* they have about the problem or issue. An example might be the topic of planning vacation times and places in advance. What are the facts surrounding this issue?

Step 4: State feelings

Again, one or both partners might have feelings about the issue that they could share, using the "I" message format. That is, each woman states her feelings prefaced by "I feel . . ." and avoids blaming the other for causing the feelings.

For this step, rather than one partners responding to the other's request, both partners toss out ideas for possible solutions. In a brainstorm, all ideas are shared—practical or not—without evaluation, in order to encourage the fullest and most creative solutions to emerge. Both partners are encouraged to get their ideas out. Avoid the that-won't-work-because mentality. Wait until later to evaluate the ideas.

Step 6: Pick a solution

Once all the ideas for a solution are out, partners negotiate around which solution or combination of approaches appeals to them.

Step 7: Reach resolution

As before.

Step 8: Clarify the agreement

As before.

In using this format, some suggestions for troubleshooting may prove useful.

- *If you get too angry to continue or the process is going off track:*

  Use the "time-out" tactic. Time-out means just that. It is a break in the action, much as is used in sports, to give the partners a chance to regroup, get calmed down, plan their strategy, and so on. Both must agree to abide by the time-out; i.e., one person must not follow the other through the house trying to re-engage her in discussion before the time-out is over. The person who calls for a time-out needs to specify how long she wants. (We suggest longer than five minutes, and shorter than twenty-four hours.) She can always reapproach her partner after one time-out and request another, if they need more time.

- *If you have a tendency to blame:*

  Practice the "I" message technique. This involves describing your feelings *as* your feelings; e.g., "I feel hurt when you . . ." It is important not to confuse "feel" with "think." "I feel that you are a creep" is *not* an "I feel" message. It is an "I think" statement. To tell the difference, look at the word which follows the word "feel." Is it a feeling or is it the word "that"? If it is "that," we know that "that" is *not* a feeling.
- *If you have trouble listening, or if either of you feels unheard or not listened to:*

  You might practice repeating the speaker's ideas back to her (or even in your own mind), to make sure that you didn't miss anything or misunderstand. The key thing is to check out your understanding of what the speaker has said before you respond with your ideas or point of view. Keep in mind that the speaker is the expert on what she said. Don't go on until she says she was heard accurately. So often we have a misunderstanding in communication that occurs very early in the process, and everything gets off on the wrong foot.
- *If you store up old resentments and then throw them into each fight:*

  Make a grievance list that contains all the things that you ever resented or were hurt about. Don't leave anything out. Then go through the list. Cross off any that you really can let go of. Now look at the others to see which ones might be suitable for the conflict resolution process. Go through the eight steps outlined to address the items on your list.
- *If you find that you are just not able to fight fair, or that your fighting styles are creating worse problems than the issues you started off fighting about:*

  Get some outside help. Go to a workshop, read a

book, see a counselor, or use whatever other interventions are likely to improve your communication skills, your understanding of yourself and your partner, and your fighting styles.

Violence

While conflict is inevitable and can be made constructive by learning healthy styles of confrontation, violence is never necessary.

Physically abusive relationships *do* exist among lesbians. Althea Smith reports that the dynamics are similar to those in abusive heterosexual relationships. The woman who is abused loses her sense of personal power, confidence, and control. Which partner is abused does not depend on size, role, or physical abilities. The woman who abuses often has low self-esteem, few anger management skills, is afraid of losing control over her partner and over herself, and believes that violence is permissable. The sequence of eruption and violence is followed by guilt, apologies, and promises of "never again." A honeymoon period of closeness is followed by a repeat of the violence. Alcohol or drugs are often, but not always, involved.

Until recently, violence in lesbian relationships has not been well documented. One reason for this is that the women have not identified the behavior as abusive. Women who grow up in families where abuse is "normal" are particularly prone to minimize and/or fail to label their partner's behavior—or their own—as abusive.

Marnie grew up in a violent family. Her mother was physically abusive, and both parents kept up a steady stream of criticism, put-downs, and threats directed toward Marnie and her younger brother. Marnie was regularly accused by them of being "stupid," "worthless," and "a dirty slut." They threatened the children with physical beatings and with being abandoned if they did not do what their parents wanted them to do. There were enough beatings to make these threats quite believable. This was all "normal" family life.

Marnie's first partner, Judy, had a "short fuse," as she described it. When Judy lost her temper she usually directed her anger at Marnie. She blamed Marnie for whatever had gone wrong—and yelled and screamed a lot. Because Judy had never physically assaulted her, Marnie did not think of Judy's behavior as abusive. Judy's yelling and the things she said were not as bad as what Marnie had grown up with. She did get scared when Judy blew up, and her feelings were hurt by Judy's attacks, but she did not realize that she was being abused. After each episode, Marnie minimized it—"It wasn't so bad," or "It didn't really bother me too much," or "That's just how Judy is." She did not label Judy's behavior as abusive—so she just put up with it.

Another reason for the lack of documentation is that even when a woman knows that her partner is being abusive, or that she herself is abusive, it is kept secret. This can happen out of feeling afraid or ashamed, or because of lack of support in the lesbian community.

Adrienne was so intimidated by her partner Helen's threats of suicide that she hardly went anywhere anymore except to work. Helen wanted her to stay home—and she did.

Randa and Jane both felt guilty and ashamed after they would "lose it" in a fight and end up screaming and hitting each other. Neither of them would even think of telling anyone. It was too embarrassing.

When Tamara finally admitted to herself that her partner Joy's behavior was abusive, she was mortified. She blamed herself for allowing it to happen. With her stance of "I should have known better; I should have stopped it before it got to this point," it was hard for her to tell even her counselor about the situation.

When Dionne summoned up the courage to tell some other lesbians about the beatings by her partner, May, they were shocked and disbelieving. "I just can't believe May would do that," and "You must have done something to provoke her" were typical responses. When Dionne finally made the break from May, she also left the area where she had lived for ten years, because she had felt such a lack of support from the community.

Although some abusive behaviors are more dangerous than others, most of them are potentially dangerous, and all show a lack of respect and an attempt to intimidate and control the partner. This abusive behavior and violence to achieve power and control over a partner is the focus of an analysis of lesbian battering by Barbara Hart. Hart recognizes that there are situations in which both partners are abusive; both may be physically violent; or one may be abusive physically while the other abuses verbally. While she opposes all violence, Hart distinguishes between incidents of violence and the phenomenon of battering. The critical ingredient in her definition of battering is that the batterer uses violence or abusive behavior to gain *power* and *control* over her partner. She defines battering as "the pattern of intimidation, coercion, terrorism or violence, the sum of all past acts of violence and the promises of future violence that achieves enhanced power and control for the perpetrator over her partner." An abused woman is battered if she is "controlled or lives in fear of her lover because of actual attacks, or threats or gestures."

How do you know if the patterns in your relationship are abusive? One way is to think of abuse as being along a line from mild to severe. At the severe end are behaviors like forced sex, choking, beating, and hitting with objects like sticks. At the milder end are behaviors like name-calling, verbal threats, and insults.

It took Dorothy some time to realize that her partner's behavior was emotionally abusive. Esther's criticism and belittling were often subtle. She constantly said things like, "Let me fix that because you'll probably break it"; "Are you sure you're really qualified for that job you are applying for?" and "You look so much better since you lost weight, but now your clothes look awful on you." No one of her comments was all that bad, but the sheer number of them and her tone of voice combined so that Dorothy felt her confidence undermined and her self-esteem dropping.

During the time they were involved with each other, Melinda thought of her partner Lynn's behavior as cruel when she got angry but not as abusive. Lynn never actually hit Melinda, and she never even threatened to. What she did do was break Melinda's things, or tear up her writing, or somehow destroy something that was important to Melinda. Afterwards she would apologize and buy Melinda a present, trying to replace what she had ruined.

One of the problems with abuse is that it escalates so that even behaviors which might be considered mild may be indications of a growing tendency. It gets worse. Another problem is that *both* partners in an abusive relationship tend to minimize the frequency, intensity, seriousness, and impact of the abuse. Abuse is always unhealthy—to give or to get.

For women who know who they are or wonder whether they are being abused—get help. Contact a counselor or a women's shelter or someone who can give you support to find the resources you need to get clear and change your situation. The book *Getting Free* (1982) by Ginny NiCarthy clearly identifies what abuse is and how to get out of an abusive relationship. *Naming the Violence: Speaking Out about Lesbian Battering,* edited by Kerry Lobel, is written by and for battered lesbians and those who work with them. (See bibliography for additional resources.)

And to therapists working with lesbians and lesbian couples, our recommendation is to check for abuse and not assume there is none because abuse and battering don't happen in lesbian relationships.

In summary, the ability to resolve conflicts is a skill. And skills can be learned. Everything we have discussed in this chapter, from expressing wants, to listening, to the eight steps for conflict resolution, gets easier with practice. We believe that each of us can learn to resolve her conflicts more constructively, and eliminate destructive conflicts and violence.

Chapter 14

Recovery

It takes the first twenty or thirty years of our lives to accumulate the experiences and develop the patterns of thinking, feeling and behaving that we spend the next thirty years trying to understand, unravel, and, in some instances, change. Although the term *recovery* has come to be associated with addiction, all of us, in a sense, are recovering from something. We may be recovering from not getting what we needed as a child to grow up confident and sure of our specialness and worth. Or we may be recovering from being married. Or we may be recovering from the effects of sexual or physical abuse, or from severe depression and anxiety, or from addiction to food, alcohol or drugs. Individual therapy, Twelve Step Programs such as Alcoholics Anonymous, and self-help reading and groups are some of the ways women seek help in the recovery process.

Aspects of all these recoveries have an effect on the couple relationship. While every person and every recovery is unique, and no couple relationship is exactly the same as another, certain patterns are common. Some of these patterns involve confusing or hurtful behavior; others are constructive, and facilitate the recovery process. In this chapter we review the impact of a number of painful experiences and offer suggestions for couples where one or both partners are recovering.

Needing and talking

In general, any woman who is in recovery is focused on

her own healing. This partner in a couple may therefore be self-absorbed. She may not have much attention left over to give to her partner. In addition, she may want a great deal of support and understanding from her lover. Her partner may be torn between wanting to be supportive, at the same time resenting the demands for her time and emotional attention. If both partners are focused on healing themselves, it is likely that both are feeling needy at the same time. This situation can lead each partner to feel uncared for and unloved by the other.

The recovery process puts less strain on the relationship when the women can be clear with each other about what they are thinking, feeling, and wanting. Self-awareness and good communication don't guarantee that this situation will be easy, just that it will be easier. But sharing these ambivalent feelings may be a problem in itself. Many women will need help to do this.

If one woman knows very little about the effects of her partner's experience and the recovery process, she will need to educate herself. She may find it useful to go to an appropriate support group meeting if it is available, and to talk to others who have gone through this experience. She could also consult with her partner's (and/or her own) counselor, and read or otherwise seek out information that will help her to understand and deal with her partner's and her own experience better.

In the following sections, we will look more in depth at some of the issues in recovering from specific kinds of experiences, and how each of these affects couples.

Incest and child sexual abuse

The statistics about sexual abuse are staggering. In her book, *The Secret Trauma*, Diana Russell estimated that thirty-eight percent of females in this country are sexually molested before the age of eighteen and that one in five is an incest survivor. In a recent survey of 1566 lesbians, JoAnn

Loulan (1987) found that the same percentage—thirty-eight percent—reported childhood sexual abuse. Some women are raped by strangers, but perpetrators are more likely to be an acquaintance. For many, the abuse occurs in the family. The abuser may be a father, a mother, a grandparent, an uncle, a brother, a stepfather, or a trusted family friend, neighbor, or babysitter. Sexual abuse may be a single incident or go on for years. It may be combined with physical or emotional abuse, or it may not.

The impact of sexual abuse in childhood varies, depending on all kinds of factors. These include how old the woman was when it happened, how long it went on, who the abuser was, whether physical violence was involved, and how adults responded if she "told."

Whatever the circumstances, sexual abuse is never the child's fault. It is the adult who is responsible. We cannot emphasize this enough. Unfortunately, children typically blame themselves for the abuse. In addition, those who abuse children often play upon this tendancy by assigning blame to the child. "It's your fault; you tempted me." Secrecy exaggerates the confusion, guilt, and shame. Usually the child is told not to tell: "It's our little secret." She may be threatened. Threats range from emotional punishment: "Mommy would be angry" to physical harm: "I'll cut you up in little pieces."

Beyond blame and secrecy, being used as a sexual object by a trusted adult inevitably produces feelings of guilt, confusion, shame, and fear in a child. The child has no "safe place." She is not safe in her family, in her home, or even in her own body. The experience is such a burden that many abused adults report that they did not remember about the abuse until they were well into their twenties or thirties or older.

There are a number of implications for lesbian couples in these patterns. One is that the odds of at least one member of the couple having a history of sexual abuse are greater than with other couples, just because there are two women. Another implication for lesbian partners is that the impact of sexual abuse is never limited solely to a couple's sexual relationship. Incest is an emotional violation. Incest survivors often have difficulty trusting and feeling emotionally safe with their lovers. This is certainly understandable since, in their experience, intimate relationships are associated with violation, betrayal, and abandonment. An abused child is forced to ignore her inner self in order simply to survive. As a result, the adult woman often does not know how to set limits based on what she wants and does not want. This may be the case in sex as well as in other areas of her life.

As for sexuality itself, survivors may place great importance on sex in their adult lives, or they may de-emphasize it. They may also do each at different times. For example, many women decide not to be sexual while they are working on the abuse issue in therapy. This decision can be expecially painful and confusing to their partners, who want to be supportive, but who also want to be intimate sexually. Partners may understand but still feel disappointed or rejected. It can help to understand that their personal attractiveness is not the issue. Also, couples can explore alternative ways of being intimate. Romantic dinners, long talks and love notes can provide occasions for intimacy without sex.

Healing from incest and early abuse is a difficult process for both the survivor and for her partner. However, the secret is out and help is available. With all the attention now being focused on child sexual abuse, many women are coming out of the closet about being survivors of childhood abuse. The good news, amongst all this bad, is that talking with each other about this widespread problem is yielding new information and new ways to heal survivors. We offer some suggestions later in this chapter. Other books address this topic in some detail. JoAnn Loulan's books (1984, 1987) include suggestions and specific exercises for lesbian incest and rape survivors, as well as for their partners. Another excellent and lesbian-affirming resource is a book by Wendy Maltz and Beverly Holman called *Incest and Sexuality: a Guide to Understanding and Healing*.

Adult children of alcoholics

Many people, including many lesbians, grew up in families with an alcoholic parent or parents. In recent years we have learned a great deal about the later impact of this experience. A number of patterns have been identified as characteristic of adult children of alcoholics (ACOAs). However, ACOAs are not the only people with these patterns. Growing up in a family where one or both parents are unavailable because of physical or emotional illness, for example, can have similar results.

There seem to be four general patterns that children adopt to deal with the stresses of growing up in such families. The oldest child often adopts a "caretaker" role. Caretaker children are super-responsible, serious, capable, and old beyond their years. "When you are six years old, and your mother is drunk so she can't make dinner, and she won't let you in the kitchen, you have to get good at figuring out how to get something to eat."

Other kids become "pleasers." They try to keep the peace and keep everyone happy. They try to meet their own needs for love by trying to meet the needs of others. "I thought if I was just good enough, or smart enough, or pretty enough, that my dad would stop drinking and be a dad again."

Some children tune out. Claudia Black (1981) calls this child "the adapter." These kids soak up the tension and emotion, but show nothing. Later, they may not even remember much of the violence or dramatic childhood incidents, because they were engrossed in watching TV or listening to records through it all.

The fourth type of response can be seen in those children who become addicted to alcohol or drugs themselves, and create "problems" for the rest of the family.

Again, the implications for the lesbian couple are broad. Growing up in an alcoholic family often means a childhood littered with broken promises; with incidents of violence or threats; with crisis after crisis; or with just plain neglect, inattention, and unavailability. Recovering ACOAs are involved in learning how to think, how to feel, and how to trust. These are all things they learned not to do growing up, as a price of survival. A woman who did not come from this kind of family background may find it hard sometimes to understand her partner's behavior.

Joan, for instance, travelled a lot with her job. Every time that her partner, Dee, offered to pick her up at the airport, Joan thanked her—and then outlined a backup plan in case Dee couldn't make it. Eventually, Dee became offended at this behavior and accused Joan of not trusting her. Joan was operating out of old habits she had developed from growing up in a family where you couldn't count on people. As a child, often something did "come up," and her alcoholic parent would fail her. Dee took Joan's behavior personally. She assumed that Joan's response was related to her and to her trustworthiness.

The need here is for Joan to see her pattern as belonging to the past, and for Dee to be clear that Joan's behavior is not a response to her. When children grow up in alcoholic (or other poorly functioning) families, they may also have little idea about what a positive relationship between adults would be like. Craziness was so "normal" in their family that they do not know what is reasonable to expect from others. ACOAs often miss the chance to learn many basics. Nobody told them, taught them, or modeled appropriate behavior for them.

Diane was never sure whether her behavior was really appropriate, especially in social situations. Her mother was alcoholic, and her father had been severely depressed as far back as she could remember. She described her mother as having been "off the wall" most of the time, and says about her father: "He never did much at all." Consequently, Diane had very few internal standards on which to base her ideas of what was okay behavior and what was not. Instead, she relied on others. If they said she was appropriate, she was. If someone said she was out of line, she figured they were right.

As a result, she had gone along with almost everything her partner Barb wanted. And Barb was none the wiser. She just assumed that Diane was in agreement with her.

Four years after they had started living together, Diane had gone into therapy because she was so depressed. It had been a long haul and a lot of hard work, but she eventually felt clearer about what she thought and felt, and more confident about expressing herself. She credited therapy and her Al-Anon program with helping her make these changes. There were times when Diane was not sure that her relationship with Barb would survive. But they weathered the rough spots. Their relationship, in fact, had improved and they both felt that the hard times had been worth it.

Not all ACOAs choose to enter therapy or to work a Twelve Step program, such as Al-Anon, as Diane did. Different people find different tools helpful in working toward their goals for themselves and for their relationships.

However, because ACOA patterns and characteristics have now been identified, more kinds of help are available. In addition to Al-Anon groups, for those whose life has been or is affected by an alcoholic, there are local chapters of Children of Alcoholics (COAs) in many cities. These are also self-help groups modeled on the Twelve Step Alcoholics Anonymous (AA) program. In many areas, private therapists and agencies offer workshops and groups specifically for ACOAs. A number of very readable books are now available. Those listed in the bibliography are useful both for ACOAs and for their partners.

Combination of abuse

Some lesbians come from a family where they got it all. They had one, or two, alcoholic parents, and were sexually, physically, and/or emotionally abused. Other women have parents or guardians who demonstrated some, but not all, of these behaviors.

Abuse can be physical and emotional, as well as sexual.

Physical abuse is being hit, punched, slapped, beaten, or punished to the point of injury. Emotional abuse is psychological injury resulting from such practices as belittling, name-calling, and threats of punishment or abandonment. Neglect may also be either physical or emotional. A physically neglected child does not receive the basics, such as food, clothing, and medical attention. Emotionally neglectful parents ignore their children, don't talk to them, don't hold them, and show no interest in them. These parents are not emotionally available.

Regardless of the type or combination of abuse, adults who were abused as children carry the after-effects of this abuse. We have discussed difficulties with trust, and with knowing what is appropriate behavior and what is not. Another major problem area is self-esteem. Abused children rarely understand that it is their parents who have the problem. Most abused kids grow up thinking they are bad. They may feel unworthy and unlovable. As adults, it is hard for them to believe that they have something to offer that anyone else would want. In the recovery process, an abuse survivor may seesaw. First she may want a lot of reassurance that she is okay to the point of appearing to be clinging; and then she may abruptly switch and push her partner away, insisting that she neither needs nor wants anyone.

And what kinds of feelings and reactions does the partner who was not abused have? Mary and Dot provide one illustration.

After Dot went into therapy, Mary learned more than she ever wanted to know about how badly Dot had been abused as a child. She felt so bad for Dot that she had been determined to protect her—in fact, to provide a totally warm and nurturing environment for her. To do this, Mary had vowed to herself that she would avoid conflict entirely, by going along with everything that Dot wanted. However, Mary had experienced great difficulty in holding back comments when Dot talked about attending her family reunion. Mary had been so angry with Dot's parents, particularly her father, that she could have cheerfully strangled him. She had not been able to understand why Dot did not feel the same way. But Dot did not; and so Mary had felt alone and stuck in her anger and helplessness.

Mary had some of the typical responses that partners have. It is common for partners to want to protect and make up for the past abuse. Partners also may be very angry with the abuser(s) and/or the parent(s) who did not protect the child. Another frequent reaction for partners is feeling impatient with the recovery process of the abuse survivor. Partners usually want the recovery to be over, so that the couple can focus on the present and their life together. Impatient partners may then feel guilty about their impatience.

Abuse survivors need to get the help they need to recover, and whatever amount of time that recovery demands. Dot needs to know that her internal timetable may not be the same as Mary's timetable for her, and that it is her own pace she needs to follow.

Partners of abuse survivors also have needs. These partners become victims of incest too, in that they cannot change the past and must deal with the consequences of the abuse in the present, on a daily basis. If Mary is to grow and change in this process, she needs to give herself permission to have feelings and to talk about her reactions. If it is not appropriate, or possible, to do this with Dot, Mary needs to seek support elsewhere. For example, Mary has every right to have her own feelings and reactions about Dot's father. However, Dot may be so involved in working out her own feelings that she has little energy for dealing with Mary's.

Partners need to practice self-care and patience. They are most helpful to their survivor partners when they validate the reality of the abuse and keep the responsibility for it on the perpetrator. Survivors are most helpful to their partners when they try to understand the partner's position and be responsive to it. They need to listen to the partner's feelings and repect them, even though it may be hard.

Survivors and partners alike need to avoid burdening

each other and the relationship to the point of burnout. It is critical to utilize other resources. Talking with friends or a counselor, or joining a support group is using "people resources." Other strategies which survivors or partners have identified as helpful include journal writing; reading about child abuse; doing physical exercise; and joining a group or organization that works for abuse prevention.

Chemical dependencies

A 1983 survey in Los Angeles by Eric Rofes found that thirty percent of lesbians were *currently* addicted to drugs or alcohol. JoAnn Loulan's data (1987) on 1566 lesbians between 1985 and 1987 indicated that thirty percent of these women considered themselves to be in recovery from alcohol or drug addiction.

Lesbians who are recovering from chemical dependencies are doing a lot of growing. They have to. This is because they stopped growing in many ways when they started using whatever drug came to control their lives. Unhooking from alcohol and/or drugs means not only a physical recovery process, but also an emotional, social, and spiritual one. People who learn to use alcohol and drugs to cope with life don't develop and use other skills. Many women report being afraid to do sober the things that they used to do while drinking—such things as dancing in public, being sexual, talking to new people, and so on. They need to learn from scratch how to deal with feelings that they used to drown, or at least dilute, with drugs or alcohol. This means having to develop new coping strategies for handling anger, pain, loneliness, and anxiety, as well as more pleasant aspects of the human condition.

Typically, this recovery process is very stressful on a relationship. In part, this is because an addict is usually involved in a relationship with a codependent partner. The addict's partner often shows a pattern of behavior that includes rescuing the addict. She often unwittingly enables her partner to continue with the addiction by being the responsible one in the couple and protecting the addict from the consequences of her behavior. Codependents can easily become martyrs, devoting themselves to their partners. JoAnn Loulan (1984) notes that codependent behavior roles—supermother, martyr, and manager—are traits highly encouraged for all women. This does not make them healthy; it may, however, make them more seductive.

Once the pattern of addict/codependent is established, change requires great patience and a lot of hard work. Both partners have to want to change. Even with desire and effort, changing this pattern is particularly hard. One reason for this is that both women are exhausted from what they have been through. Also, much anger, hurt, and resentment has been built up on both sides. These feelings need to be dealt with at the same time that both women are learning how to live addiction-free lives. That is a lot to have on the table at the same time.

Resources for supporting changes include AA, Al-Anon, and Narcotics Anonymous (NA). These organizations have gay and lesbian meetings in many geographical areas. There are also some treatment programs specifically for lesbians and gays; and many counselors specialize in working with those recovering from alcohol and other drug addictions.

It can be very useful for couples to try to identify which issues and problems in their relationship are related to the recovery process and which are not. While this is not easy to do, it is a great help to know that those related to recovery will pass.

This is not to say that all couple relationships survive. Sometimes the experiences of the recovering woman and the reactions of her partner stress the relationship beyond the breaking point. Sometimes the pace of the changes is too fast, or too slow, or too much for the other partner to manage.

Inevitably the couple relationship will change when one or both partners are involved in the kinds of recovery processes we have described. It may emerge as a fuller and more satisfying couple relationship. Or it may become a friendship. Partners need to realize that the pain and struggles of recovery will pass; that the recovery process is a healing that ultimately expands potentials for intimacy and a balance of separateness and togetherness in relationships.

Chapter 15

Disability

When we hear the term "disabilities," most of us think about people with the most obvious disabilities. We may picture a person who uses a cane or a wheelchair, for example. We frequently do not include those who have dyslexia or asthma, or are color-blind. We likely don't think about those who have lost or are losing their hearing or vision, or who have other disabilities that do not have obvious symptoms. Disabled people are often treated as if they are sick. Just because a person has a disability does not mean she is ill. Many individuals who are deaf or who use wheelchairs, for example, are as healthy as their non-disabled peers. Likewise, people with a chronic illness are not necessarily disabled. However, someone with a chronic illness may become disabled by that illness. Disability and illness are different. That is why it is important to distinguish between the terms *disability* and *chronic illness*.

Disability refers to loss of the ability to carry out a specific function. JoAnn Loulan (1984) describes a person as being disabled if she experiences physical or sensory limitations and loss to any degree that either consistently or intermittently affects her functioning, her self-esteem, and the quality of her life. Because this definition focuses on the person's experience of being physically different, it includes disabilities associated with chronic illnesses or other disabling conditions which may not have visible signs, at least initially.

In her book, *We Are Not Alone*, Sefra Kobrin Pitzele re-

This chapter is based on a manuscript by Vickie L. Sears

ports that one-third of the adult population in the United States suffers from chronic illnesses. By definition, these illnesses are permanent and cause substantial modification of a person's lifestyle, goals, vocational choices and opportunities, recreational activities, and interpersonal relationships. Depending on the illness, it may be relatively easy or very difficult to diagnose; it may progress rapidly or very slowly. There may be periods of remission that are relatively symptom-free as well as periods of acute illness.

Because those who have chronic illnesses typically also have temporary or long-term disabilities, they have problems similar to those in the disabled community. Accessibility to buildings and to transportation is one such problem. However, there are differences too. For example, many members of the disabled community have adjusted to their disability. Perhaps they were born with it, or acquired it early in life as a result of an acute illness or accident. Chronic illness, on the other hand, often occurs in adulthood, and the adjustment process is ongoing, because illnesses are often progressive.

We realize that there are many terms which have been used to "name" the world of the disabled. There is debate in the disabled and ablebodied communities about which words to use. Some would say "physically challenged." Others prefer "other abled," "differently abled," "handicapped," or "disabled." We have chosen to use the term "disabled." We also realize that our discussions do not begin to cover the breadth and the depth of the topic of disability. Because our focus is on lesbian couples, our emphasis is on the impact of disability on the couple relationship. We want to acknowledge that there are many important issues which we may only mention or cover briefly.

Stereotypes

The word *ableism* is the most common phrase used to describe prejudices toward disabled people. Some common stereotypes about the disabled are:

- They are not pretty to look at.
- They are not healthy.
- They are not capable of being employed in meaningful work.
- They are nonsexual.
- If they are sexual, they ought not to have children.
- They are dependent and make their children dependent.
- They are brave in coping with adversity.
- They do not like to talk about "it."
- They like to be asked about "it."
- They need help with everything they do.
- They "suffer in silence."

While the lesbian community may like to think of itself as more sensitive than the rest of society, we are not free of ableistic stereotypes and attitudes. These attitudes affect how lesbians who are disabled are treated, and how their partners are treated.

Being seen as dependent can result in well-meaning friends', or even partners', providing unnecessary help. Unasked, they may push a wheelchair, or explain to a store clerk that their friend is deaf. At the other extreme, they may set a disabled women on a pedestal for being "brave" and "long suffering." This can mean that the woman has no room to complain on days when she is just feeling crabby and out of sorts. Being regarded as a "super-cripple" can put pressure on the disabled woman to keep up this image; she may not feel free to ask for help when she needs it.

It is not uncommon for ablebodied partners to be thought of as strange because they are lovers with a disabled woman. At other times they may be glorified as "noble" or "good" for choosing a disabled women as a partner. When these couples are out in the world together, they may have to deal with incidents of rude or discounting behavior.

Sarah and Carol were in the bar one night, when a friend of Carol's came over to their table. Sarah had only met this woman briefly, on one previous occasion. Although the women clearly meant to include both Sarah and Carol, she made eye contact only with Carol and directed all the conversation to her. She invited them to a party, and asked Carol if they could come and if Sarah could get up the stairs. *Sarah* answered that indeed she could.

Because she used a wheelchair, Sarah was treated as "less than": less than present, and less than competent to speak for herself. Her partner was the spokeswoman, the one to talk to, the one who could make decisions. Sarah understood what was happening. She realized that part of the woman's rudeness was due to her discomfort at being so close to someone who was disabled. Carol also realized what was happening, and wisely let Sarah speak for herself. It is not, however, the disabled woman's responsibility to adjust to the discomfort of the ablebodied. It is the responsibility of society and of the lesbian community to acknowledge and correct our prejudices and our discrimination.

Dealing with these incidents, with stereotypes and misconceptions, requires partners to communicate with each other. They need to express their thoughts and feelings and listen to each other in order to evaluate how they handled a past situation as well as how they can handle possible incidents in the future.

Impact of disability on the couple relationship

There are a wide variety of circumstances that influence the ways that disability will affect a lesbian couple. What kind and degree of disability is it? What is the history of the couple relationship? How visible is the disability? How well are the partners able to communicate and deal openly with the issues that arise?

There is another critical factor. Was the disability present before the women became involved or did it occur during the course of the relationship?

Susanne had been hard-of-hearing as a child, and was deaf by the time she was ten years old. She was in her mid-thirties, and well prepared to be in a relationship, when she met Liza. Over the years, Susanne had worked through a great many of her feelings about being deaf. She had also dealt with the reactions of lovers, both hearing and deaf. For her part, Liza was excited about her progress in learning to sign. She was much less excited about discovering her ableistic assumptions and insensitivities. But she was working on them.

Keeping the power balanced in their relationship was one of the most difficult challenges that Liza and Suzanne faced. For example, Liza interpreted telephone calls for Suzanne. The trade-off was that Suzanne did more housework. Another trade-off that helped balance the power in the relationship was the partners' agreement about choosing television programs. If Liza's choice was not captioned, and something Suzanne wanted to watch was, they would go with Suzanne's choice. It was an ongoing process to try to sort out which issues called for trade-off negotiations and which were conflicts that had nothing to do with Suzanne's being deaf. Susanne's experience in dealing with her own and with previous lovers' reactions to her deafness did not mean that issues never arose. However, it did help the couple relationship, and Liza, to have the benefit of Suzanne's past experience. It is a very different situation when a partner is diagnosed as having an illness, and thus newly incurs a disability during the course of a relationship, as was the case for Marilyn and Jill.

Chronic illness

Marilyn had been concerned about feeling weak and tired, having blurred vision and pain in her left eye, and sometimes falling or feeling as though her limbs would not hold her. These symptoms had come and gone over a period of months. When she lost control of her bladder on two separate occasions, Marilyn summoned her courage and went to the doctor. After an exhaustive series of tests, she was told that she had multiple sclerosis (MS). In some ways she was relieved to get a diagnosis; she now had a name for what she had been experiencing. But she was afraid to tell Jill. They had been lovers for five years, and had shared many difficult and joyous times. But Marilyn was uncertain how Jill, who was something of a "jock," would take the news that eventually Marilyn might have to use a wheelchair.

Regardless of how Jill or Marilyn reacts to the news of the diagnosis, they will likely go through stages in their adjustment to Marilyn's diagnosis. These stages have been described as shock, denial, anger, depression, and acceptance. Not everyone experiences all of these stages, nor do they follow each other in a predictable, orderly fashion. But it can be helpful to know that the feelings associated with these stages are the normal reactions to grieving a loss. Whether we are dealing with the death of a partner, the loss of our sight or mobility (or our partner's loss), we seem to experience stages in the adjustment process. In phasic chronic illnesses, like multiple sclerosis or Epstein-Barr virus, the need for grieving can be more easily ignored or denied because there are periods of remission where the person feels fine. Then, when she experiences a relapse, she may feel overwhelmed with despair. People who have chronic illnesses sometimes take a long time really to know how much loss there is and the losses which need to be grieved. Like denial and anger, hope comes and goes. Different losses may be grieved at different phases of a disease. A person in the early stages of diabetes, for example, will likely not yet have to grieve the loss of sensation in her fingers or toes because these symptoms occur in the later stages of the illness. Grieving often progresses from numbness, to disbelief, to pain and anger, to self-absorption about the loss, to acceptance and reinvolvement with living. Different people move at different paces through the grieving process.

. . . .

Shock and denial stage

At first, both Marilyn and Jill were in shock. They weren't sure what to do or who to tell about the news. Even when they went through the motions of going to work or reading about MS, neither felt totally "there." Marilyn described it as her numb period. She was still numb when Jill entered her denial phase. Jill tried to convince herself, and Marilyn, that the test results had been a mistake. Then she decided that even if Marilyn did have MS, the course of her illness was not going to be the same as that of other people. Marilyn would definitely never need a wheelchair. For her part, Marilyn's journey through the denial stage was somewhat different. She avoided talking with anyone about what was going on. She tried to ignore her symptoms and pushed her physical limits even when she didn't need to.

Anger stage

Denial was followed by anger. Marilyn ranted and raved about her doctors and her rotten luck. "Why me?" she would shout over and over again. She was angry at everything and everybody. She was furious with her body for betraying her, with healthy people for being healthy, with friends who didn't mention the MS and with those who asked about it. She alternated between being sarcastic with Jill and feeling guilty for taking her anger out on her partner.

In fact, Jill had a much easier time with Marilyn's anger stage than she did with the depression that came later. She understood Marilyn's frustration and rage. Now that she realized more of what this illness meant, she experienced a mix of feelings. Like Marilyn, she was angry. "It's not fair," was her main theme. She felt relieved that she was healthy and then felt guilty about feeling relieved. Mostly she was afraid of what the illness would mean for them both, and for the relationship. Both Jill and Marilyn wisely sought out a number of support people. They recognized that they each needed to express their feelings but that they also needed to respect each other's limits. They did not want to burn each other out. In addition, Jill started jogging and Marilyn began to keep a journal.

Depression stage

It was the depression stage that put the most stress on their relationship. Marilyn sought out a counselor in part because Jill was no help to her at all. Jill was critical of what she saw as Marilyn's "giving up on life." She responded to her partner's sadness by trying to cheer her up. In the process, she gave Marilyn the message that her feelings were not valid. When Marilyn was not cheered, Jill got irritated with her. The counselor helped Marilyn to understand that her depression was a reaction to real events, to the losses and life changes she was going through. In these sessions, Marilyn was able to express her feelings and to plan ways to cope with her depression. It took some time before Jill trusted Marilyn's counselor. She was glad that Marilyn had this outlet but she felt that she had failed her somehow. If she had been a better partner, Marilyn wouldn't need a counselor. Eventually Jill was invited to attend some sessions with Marilyn. She was able then to acknowledge her feelings. They talked more openly about what they could and could not do for each other.

During these hard times, it was almost impossible to imagine that it would ever be any different. The partners had read about the acceptance stage, but had little hope of getting there. It took great effort for them both to keep from losing hope completely and from dwelling in the past, wishing things had not changed.

Acceptance stage

For Marilyn, the movement toward a state of acceptance was one of listening to herself and to her feelings. This meant staying, for a time, with both her physical and emotional pain. And then sharing it with her partner. Marilyn took responsibility for her own self-care as much as possible. She did what she could do, and started to ask for help when she needed it. She and Jill learned all they could about MS. They began to find room for humor and celebration again in their lives.

By taking stock of what she *could* do, rather than focusing on what was lost, Marilyn learned to be realistic about herself and her abilities. She saw herself as valuable. She was more able to be attentive to the needs of other people because she was not as self-absorbed as she had been in the initial stages of her adjustment to her illness. She described her acceptance as allowing her to trust herself again. It filled her life, pushing out bitterness, anger, and defensiveness. No longer did the effects of MS interfere with her whole life. She recognized that her illness was not her identity, but only a part of who she was.

Once she reached some degree of acceptance, Marilyn was more able to deal with the anger and depression she felt periodically. Just because she had reached the acceptance stage, however, did not mean that she never had negative feelings, or bad days. She often needed to remind herself, and Jill, that acceptance was not a capitulation to her disease and disability. For her, it was taking it in as a part of her life and learning to manage it. She refused to be condemned or useless.

Eventually, Marilyn needed to use a wheelchair. She and Jill both went through a mini-version of each adjustment stage again. After some denial, they saw some new problems that they had not counted on. They realized that they would have to move from their home, or do some very costly renovation. The front door would have to be enlarged. The bathroom was inaccessible and so were the kitchen cupboards. The basement was impossible. They went through being angry and depressed about the cost, and about how the world is set up for ablebodied people. Sometimes they were in the same phase, both angry or both depressed. Sometimes not. When they surfaced from their upset, they decided to stay put. The best plan seemed to be to apply for a bank loan to make their current home as accessible as possible.

Pain

Many women who have disabilities are not ill, and are not in pain. However, one of the realities of many chronic illnesses is physical pain. Pain is not easy to live with. It is exhausting, especially if it is a daily experience. Tolerance for pain varies with individuals and with emotional states, but it is easier to respond to if it is predictable.

For example, if Marilyn knows that her arm is going to hurt when she extends it fully, she will be prepared. She may not experience the pain as intensely if she can anticipate it. She has the choice of using her pain in an angry and manipulative way; by getting upset and trying to make her partner and friends feel badly and/or responsible. Another option is to use her pain as a teacher to tell her about her limits. Some of these limits she may try to push past; some she may not. She may also choose to work with visualization and meditation or to distract herself from the pain with movies, music, or books. What is crucial is that she acknowledges the pain and learns to live with it. It is also important that Jill knows what Marilyn's limits are and respects them.

Like many partners, Jill has to deal with the fact that she has no control over what is happening to Marilyn. She cannot fix Marilyn and she cannot make the pain go away. For many, the sense of helplessness in the face of their partner's pain and deterioration is very hard. Jill found it difficult to see Marilyn in pain. She knew she could not make the pain go away, but it was very hard for her to accept that. For Jill, acceptance of her own helplessness was the hardest thing to manage.

Self-esteem and internalized oppression

Those born with disabilities who learned that they were "all right" and could "do anything," and who always saw themselves as different but equal and healthy, are likely to have high self-esteem. Similarly, those who have a positive sense of themselves may more easily regain their self-esteem in the event that they acquire a disability in later life. It can be more difficult for those whose self-esteem was not high to begin with.

In order to build, or regain her self-esteem, a disabled woman may need to become a warrior. She may have to fight to be seen as sexual and able to have and raise children. She may battle cultural images of what is beautiful. She may have to combat the fears of others about her dependency. She may have to fight for her chance to work and to be autonomous. And she may have to wage war with herself to continue to love herself and live a full life.

Accepting a stereotype held by those in the ablebodied world—whether it be the pitiful, complaining, and dependent "cripple" or the extraordinary, brave, and ever-smiling "super crip" image—leads to internalized oppression. Either image denys the uniqueness of the individual's feelings and reactions. Adopting any "role" separates the person from herself and from her loved ones. The attitude that "My body is weird sometimes, but I'm just fine thank you very much" is one which does not make the illness or disability into an identity. This balance gives both women in a couple room to share, stretch and grow with each other.

Children, work, and independence

Historically, disabled women have been discouraged from having or rearing children. Although there may be nothing to prevent this, some things need to be considered. These include other peoples' prejudices, physical aspects of pregnancy, the nature and costs of environmental adaptations to be able to care for a baby, and modifications in strategies to discipline the child. For example, children of women with mobolity disabilities often have to learn to be reponsive to verbal instructions. Because of her crutches or wheelchair, the mother may not be able to get to the child as quickly as an ablebodied mother could. Children develop an awareness of their parent's capabilities. Ablebodied partners of disabled women may not rely on verbal instructions as much, but they do need to reinforce the child positively for responding to them.

Like their heterosexual counterparts, lesbians who have disabilities must function in a society that has refused, for the most part, to acknowledge their presence and their particular needs. As a result of both physical and psychological barriers, they are often unable to communicate, move around, or work to their fullest capacity or satisfaction.

Recent technological advances and changing attitudes allow more work opportunities for disabled people. Many find themselves fully accepted and in well paying jobs which they enjoy. However, others experience the barriers of employers' reluctance to hire; or they become "token" after being hired. If one partner is no longer able to work, some of the problems are financial: lost income and increased medical expenses. And some of the problem is emotional: the loss of identity associated with working and with the job. In addition, the application for retraining programs or for government assistance may be frustrating and discouraging. The working partner may feel burdened and overwhelmed, too. These kinds of problems need the same kind of approach as many of the others we have discussed. We recommend sharing feelings and listening to each other.

There are more tools now than ever before to help disabled people maintain their independence. For the deaf there are special devices called TTY's that allow communication over the telephone, more sign language interpretation at concerts and captioning on television, and flashing lights that signal the doorbell, for example. There are computers with vocal modems for the visually impaired, more ramps and elevators and wheelchair-accessible public transportation. Improved accessibility allows disabled women and their partners to attend more of the same social and cultural events as everyone else. However, when lesbian businesses and organizations do not make their events and services accessible, it is hard for lesbians who are disabled to be with other lesbians and to feel involved in and supported by the lesbian community.

Support systems

Whether one partner is disabled or not, no one person can meet all the needs of another. Both partners in a couple relationship need a variety of support systems. When an ablebodied woman becomes partners with a woman with a disability, her friendship patterns may change. It depends on the kind and the degree of the disability, but some of her friends may be uncomfortable with her partner, and the friendships die out. Or new individual and couple friendships with ablebodied women just don't seem to develop as expected. And for the partner with a disability, there is the reaction of her friends in the disabled community to her new partner.

Family, both biological and chosen, is an important support system for most of us. This can be especially true when a couple discovers that one partner is seriously ill. When Maxine was diagnosed with AIDS, she told her lover Barb that she was sure her family would disown her. She had never told them about her past history with drugs, much less about being gay. As it turned out, most of her family was extremely supportive. Barb was particularly grateful to Maxine's parents for the financial help they gave. She had been worried because she knew that she couldn't keep up with the bills after Maxine couldn't work anymore.

To their dismay, Barb and Maxine discovered that some of their friends began to disappear. Even though they knew that some of these people just couldn't face their fears and their own vulnerability, it still hurt. They also realized that they themselves had pulled away from friends. Part of this was the result of being preoccupied with adjusting to the news and finding out about what resources and support groups were available. Part of it was also due to not wanting to deal with friends' feelings and reactions.

This couple decided that what they each needed was a broad support system. They wanted some of the same people but some different ones too. They made a game of assigning people to categories. Category l was those people who could hear the full story or update each time you saw them. Category 2 people could hear a shortened version of the story. Those in category 3 were only able to hear positive news, and category 4 folks couldn't hear much past "everything is fine." They were aware, too, that their support people would shift around and be in different categories at different times. However, this game helped them to keep their expectations realistic. It also encouraged them to continue to ask for support from someone, even though she or he had not been very available at one particular time. That person might move into a different category at any time.

Sex

Because the illness was AIDS, it had a major impact on Barb's and Maxine's sexual relationship. As soon as Maxine was diagnosed, they began to use safe sex practices. Then there was the issue of whether or not Barb would get tested. Until she did, and turned out to be negative, Maxine was dealing with her guilt about possibly infecting her lover. Even after the test, Maxine wasn't sure she wanted to be sexual at all.

For many couples in which one or both partners are disabled, sex and sexual issues are basically the same as they are for any other couple. For others, there may be particular considerations or accommodations. But there is no need to buy into the myth that being sexual is impossible. It is true that having to change some modes of sexual expression can alter the response cycle, arousal, and sexual feelings. This may be particularly the case for women with a new injury, illness, or disability. Fatigue and pain can change or diminish sexual feelings. Lifestyle changes in work, money, or play may also affect sex, since being sexual is an expression of the whole person. A woman's worry about somehow causing pain to her disabled partner can also alter sexual expressions and feelings. The best thing partners can do is talk about what being sexual means to them, explore what will heighten their pleasures together, and then enjoy each other.

In the following sections we have outlined suggestions and hints for ablebodied and disabled partners (adapted from Vickie Sears, 1987b). We have included them knowing that they will apply for some but not all couples, depending on the nature of the disability.

Suggestions for an ablebodied partner

- Learn about your partner's illness or disability on your own, as well as from her.
- Be aware of your ableisms.
- Talk about your fears and feelings.
- Be considerate of your partner's energy level, her physical and sensory limitations, and her emotional resource limits.
- Have a separate support system for yourself, as well as sharing feelings with your partner.
- Remember that your partner's body is hers. You cannot fix it. You can just be her lover and help her when you can and when it is appropriate.
- Know the attitudes and impacts your partner faces as a disabled women from the medical profession and from society.
- If you are angry about the treatment of people with disabilities, think about doing something political about it.
- Remember that your partner's problems are not more important than yours. Ask for what you need.
- Get counseling if you need it.

Suggestions for a disabled partner

Adjustment to chronicity in an illness or a disability is ten percent physical and ninety percent emotional. Loving yourself is a major factor influencing your stress level, your body/emotional/spiritual self-management, and your behaviors. Loving yourself, whatever you look or feel like, makes healing more possible. It also makes it more possible to be attentive to other people and to experience loving feelings for them. A chronic condition brings stress which lowers your ability to cope with the condition and even means that it will take less stress to cause stress. What your body does in a stress reaction is to make more sugar in your blood, muscles, and brain. This, in turn, creates a faster heart rate, dilates your pupils, increases your blood pressure, and then releases norepinephrine into your system which, in itself, produces anxiety. Around and around it goes, circling in on itself. So, what to do? Try to love yourself! Be gentle and kind to yourself. Talk with your lover about the things that are going on with your body and spirit. Listen to her. Meditate and do deep muscle relaxation. Exercise as much as you can, because the weakness created by its lack breeds on itself. Be aware of your physical and energy limits and tailor your activities to suit you. Let your partner do the things she wants to do without you, if you are not able physically to share the activity. Remember you are a sexual and loving being. *Listen to your body and spirit and believe that you are not your illness*. Ask for what you need. Remember that you may not always get your needs met, but it is fine and powerful to ask. When your lover cannot meet your needs, get them met by someone else where possible. Do what you need to do to take care of yourself, including withdrawing so long as it does not go on too long and doesn't put you in a vacuum. Listen to your lover and her needs too. She cannot be an extention of you. She cannot live in a vacuum either. Accept yourself fully, with realism, and you will create a positive self-image in which you and your partner can share.

Further hints for a disabled partner

- Talk about your feelings and fears.

- Teach your partner about your illness or disability, including your potentialities.
- Check out your anger at your partner for not being disabled, if she is ablebodied.
- Maintain your independence but also ask for help if you need it.
- If you are angry about the treatment of people with disabilities, think about doing something political about it.
- Make certain your legal affairs are in order if you want your partner to have your possessions or have the right to make medical or burial decisions should you become unable to do so.
- Have some separate friends from whom you can get special support.
- Get counseling if you need it.

A disability or illness may require a couple to meet challenges that the ablebodied world neither understands nor appreciates. No one can predict exactly how the couple relationship will be affected, but partners can learn to anticipate some of the problems and prepare strategies to deal with them. As with other couples, self-awareness and open, caring communication are key.

Chapter 16

Growing Older Together

Elizabeth and Charlotte were giggling again. They had gotten into the habit of laughing at the odd things that happened to them because of their age and because of other people's assumptions. Today it was about the young intern at their physician's office; he had been a little shocked when he saw Elizabeth's black lace underwear and had stuttered a bit when he asked her to remove it for an examination. They figured he expected white cotton briefs with no hint of being sexy. Charlotte and Elizabeth were used to that kind of ignorance. They had been teaching themselves and learning about the issues of aging since they had become lovers thirteen years before. They had already faced: retirement, some mild and some serious health problems, their changing sexual needs, problems with their aging parents and adult children, and changes in their financial status. They were ready with their wills and powers of attorney; and they knew that they would face more changes, especially in their needs for housing and personal care. They knew that one of them probably would have to face life alone eventually.

Growing older brings with it new challenges and problems. It can also bring new joys and freedom. Western culture, with its ageist assumptions, has focused on physical change and has ignored the more positive aspects of aging. We have been innundated with horror stories of how older people become incapacitated and dependent, when, in fact, the majority of old people live independently. Eyes do change, bodies slow down, reaction time slows, people usually lose some hearing, and skin is less elastic. The youth-oriented culture sees natural changes like these as something to be ashamed of or corrected by plastic surgery. How much more appropriate to see, instead, the beauty of experience in the lines on a woman's face.

Families also change as we age. Parents grow old and die. Siblings marry, divorce, have children, and sometimes die before us. If we have children, they develop their own lives, joys, and problems; sometimes they move back in with us—or they may never have left. We may become in-laws and grandmothers and, thus, face new coming out issues. With these changes in our families, we can become freer to be our own selves. Often when our parents die, patterns from our families of origin that have hindered us may ease or resurface, perhaps giving us another chance to develop a life that is healthier and more nurturing. Coming out to new family members is sometimes easier when we are older, because we have less to lose: child custody, job security, and parental approval may become less crucial.

Older couples

How old is an older couple? Fifty? Sixty? Seventy? Eighty? A few decades ago, women in their forties identified themselves as "older." Now some women in their sixties do not. How each identifies herself probably depends on how fit she feels and whether she has had to deal with the physical problems that society equates with old age. Barbara MacDonald's *Look Me in the Eye* is an excellent discussion of one woman's growing older as a lesbian.

Older lesbians who have been together for a long time, as well as those who have been together for only a short while enjoy certain advantages. If a couple is in a long-term relationship, they can enjoy the shared memories and the richness of a long history together. If they are in a new relationship, they reap the benefits of being mature and knowing what they want out of life and with whom they want to share it. Still, aging can sometimes present a couple with difficulties when one partner is considerably older than the other. (See Chapter 11.)

Sally and May had been together for forty-five years; they had met in the army during World War II. They were not officially out to any of their family members, but were treated as a family unit by everyone because they had lived together for so long.

Helen and Sarah became lovers on Helen's seventieth birthday. Two months later they were trying to find ways to justify living together. Sarah's daughter, Nan, could not understand why her mother wanted to move in with a virtual stranger and leave the cozy apartment in Nan's house.

Lesbian couples in their fifties, sixties, seventies, eighties, and nineties may all identify as older, but there are tremendous differences in these women's experiences and histories. Women in their nineties were born in the late 1800s and women in their fifties were born in the 1930s. Their childhoods were radically different, just as their adult years have been. *Long Time Passing: Lives of Older Lesbians*, edited by Marcy Adelman, is a wonderful collection of interviews and a good example of the differences that exist among older lesbians.

Those women who volunteered for World War I found a way to be somewhat independent. There was not another chance like that until World War II. But right after World War II there was a strong push for women to go back to being housewives and dependent on men. Only the strongest or most wealthy could maintain independence. The way couples perceive themselves and live their lives depends to some degree on the decades through which they have lived and when they became a couple. Many more couples would have called themselves lesbians had they been born later and had more support for their lifestyle and words to describe it.

There are also many couples who call themselves lesbians but who are so closeted that people do not think of them in that light. This makes it very difficult to meet and socialize with these women even if one is their peer. It is even harder for younger lesbians to meet these women, because their friendship circles do not overlap very much and also because some older women prefer spending their social time with peers, ignoring young women. Many young lesbian couples want to meet and spend time with older lesbians because they want to know what older couples look like, what they do, and how they have survived in this culture. As younger women spend more time with older couples, they confront the sexism and ageism that have kept them from appreciating the gifts of older women.

How out to be

Marilyn and Ellen fell in love with each other when both were twenty-three. Ellen left the relationship, married, and birthed three children. When the youngest was sixteen years old, Ellen at last joined her life with Marilyn's. Marilyn had lived a totally closeted lifestyle, as befitted a teacher in the 1950s. Ellen rented the apartment next door to Marilyn's as a protective cover, but they really lived in Marilyn's place for seven years. They never went to lesbian events, rarely even visited women's bookstores. Neither took part in the social life at the work place of the other. They knew only one other lesbian couple. Marilyn's retirement, an early one brought on by ill health, placed new stresses on the couple. Their social isolation meant that they had no outside support for their relationship and no one to turn to for help.

Many older lesbians became aware of their lesbianism at a time when only a handful of very brave or very rich women could afford to be out to the world. As a result, many older lesbians developed a closeted lifestyle that has persisted. As it becomes easier to be out, more and more older lesbians are telling friends and family—but many others are too worried about the risks. Some fear losing their contact with their grandchildren; some are afraid that their families will try to separate them from their partners in their attempt to help out. Others fear losing their jobs or the status their careers have given them. Other older lesbians have only recently come out to themselves. They may not yet feel free to come out to the world.

When an older lesbian couple is not out, the heterosexual community assumes that they are two unmarried/divorced/widowed women who have made the best of their lonely situation. Sometimes people try to act as matchmakers for them with eligible men. But usually they are treated as a couple, in that they are invited places together, asked to host things at their home, and are often assumed to be spending time together. This may work out very well.

Spousal rights

However, a problem can come when one member of a closeted couple is gravely ill or dies. The other woman is rarely accorded the same concern or rights, such as hospital visitation, as a heterosexual spouse would be given. In the case of death of one of the partners, the survivor's depression may not be treated as seriously as when a husband dies.

As with all lesbian couples, older partners sometimes have to face each other's families after death or during the course of a debilitating illness. If a couple has not been out to their families, partners may have more difficulty maintaining their rights. Grown children and grandchildren often will not believe that their aged parent/grandparent had a woman lover. Being out is no protection, of course, only an advance warning to the families and an opportunity to work through potential problems before they arise. The couple, whether closeted or flamboyantly out, need powers of attorney and wills that protect their interests.

Rachel and Margaret met when they were both seventy. Within six months they had moved in together. Neither was out to her family, and they were both afraid that in case of death the other's family would intervene and take over all the decisions and property. They decided to see a young woman lawyer whom Rachel had heard speak on gay rights. They drew up will and powers of attorney. Then they came out to their families. Rachel's children wanted to have her declared incompetent. Margaret's family was generally supportive. In fact, it was Margaret's son John who was able to persuade Rachel's daughters to drop the incompetency proceedings.

Families need time to adjust to the change they think has just happened in their older family member. The older woman may always have been a lesbian, but her family is discovering the fact for the first time, about someone they thought they knew well. Family members may react first and settle down to thinking later, as Rachel's did. Sometimes the families never become tolerant or supportive, and the lesbian couple may lose their contact with those people. Sometimes the family may be delighted that the older woman has found someone she loves. These possibilities need to be weighed when an older couple, or any of us, makes the decision to come out.

Health

While the stereotype of older people is that they are sickly, aging women are often both healthy and active. Most of us will be able to be involved in activities and interests throughout our projected lifespan of well into the seventies. Even if the women in a couple are healthy, however, some of the physical changes that accompany aging need to be acknowledged. Slowed reaction time, for instance, may necessitate leaving ample time to go somewhere, because the women drive more slowly than they used to. It is important to note that as with all problems that couples have to deal with, the more couples can talk about their experiences of changing or about impaired health, the easier it is for the women to adjust to whatever they face.

Elizabeth's physician told her that she had to change her eating habits and that she should exercise daily, or she would not live to retire. Carrie, her new partner, was a fitness instructor and a nutrition buff. Together they developed a food plan and an exercise routine that gradually moved Elizabeth toward improved health. The interesting side effect of this was Elizabeth's discovery that her long buried love of art was still alive. She began to paint again, and she blossomed. She and Carrie were delighted.

Sometimes, dealing with our physical aging has wonderful by-products for our emotional selves. As we slow down because of the normal process or because of some condition, we focus on aspects of our being that we may formerly have ignored, thereby allowing ourselves to grow in unexpected ways. Many people actually get busier when they retire. Some have been so burdened by their jobs that they have really stopped living. When they quit work they come alive.

Sexual activity

One assumption made about older women is that they are not sexual beings.

Roma and Natalie had been lovers for three years, and they were enthusiastic about sex. Roma came out when she was fifty-five and told everyone she was making up for lost time. Natalie had always enjoyed sensual activities; she now gave herself to discovering new ways to indulge her senses.

Charlotte and Nancy had been lovers for thirty years. They loved to touch each other and took joy in noticing how their bodies and responses had changed over the years. Each knew exactly how too pleasure the other. They did not have genital sex often, but they enjoyed sex together even more than when they had first met.

Another assumption is that older couples do not have sex, and that they stay together out of friendship or convenience. While this is true for some couples, others report that their sexual lives grow richer as they age.

Work and retirement

As women age, we often learn more about our interests

and skills. Jobs that suited us when we were younger may no longer meet our needs. Some older women decide to move into a new career or to expand a hobby into a money-making venture. One woman we know was a Head Start teacher in her thirties and then worked with disadvantaged families through a hospital-based program. When she was in her fifties, she realized that she was tired of working for others. She went back to school and earned a degree in social work and set up a business as a consultant for hospitals and state organizations which worked with poor families. As a happy side effect, her excitement about her new work had a stimulating effect on her partner and gave an added zest to their relationship.

When one member (or both) of a couple retires, time and money may be big issues. The retiree may have a lot more time and—depending on her interests—may get bored or, on the other hand, be eager to make use of her new free time. If she wants to take over the home responsibilities, her partner may see this as a boon, or as an encroachment. If she wants to do more things away from home this, too, can be a source of conflict or pleasure. A retired woman may need help in adjusting to the loss of her work-related identity and to a potentially diminished self-esteem. Sometimes a partner has a whole list of things she wants to do when she retires. This could include reading, volunteer work at the local hospital, sewing, car mechanics, and so on. If she doesn't have any interests, she may end up doing nothing, and feel bored, depressed, or angry.

Rhoda and Marge had been lovers for twenty-six years. When Marge retired, they almost broke up. Marge had always been the main wage earner, with Rhoda's getting a job outside the home every now and again when they wanted to do something special. In general, Rhoda took care of the house. When Marge had no job to go to she sat around the house and got in the way of Rhoda's routine. They saved their relationship by moving to Arizona and becoming caretakers at a mobile home park. Marge did the maintenance work, while Rhoda took care of their trailer and their garden.

Retirement is usually a dramatic enough shift to require renegotiating some aspects of a relationship. Money may be one of the factors that forces such a renegotiation for a couple when one or both retires. If the retiree's income drops significantly and her partner's income is not enough to absorb the loss, they will have to adjust their lifestyle. Some couples decide to share their living space with others to save money or to buy food in bulk with other households. Some women do odd jobs to raise extra money, if they have skills that are in demand. Since women are generally underpaid, older women may not have saved enough for a comfortable retirement. As a result, it is imperative that we plan ahead. The Canadian government underwrites a larger portion of costs than does the United States government, so older Canadian women may be in better financial shape than their American counterparts. But in general, poor, older women have to take whatever is available to augment anything they have managed to save. For women with more money available for advance planning, there are some accountants and financial advisors, especially in large urban areas, who specialize in helping lesbian couples plan their financial futures.

Supportive care

As lesbians age, we may need help to continue living independently. There are a variety of services available that bridge the gap between total self-care and institutional care. Sometimes older couples rent a room to a younger person in exchange for help in cleaning, yard work, personal hygiene care, or cooking. In many cities there are agencies that offer free or low-cost help with household maintenance. Some older couples move into homes that require less maintenance than their previous homes. Sometimes one or both of the partners become physically impaired and cannot move around easily. The couple may be able to move to another home that accomodates wheelchairs, or otherwise makes it easier for the disabled partner to move about. Meals on Wheels (meals brought to seniors at their homes) exists in many cities in both Canada and the USA. If an older lesbian couple is out in their local lesbian community (or even if they aren't), there may be ways they can get help from individual lesbians or lesbian resource centers. It might be donated help or it might be in exchange for something the older women can offer the younger women. Again, the more money the couple has available, the more options they have for taking care of themselves; and there are also some ways for women with little money to get the assistance they need to remain in their own homes.

Retirement homes

Older lesbian couples may need to go to retirement homes either together, separately, or together at different times. Older people are sometimes exploited and even abused in these institutions; and since older women, especially women of color, are among the poorest groups, they are the least likely to be able to afford good care. We lesbians run the additional risk of not being allowed to live together as a couple. Nursing homes offer the same dilemmas and often more regimentation. Obviously, we need to do a lot of research and planning before moving into one of these facilities.

Depending on cultural background and individual family styles, an older lesbian may be expected to move in with her family when she has trouble taking care of herself. It is important to be very clear with our families about what we want to do if we need to move out of our homes. If a couple is out, they may be able to get help from the lesbian community—or at least emotional support—while they wade though the bureaucratic process. There are creative ways to deal with the various situations we face as we age; but because society does not acknowledge older lesbian couples, we have to be clever, persistent, and knowledgeable about our rights.

Mary and Sandra moved into a retirement home in Seattle. They chose that city because of its large lesbian community and because the weather was warmer than in their native North Dakota. Before they moved, Mary wrote to the local lesbian resource center. She learned about the older women's group and talked with the facilitator of that group. When Mary and Sandra arrived in Seattle, another lesbian couple in their eighties, met them at the airport and helped them move into the retirement home.

Dying

The last of our developmental tasks in this world is dying. This process can be as full of love and growth as any other stage we go through. As we age we reminisce, a kind of pulling together of the strands of our lives. When we are part of a couple, the memories include the stages of our relationship and the changes we have gone through together. This can create a special kind of richness that comes only after a long life. Sometimes a woman who has had a hard time being close to other people, allows others to get closer to her when she knows that she is dying. This can add still another dimension to her life and relationship.

Death can also come unexpectedly, leaving little or no time for a couple to process its meanings and impact. This is harder and leaves the survivor to do the grieving process alone that in other, more expected deaths, the couple can do together. But in this case, as well, the process of saying goodbye can be nurtured by friends, family, and the survivor's memories of the couple's life together. We talk more about a partner's dying in Chapter 17.

The older couple's interaction with the lesbian community

While the lesbian community in general may be better at confronting its ageist attitudes, there still exists ageism that can make the older lesbian invisible. Older lesbians who are out are frequentally not acknowledged, sought after, or listened to. Especially when ageism is compounded by racism or classism, the older lesbian may feel alienated from the very group she reaches out to.

As do all lesbians, older lesbians need to have the opportunity for contact with other lesbians, both young and old. One couple we know say they rely on younger lesbians to keep them alert to the changes in the world. Older lesbians have the right to active social and family lives. Activities in the broader lesbian community need to be accessible to and comfortable for older women.

Some older lesbians have started support groups for older lesbians, to help them meet each other, socialize, and discuss issues pertinent to older women. Many cities have groups for lesbians over forty or fifty. We recommend that couples ask friends or advertise in lesbian and gay publications, to start their own support groups if none are available. In general, those who have been able to come out beyond their small circle of friends enjoy the additional support from women who have had similar experiences. The Old Lesbian Conference in California in the summer of 1987 illustrated that resources are beginning to open for older lesbians. They include OWL (Older Women's League); the Gray Panthers (individual branches may or may not be open to lesbians); Old Lesbian Network; SAGE (Senior Action in a Gay Environment) in New York City; GLOE (Gay and Lesbian Outreach to Elders) in San Francisco; and *Broomstick*, a national magazine based in San Francisco.

It is, however, also important for the younger lesbian community to sensitize itself to older lesbians. Some groups have invited older lesbians to speak to them as a beginning step. Whenever women form committees or participate in political action, older lesbians need to be included, because they bring a perspective no one else has. They often save time, because they have done a particular task or have been through a situation before. It is important to see older lesbians as the whole people they are. They have interests and ideas that are valuable in discussions and activities other than those directly related to aging.

All of us are aging; and in time, there will be many more out, older lesbians who will have a stronger voice within our communities. However, the lesbians who are older now need nurturance and respect for their life experiences—in part because their pioneering made the present-day visibility of the lesbian community possible.

Chapter 17

Endings

There are two ways a relationship can end: either through a breakup, or through the death of a partner. In either case, we experience loss and the recovery process involves grieving for this loss.

Breaking up

Women take their couple relationships—and breaking up—very seriously. As women, we are trained to define ourselves by our relationships. We are Edna's daughter or Mary's sister, Teresa's partner, or Janice's old lover. There is a lot of pressure to be in a relationship in order to be okay. If a relationship ends, a woman often feels she herself is not okay and there may even be a loss of identity—"If I am not in a relationship, I don't exist."

Sometimes it appears that lesbian couples don't stay together as long as other types of couples do. While we are not aware of any confirming research data, there are at least two factors that may contribute to this impression.

The first is the invisibility of long-term lesbian couples. Couples who have been together for fifteen, twenty, or more years are often invisible, even to other lesbians. Some of these couples are closeted. Others socialize almost exclusively within small friendship networks made up of other long-term couples. These couples have great stability, but few people know about it.

The second factor is that lesbians tend to define their relationships with a capital R very early in the game. Within two months, or even two weeks, both women may feel that they are a couple in a "Relationship." They talk long-term commitment and often begin living together. Later, some couples may discover that the relationship is based primarily on physical attraction or on the desire to be in a "Relationship." There may in fact be little basis for a long-term partnership. Now what? They have to break up. These endings are mourned in the same way as the breakup of a long-term relationship would be. Instead, many of these breakups could be more realistically viewed as the end of dating relationships that did not progress beyond the Prerelationship stage.

Tradition has it that a relationship is forever. So when a relationship ends, partners often feel a sense of failure. Either the failure is in picking the wrong person, or in not being a good enough partner oneself. Both women feel bad because their expectations have not been met, and their ability both to make a good choice in partners and to be successful in a relationship have been called into question. Since we have these lifetime expectations—often without even realizing it—we are poorly prepared for ending. Lacking the skills and attitudes required for what Emily Coleman and Betty Edwards call "caring closure," we feel helpless, disappointed, guilty, angry, and panicky.

Slowing down the early stages of a relationship is a good way to reduce the chances of going through a painful breakup. Taking time to get to know each other leads to a clearer assessment of compatibility and a more realistic prediction for the future of the relationship. Laura Brown (1984) labels this process as getting and giving "informed consent." Both partners need to inform themselves and each other about who they are and what they want and expect in this relationship. The women then consent to be in the relationship based on clear information, rather than on assumptions, hopes and illusions. A couple who sees this period as dating, or "informed consent," or the Prerelationship stage will likely feel less a sense of failure if they can realistically say, "I decided that I didn't want to get involved with Sue; we didn't want the same things from our relationship," or "There just wasn't enough in common to share with Elaine."

Reasons lesbian couples break up

Lesbian couples are not always able to withstand the many pressures from within the relationship and the lack of support from the outside world. Women expect a lot from their partners in a lesbian relationship. The feeling is one of "Here at last is what I've always wanted. Because she is a woman too, she will understand me and meet my emotional needs." These expectations involve a lot of assumptions, and they put intense pressure on the partners. Hostility from the broader culture is a given. The negative impact that the lesbian community itself may have is less obvious. There are particular pressures, for example, on lesbians who are involved in long-term partnerships. They may be viewed as a "perfect couple." Friends may want to believe that such relationships are possible, so they will not hear about any problems the perfect couple may be having.

Ginny and Donna broke up after eight years of what looked to their friends like an ideal relationship. In fact, neither partner had been very satisfied for the last two years. Donna was deeply disappointed that Ginny was not more emotionally supportive. After years of relating to men, Donna had expected that in a relationship with another woman she would get all the understanding and support she felt she had missed. For her part, Ginny was frustrated with what she saw as Donna's demands on her time and energy. Ginny's life had changed dramatically in the last few years. She was laid off, went back to school for job retraining, and began a new job in a nontraditional field. She liked the work itself and the pay, but having to deal with open homophobia, sexism, and racism on the job was an incredible strain. A good deal of the time she was both physically exhausted from work and emotionally drained from dealing with her coworkers. She knew she wasn't putting a lot of energy into the relationship. She kept telling Donna—and herself—that things would be better after the job settled down.

But it was only when Donna began an affair with an old friend, Sue, that her relationship with Ginny just seemed to blow apart.

Let's look at this. One of the major pressures from inside a relationship is our expectations of our partner, or our sense of how relationships are supposed to be. In this example, Donna expected Ginny to be more emotionally supportive because she was a woman. Outside pressures came into play with Ginny's stressful job. For her part, the more strain she had at work, the more Ginny wanted her relationship with Donna to be a safe haven. She expected Donna to be more supportive, or at least patient.

Having their lesbian friends view them as a perfect couple was also a pressure. When their friends romanticized and idealized their relationship, Ginny and Donna were cut off from support. They were not allowed to have, much less talk about, any difficulties.

After a long-term couple does break up, each partner often has fears about their friends' taking sides. In our example, Donna alternates between feeling guilty and feeling justified about her involvement with her new lover, Sue. Since she blames herself for causing Ginny a lot of pain, she avoids their mutual friends. She knows some of them have taken sides and are angry with her; she sees others as possible supports for Ginny and wants very much for Ginny to get the emotional support she needs.

It is true that friends may take sides when a couple breaks up. However, Donna almost guarantees that this will happen. In effect, she rejects these former friends by assuming they would be unsupportive. First, she decides that Ginny needs support more than she does, and, second, that their friends would do better to give Ginny support. In making this decision, Donna cuts herself off from support, and cuts the friends off from the information that could balance their view of the situation. She is mind reading what Ginny needs and what their friends think.

Of course, one or both partners in a breakup may be so hurt, or so angry, that they *try* to get friends to take their side. Even when this is not the case, mutual friends may take sides anyway. This is very painful, because it means that one or both partners are losing friends as well as losing their partner relationship. Some strategies may help prevent this. The couple breaking up can talk to their mutual friends together, at least initially, about the breakup. They can each try to be fair to the other when they talk to friends individually. They can ask friends specifically to avoid taking sides. For their part, friends can listen to the feelings and distress of each partner with understanding and without harsh judgement. Sometimes, however, losing friends is unavoidable. Their values, loyalties, or feelings are so involved that their alliance is solidly with one partner over the other. When this happens, there may be no choice but to accept and grieve the loss. Perhaps with time, the rift can be bridged and the friendship healed.

Dividing up friends is one problem, particularly when the community is a small one. Another issue is meeting the former partner at social events, in public places, and so on. This can be particularly touchy if one partner has a new relationship and the other does not. Some women decide to divide up the territory. They agree to avoid going to certain places knowing the other may be there, or they agree to check in with each other, and negotiate who will go to what event. Others may avoid going out at all because there is no prior arrangement to avoid confrontation. Some former partners continue to have contact with each other while others take a break because it is too painful, or they are too angry. There is no one right way; but often there is a best way for the particular women involved. Ideally, the former partners should communicate with each other to discuss and agree on these practical issues.

• • • •

But why?

There are various ways to explain what went wrong in a relationship.

Hilda blamed her partner LouAnn completely for their relationship ending. To hear Hilda tell the story, LouAnn was totally a villain and Hilda an innocent victim.

Simone described life as being like a lottery. She figured she had just had bad luck so far. She kept hoping she would get a better deal on the next round.

Ellen explained that her relationship with May ended due to circumstances beyond their control. She herself had a stressful job and their apartment was so small that they couldn't avoid all those fights. There was really nothing they could have done.

These three women use different explanations for their relationships not working out. What they have in common is that they have no sense of control or power in the situation. Bad luck and forces-beyond-our-control explanations, like those of Simone and Ellen, do not allow for learning how to make the future work out better. Similarly, when Hilda blames LouAnn, she feels victimized. Blaming can be used to justify vengeful behavior and even destructiveness. It also makes it hard to let go of the relationship. Hilda can't learn how to improve her relationships in the future unless she gets clearer about her contribution to what happened.

While Hilda takes too little responsibility for the ending of her relationship, Sara takes too much.

Sara blamed herself for not being a better partner to her lover, Betsy. She went through lists of "if onlys," replaying how maybe it would have worked out if only she had said or done something differently.

The fact is that each partner makes a contribution to the relationship's ending. No one person is responsible for the partnership's working—or not working. In order for each partner to understand her contribution, the problems in the relationship have to be separated from the stress of the ending. This is not an easy task.

Ginny and Donna, our first example, confronted some major stresses in ending their relationship. One of these was Donna's involvement with Sue; another was their merged financial affairs; a third was the mix of feelings they both had about the break-up.

Sometimes another involvement is used as a means of ending a relationship. A woman may believe that she needs the support or the distraction that a new relationship provides in order to end the old relationship. She may be dissatisfied and want out of the relationship, but unable or unwilling to deal directly with her dissatisfaction. Another involvement may appear to be the only acceptable justification for the breakup. This process is not always a conscious one; it may become more clear to a woman after some time has passed. When a relationship ends in this way, both partners are likely to feel bad. The woman who initiates the breakup is likely to feel guilty, while her partner is likely to feel rejected. The woman who is "left," or who does not have a new lover, may feel worse, if pain can be quantified. But both feel pain.

The guilt that Donna felt and the rejection and anger that Ginny experienced contributed to their difficulties in sorting out their financial separation. Their finances were completely merged. They had never made any plans, or even discussed what they would do if the relationship ended. After Donna moved out, Ginny was very angry. She refused to talk to her ex-lover about making arrangements about the car, the house, and the furniture they owned together. Donna's leaning was just to let Ginny have it all; but she was hurting for money. She was paying for an apartment for herself, as well as her share of the mortgage payment on the house where Ginny still lived. At one point, they had a big fight over the new VCR they had recently bought for the house. This purchase had been made on Donna's credit card. Ginny refused to contribute anything toward the monthly payment, to give Donna the VCR, or even to discuss it.

The third stress that this couple faced was dealing with

the mix of sometimes contradictory feelings about the breakup. Ginny was surprised to notice that in addition to pain, she felt some relief when Donna finally moved out. No more did she have to deal with Donna's demands and her sulking. She could come and go—and sleep—as she pleased, without worrying that she was not putting enough energy into her relationship with Donna. She was angry with her ex-lover; but she also idealized her. She wondered if she would ever find someone as kind and thoughtful as Donna had been. For her part, Donna had been desperate to leave. Once away, she missed Ginny terribly. She began to doubt her decision to break up, particularly when she remembered the good times. In addition, Donna was alarmed to find herself beset by fears. She was afraid of being hurt in her new relationship, of having to take care of herself, of sleeping alone, and just of being on her own—without Ginny.

Successful endings

It is important to recognize that there is no easy way to break up and no way to make the ending totally painless. Even endings that are mutually agreed upon by both partners are likely to have a bittersweet quality. While both women may feel satisfied and even good about the decision to break up, both are likely to experience pain, fears, and ambivalence.

According to Emily Coleman and Betty Edwards, to end a relationship with grace and caring requires skills and attitudes that are not common in our society. We must learn to regard endings as a part of the natural flow of life. Endings are also beginnings. They point out that days end, meals end, vacations end, projects end, school programs end, and we adjust to these events. So, too, relationships end—at least in their previous form. Forever is not necessary in order for a relationship to be valuable and worthwhile.

Another attitude that needs changing is our reluctance to discuss the possibility that a relationship may come to an end.

Many couples avoid talking about a breakup because it feels like an invitation to disaster. They get upset at the idea of making agreements. In fact, discussions about parting are acts of caring. Advance planning can go a long way toward avoiding conflict if the relationship does end.

Having a clearly spelled out agreement or contract can ease the difficulty and minimize the messiness of ending a relationship. Clear agreements about how to make ending as easy as possible are important when a couple makes an exclusive commitment, or when a couple moves in together. The best time to negotiate how you will divide any property held in common, or whether or for how long you will go to counseling or seek clarity from your spiritual community, is well in advance of when you need to make these decisions.

Breaking up clearly involves many of the same skills that help to develop a satisfying relationship. Good communication, conflict resolution skills, goodwill, trust, and shared goals are some of the main ingredients. If you are having difficulty negotiating the terms of the breakup, consider engaging a counselor, a mediator, or an attorney. Continuing to fight without resolving anything can build unnecessary hurts and resentments which may interfere with having another satisfying relationship after the breakup.

And what kind of relationship do you want to have with each other after the breakup? What kind of commitment are each of you willing to make toward that goal? If you both agree that you want to be friends, you need to negotiate the terms of your friendship. What are your wants and expectations? How much time are you each willing to spend to work out this transition from lovers to friends? Do you need to consider having a third party—a counselor, for example—help in this process? Does either one of you need some time apart, without contact at all?

In making the transition from being to not being in a couple relationship, doing something special can be important to bring closure to the relationship.

Vanessa set aside a special time to pack up all the pictures, presents, and mementos that reminded her of Sun-Li. She decided not to throw anything out—yet. So she stored the boxes in the basement until she would be ready to sort through them.

Monde cleaned the whole apartment and rearranged all the furniture after Louise moved out. To her this symbolized making the place hers again.

Candace and Rebecca asked their minister to conduct an ending ceremony with them. They found it affirming to acknowledge the good things about the relationship and about each other. Doing this helped them feel more positive about ending their relationship.

Vicki decided to take a trip to the desert by herself after Angela announced that she wanted to end their relationship. The desert had always been a place of cleansing and healing for Vicki. While she was there, she designed a healing ritual for herself which allowed her to let go of some of her pain.

After the end of her five-year relationship, Esther's friends gave her a "starting over" shower. They wanted an event to mark the end of her relationship and the beginning of her new identity as a single person.

Dealing with loss

After the loss of a relationship, there are phases in the recovery process and tasks of mourning that need to be accomplished. First we will look at this process after a break-up and then when a partner dies.

According to William Worden, in *Grief Counseling and Grief Therapy*, there seem to be three parts to the grieving process. The first is *shock and denial*. In the earlier situation with Ginny and Donna, Ginny was convinced at first that Donna's leaving was a bad dream. She was sure that Donna would come to her senses, return to their home, and everything would be okay. As she began to realize that Donna was not coming back, she accomplished the first task in the grieving process. She began to accept the reality of the loss. Instead of denying that the relationship was really over, she realized that Donna was, in fact, not coming back. When she fully realized that the relationship was over, Ginny then became furious with Donna for leaving and angry with herself for "wasting all those years." She felt betrayed and abandoned. Sometimes it seemed to her that her heart was breaking. She couldn't remember ever feeling so depressed. This period of *anger and depression* is the second phase of recovery, and the task is to experience the pain of the grief. Ginny needs to be patient and treat herself gently during this period of healing. Eventually, she can accept the end of the relationship with Donna and adjust to living without her. The last task in grieving is *moving on*—reinvesting energy in other relationships.

There is no set amount of time for the grieving process; usually it proceeds by degree. One sign of progress is being able to think of the person without intense pain. Gradually Ginny will begin to feel a little less sad, a little less hurt and angry. However, she will probably not feel good as fast as she would like. She may expect that she should be getting over the relationship with Donna faster than she is. She may desperately want to be done with it, yet not feel done.

At this stage it is tempting to get involved in another relationship to distract oneself from the pain of grieving. Frequently friends become uncomfortable with their friend's grief and may try to match her up with someone, or try to get her to stop feeling her pain. Worden believes that it takes four full seasons of the year before grief over the loss of a close relationship begins to abate.

There can be many complications in the mourning process. Often one loss reactivates previous losses.

As Ginny grieved for the end of her relationship with Donna, she also grieved for the death of her father. When he had died five years previously, she went numb and never did express much feeling, even though she felt close to him. She hardly cried at all.

This is very common. Sometimes when she cried about Donna, she was aware of how much she missed her father.

Some of her tears were for losing him. Sometimes it seems that we each have a deep reservoir of sadness and pain. Any particular loss can tap into this well of unshed tears. Asking "When is mourning finished?" is like asking "How high is up?" There is no ready answer. This is true for breaking up as well as for the death of a partner.

When a partner dies

Laverne and Pamela had been together for fourteen years when Pamela was killed in a car accident. Two years later Laverne had not yet finished grieving her partner.

At first she was in shock. Weeks after the funeral she kept imagining that she saw Pamela on the street, or that she heard her car in the driveway. She had to keep reminding herself that Pamela was not going to return. Just as it took time for Ginny to accept Donna's leaving, Laverne had to work hard to accept the reality of Pamela's death.

For some time Laverne just felt numb; she felt nothing. Then when she started to feel the pain, she threw herself into her work to try to distract herself. She thought about moving to another city and then decided that the geographical cure probably wasn't much of a cure at all. She wondered "Why me?" a lot. She found herself being angry with Pamela for dying and at other people because they were alive and Pamela was not. Luckily, she had a strong network of friends who were very supportive as she finally allowed herself to feel the depth of the pain, sadness, and rage. Only after she had allowed herself to be aware of her feelings was Laverne able to move on to the final task of mourning. This was the task of adjusting to an environment where Pamela was missing. She had to take care of things that Pamela had attended to for years. Over time, they had gradually divided up chores based on their time and interests. Pamela had always balanced the checkbook and done most of the yard work. Laverne was shocked at how helpless and inadequate she felt in handling everything herself. But she did it. She was late getting the storm windows up, and the lawn was pretty scruffy the next summer; but she managed. During this time, she was amazed at how sad and angry she continued to feel about Pamela's death. All their plans for the house, and for travelling, were shattered; Laverne was left alone.

Laverne's good fortune in having a network of friends to provide support was particularly important because she was closeted at work. One of the complications of lesbian relationships is that the couple usually does not have the support that a heterosexual couple takes for granted during the course of a relationship and in the event of a partner's death. People at work did not learn of Pamela's death. If they had, their condolences would not have been based on an understanding of the nature and depth of the relationship. They would have wondered that Laverne was so upset; after all, they were "just friends."

Other complications in grieving over the death of a lesbian partner can be the attitude and behavior of the family of the deceased partner. If a will exists that specifies desired funeral arrangements and property disposal, potential problems can be avoided. Without such precautions, the remaining partner may risk being excluded from decisions about funeral arrangements and other post-mortem issues. In addition, family members of the deceased have been known to swoop in and remove possessions from their daughter's home—including things that belonged to the remaining partner. Having a will ensures the partner some legal protection in the event her lover's family is antagonistic.

If we do not like to think about the "what ifs" in breaking up, how much more do we avoid the "what ifs" concerning death? But once again, advance planning, such as having a will, can prevent adding unnecessary legal and other hassles to the already difficult mourning process. In the absence of a structure of legal and societal agreements established for married people in the heterosexual world, lesbians as individuals and as a community can assent to having their status as couples be ignored—or we can create a structure for ourselves.

Chapter 18

Beginning Again

Succeeding in a new relationship depends in part on understanding our previous ones. If we ignore the past or fail to understand it, we run a greater risk of repeating past mistakes. So finishing unfinished business from previous relationships is important when we choose new partners and begin new relationships.

Understanding the past

In the chapter on endings we discussed the tasks of building a new identity and of grieving the loss when a relationship ends. Our third task, understanding the past, involves analyzing what went wrong—and what went right—as we come to terms with the old relationship. When we try to understand why a relationship ended, it is hard to be objective. Even after we have overcome our strong emotional attachments, we may still blame our partner or ourselves for the breakup. It is more helpful, instead, to develop a balanced and clear assessment of the whole relationship. In this assessment, the most important thing to recognize is that both partners contributed to the good and to the bad in the relationship.

To understand the past, it is useful to write down a short history of the relationship. In this history try answering these questions:

1. What did you like and/or admire in her when you first met?
2. What were the most significant positive experiences in your relationship?

3. What did each of you do to make the relationship work?

4. What were your greatest sadnesses? Your feelings of failure?

5. How did she contribute to these failures? How did you?

6. What still makes you feel angry? Guilty? How might you have contributed to creating these feelings? Your partner?

7. In what ways has the relationship added to your life?

8. What did the experience teach you about yourself? About relationships? How will this knowledge help you with your next relationship?

After you finish writing your history, check it for objectivity. If you think it is biased or that it will not help to guide you toward more successful future relationships, it is worth your time to answer the questions again.

By its very nature, a relationship involves the behavior of two people. Partners work together to produce what is positive in the relationship, and must share responsibility for what goes wrong. In looking back, we can't do anything about our former partner's mistakes. But we can learn from our own. We need a balanced and clear view of the history of a relationship so that we can avoid mistakes made in the past and create a relationship in the future that is more like what we want.

Choosing a new partner

Finding a good partner takes a combination of imagination, planning, thought, a willingness to extend onself, and good luck. We can't count on stumbling onto opportunities —we have to help create them.

Meja decided that if she was going to meet any new women she was going to have to find them herself. No one was going to come knocking on her door. So she volunteered to do some work at the local Women's Center.

Cecilia complained to her friend Elena that the only women she met drank too much. When Elena asked where she went to meet women, Cecilia laughed and said that she went to the bars.

Fiona decided that she wanted to meet women who were physically active so she joined a volleyball team and enrolled in a backpacking class.

The people we meet are the ones we arrange to find, whether or not we are aware of making the arrangements. Three good steps are: define the kind of women who interest you; figure out where they are likely to spend their time; and then arrange to be there to meet them.

Richard Stuart and Barbara Jacobsen suggest writing a "Personals" ad to help clarify what you want in a prospective mate. The idea is not actually to place the ad in a paper (although you may do that, too), but to use it as a tool to get clearer about how you see yourself—as well as what you expect from a partner. In this ad, describe the kind of person you want under the section "Who I want to meet." Specify your strong preferences or requirements. These may include age, religion, occupation, personal qualities, and anything else you consider important. Then under "What I offer in return" write an honest description of yourself. When you finish your ad, look it over. Underline the most important words in your description of yourself and the partner you are seeking. Have you been accurate about yourself? Have you been too idealistic about your prospective partner? Are the two descriptions compatible?

Once we know what kind of person we want, we can either trust to luck to run into her, or we can put some effort into the search. We can give parties rather than waiting to be invited; we can risk the chance of rejection (or success) in dating, rather than avoiding the risk; we can initiate a conversation with a stranger at a party rather than waiting for her to speak to us; we can give others a chance rather than eliminating them quickly as unsuitable.

If this last description sounds like you, try this: decide on three characteristics that are essential in a partner. No, not ten or twenty, just three. So if the essential ingredients are *single*, *over thirty*, and *politically active*, eliminate only those women who don't have these three characteristics. Give yourself a chance to get to know *any* woman who *does* meet the three essentials. This way you avoid writing women off before you get a chance to know them. Even if they do not turn out to be appropriate partners, they may become (or have) friends.

So now that you have met someone who interests you, what next? Keep the following guidelines in mind in choosing your new partner:

Guideline 1:

If there is anything that you very much want in a partner, look for someone who has it already. We cannot trust the power of our love to create what is not there initially.

Charlene was concerned about Zizi's eating patterns before they moved in together. However, Charlene was sure that she could influence her partner to stop, or at least to cut down on her compulsive eating. Needless to say, Charlene could not stop Zizi's eating; Charlene got discouraged and hurt; and Zizi got angry when she found out about Charlene's attempts to improve her.

It was important to Esther that her partner really did want to live with Esther's children. She had learned the hard way that some people just did not want children in their lives. Before she got serious about Chris, she carefully checked out how Chris felt about this.

Guideline 2:

Love is not enough.

Rene was convinced that what she felt for Sue was true love. We would say, instead, that she was infatuated. She was totally ecstatic about Sue, even though she hardly knew her; she got more interested in Sue as Sue showed less interest in her; she was obsessed with thinking about Sue—everything and everyone else in Rene's life was unimportant by comparison.

Love is a deeper emotion than infatuation. Though not as intense, love has a better chance of resulting in long-term satisfaction because it is based on accurate knowledge of our partner and genuine and mutual sharing of interests and values.

Since we have rejected the idea of love as infatuation, let's define what we *do* mean. Love is a feeling of our partner's being as important to us as we are to ourselves. Love *is* essential for a good couple relationship, but it is not enough in itself. If two people are not compatible in their ways of handling the details of daily life or if their goals and values are very different, love may not be enough for a satisfying commitment.

Ingrid loved Kerry very much, but she did not at first realize how determined Kerry was to have children. This was not something that Ingrid wanted and so eventually they parted.

It was hard for Adrian to believe that her relationship with Dora didn't work out because they couldn't live together comfortably. But it was true. Their approaches to chores, paying bills, and the details of running a household were very different—and they were both "set in their ways," as Dora described it. Because they each wanted to be able to live with their partner, the relationship ended.

After a year of being with Norma, Bella saw more clearly how different they were. Norma was focused on security and work, while Bella valued travel and a sense of adventure. She wished she had seen this earlier . . .

Guideline 3:

Similarities and differences are both important. A balance is best.

Some of us believe that opposites attract. While there may be some truth to this, those who bring very different values and goals to a relationship have sources of potential conflict. Similarity, on the contrary, provides for comfort and a sense of understanding and being understood. But too much similarity can be boring. We need someone who shares our important values and goals, but who is different enough to make life interesting and to broaden our perspectives. Similarities may make life easier, but differences make it stimulating. The trick is to find the balance.

Before they moved in together, Rachael and Sumiko had a session where each outlined to the other what her personal goals were, so that they could compare notes. They discovered that financial security and spending time together were the highest goals for each of them. That made them feel alike—and close—but there were also differences. Physical fitness and exercise were important to Rachael. Sumiko really didn't care about that at all. On the other hand, a commitment to spiritual meditation was crucial for Sumiko and not for Rachael. In this case, they valued these differences. They also decided to have a yearly review of these goals to make it clear that there was room for each to change her priorities over time.

Guideline 4:

We can learn from the past and apply our knowledge to the new relationship.

In starting a new relationship, we bring together the past, the present and the future. By coming to terms with our past relationships, we can understand ourselves better and avoid making the same mistakes again. By getting clear in the present about what we want in a partner, we increase our chances of recognizing her when we find her. And by taking an active role in arranging to meet potential partners, and realistically assessing our compatibility with them, we are much more likely to build a satisfying relationship.

Whether we have one long-term relationship or a number of relationships, lesbian couples are similar to other types of couples. We all bring our personal histories into our relationships. Many of us struggle to improve our communication and enhance the intimacy between us. Most of us search for a balance between work and play. We all go through stages as our relationships age and mature.

As lesbian couples, we also face some unique problems and challenges. We cope with homophobia and having to decide whether we can even acknowledge our partners publicly. We sort out how to have children together and how to get societal recognition of our relationships. We design our own rituals and events to celebrate and affirm the nature of our relationships. The amazing thing is that we do all of this without much societal support.

We are impressed with the creativity that lesbians bring to couple relationships. One of our goals has been to acknowledge the community of lesbian couples in its diversity and possibilities; another has been to help lesbian couples enhance their intimate relationships. We need to celebrate our couple relationships and take them seriously: they are both a gift and a commitment.

Bibliography

Abbitt, D. and B. Bennett. "Being a Lesbian Mother." In *Positively Gay,* edited by B. Berzon and R. Leighton. Millbrae, Calif.: Celestial Arts, 1979.

Ackerman, R.J. *Growing in the Shadow: Children of Alcoholics*. Pompano Beach, Fla.: Health Communications, 1986.

Adelman, M. *Long Time Passing: Lives of Older Lesbians*. Boston: Alyson Publications, 1986.

Bach, G.R. and P.Wyden. *The Intimate Enemy: How to Fight Fair in Love and Marriage*. New York: Avon, 1968.

Barbach, L. *For Yourself: The Fulfillment of Female Sexuality*. New York: New American Library, 1975.

Barbach, L. *For Each Other*. Garden City, N.Y.: Anchor Press/Doubleday, 1982.

Bass, E. and L. Thornton. *I Never Told Anyone*. New York: Harper and Row, 1983.

Bernhard, Y.M. *Self Care*. Berkeley, Calif.: Celestial Arts, 1975.

Berzon, B. "Sharing Your Lesbian Identity with Your Children." In *Our Right to Love: A Lesbian Resource Book*, edited by G. Vida. Englewood Cliffs, N.J.: Prentice-Hall, 1978.

Berzon, B. and R. Leighton. *Positively Gay*. Millbrae, Calif.: Celestial Arts, 1979.

Black, C. *It Will Never Happen to Me*. Denver: M.A.C. Printing and Publications, 1981.

Black, C. *Repeat After Me*. Denver: M.A.C. Printing and Publications, 1985.

Bloom, L.Z., K. Coburn, and J. Perlman. *The New Assertive Woman*. New York: Dell Publishing Co., 1975.

Blumstein, P. and P. Schwartz. *American Couples*. New York: William Morrow and Co., 1983.

Borhek, M.V. *Coming Out to Parents*. New York: The Pilgrim Press, 1983.

The Boston Women's Health Collective. *The New Our Bodies, Ourselves*. New York: Simon and Schuster, 1984.

Brehm, S. S. *Intimate Relationships*. New York: Random House,

1985.
Bridges, W. *Transitions: Making Sense of Life's Changes*. Reading, Mass.: Addison-Wesley, 1980.
Briggs, D.C. *Your Child's Self-Esteem: The Key to Life*. Garden City, N.Y.: Doubleday and Co., 1975.
Briggs, D.C. *Celebrate Yourself*. Garden City, N.Y.: Doubleday and Co., 1977.
Brown, L.S. Personal communication. 1984.
Brown, L.S. "Sexual Issues in the Development of Lesbian Couples." Paper presented at the meeting of the American Psychological Association, Toronto, Canada, 1985.
Browne, S., D. Connors, and N. Stern. *With the Power of Each Breath: A Disabled Women's Anthology*. Pittsburg: Cleis Press, 1985.
Burns, D.B. *Intimate Connections*. New York: Signet, 1985.
Butler, P.E. *Talking to Yourself: Learning the Language of Self-Support*. San Francisco: Harper and Row, 1981.
Butler, P. *Self Assertion for Women*. rev. ed. San Francisco: Harper and Row, 1981.
Campbell, S.M. *The Couple's Journey: Intimacy As a Path to Wholeness*. San Luis Obispo, Calif.: Impact Publishers, 1980.
Campbell, S.M. *Beyond the Power Struggle*. San Luis Obispo, Calif.: Impact Publishers, 1984.
Chesler, P. *Mothers on Trial: The Battle for Children and Custody*. Seattle: The Seal Press, 1987.
Clark, D. *Loving Someone Gay*. New York: New American Library, 1977.
Clark, J.I. *Self-Esteem: A Family Affair*. Minneapolis: Winston Press, 1978.
Coleman, E. and B. Edwards. *Brief Encounters: How To Make the Most of Relationships That May Not Last Forever*. Garden City, N.Y.: Anchor Books, 1970.
Colgrove, M., H.H. Bloomfield, and P. McWilliams. *How To Survive the Loss of a Love*. New York: Bantam Books, 1976.
Cramer, D. "Gay Parents and Their Children: A Review of Research and Practical Implications." *Journal of Counseling and Development* 64 (1986): 504-507.
Cuming, P. *The Power Handbook: A Strategic Guide to Organizational and Personal Effectiveness*. New York: Van Nostrand Reinhold Co. , 1981.

Curry, H. and D. Clifford. *A Legal Guide for Lesbian and Gay Couples*. 4th ed. Berkeley, Calif.: Nolo Press, 1986.
Doress, P.B. and D.L. Siegal and the Midlife and Older Women Book Project in cooperation with the Boston Women's Health Book Collective, eds. *Ourselves, Growing Older: Women Aging with Knowledge and Power*. Boston: Simon and Schuster/Touchstone, 1987.
Eichenbaum, L. and S. Orbach. *What Do Women Want: Exploring the Myth of Dependency*. New York: Berkeley Publishing Co., 1983.
Faber, A. and E. Mazlish. *How To Talk So Kids Will Listen and Listen So Kids Will Talk*. New York: Avon, 1982.
Fairchild, B. and N. Hayward. *Now That You Know: What Every Parent Should Know about Homosexuality*. New York: Harcourt, Brace, Jovanovich, 1979.
Fisher, B. *Rebuilding: When Your Relationship Ends*. San Luis Obispo, Calif.: Impact Publishers, 1981.
Finkelhor, D. *Child Sexual Abuse: New Theory and Research*. New York: Free Press, 1984.
Fortune, M. *Sexual Violence: The Unmentionable Sin*. New York: Pilgrim Press, 1983.
Garcia, N., C. Kennedy, S.F. Pearlman, and J. Perez. "The Impact of Race and Culture Differences: Challenges to Intimacy in Lesbian Relationships." In *Lesbian Psychologies*, edited by The Boston Lesbian Psychologies Collective. Urbana, Ill.: University of Illinois Press, 1987: 142-160.
Gil, E. *Outgrowing the Pain*. San Francisco: Launch Press, 1983.
Golumbok, S., A. Spencer, and M. Rutter. "Children in Lesbian and Single-Parent Households: Psychosexual and Psychiatric Appraisal." *Journal of Child Psychology and Psychiatry* 24, (1983): 551 (abstract).
Gonsoriek, J.C. *Homosexuality and Therapy: A Practitioner's Handbook of Affirmative Models*. New York: Haworth Press, 1982.
Goodman, B. "Some Mothers are Lesbian." In *Women's Issues and Social Work*, edited by E. Norman and A. Mancuso. Itasca, Ill.: Peacock, 1980.
Gordon, T. *P.E.T.: Parent Effectiveness Training*. New York: Peter H. Wyden Inc., 1970.
Gottman, J. et al. *A Couple's Guide to Communication*.

Champaign, Ill.: Research Press, 1976.
Gravitz, H.L. and J.D. Bowder. *A Guide to Recovery: A Book for Adult Children of Alcoholics*. Holmes Beach, Fla.: Learning Publications, 1985.
Green, G.D. "Mental Health Considerations of Lesbian Mothers." In *Gay and Lesbian Parents,* edited by F. Bozett. New York: Praeger Publishers, 1987.
Green, R. "Sexual Identity of 37 Children Raised by Homosexual or Transexual Parents." *American Journal of Psychiatry*, 135 (1978): 692-697.
Hall, M. "Lesbian Families: Cultural and Clinical Issues." *Social Work*, 23 (1978): 380-385.
Hanscombe, G. E., and J. Forster. *Rocking the Cradle: Lesbian Mothers—A Challenge in Family Living*. Boston: Alyson Publications Inc., 1982.
Harris, M.B. and P.H. Turner. "Gay and Lesbian Parents." *Journal of Homosexuality* 12(2). (1985/86):. 101-113.
Hart, B. "Lesbian Battering: An Examination." In *Naming the Violence: Speaking Out about Lesbian Battering*, edited by K. Lobel. Seattle: The Seal Press, 1986: 173-189.
Herman, J. and L. Hirschman. *Father-Daughter Incest*. Cambridge, Mass.: Harvard University Press, 1981.
Hollibaugh, A., and C. Moraga. "What We're Rollin' Around in Bed With: Sexual Issues in Feminism." In *Powers of Desire: The Politics of Sexuality*, edited by C. Stansell and S. Thompson. New York: Monthly Review Press, 1983: 314-405.
Hotredt, M. and G.L. Mandel. "Children of Lesbian Mothers." In *Homosexuality: Social, Psychological and Biological Issues*, edited by W. Paul, J. Weinrich, J. Gonsioriek, and M. Hotredt. Beverly Hills, Calif.: Sage, 1982.
Hughes, N., Y. Johnson, and Y. Perrault. *Stepping Out of Line: A Workbook on Lesbianism and Feminism*. Vancouver, B.C.: Press Gang Publishers, 1984.
Jacubowski, P. and A. Lange. *The Assertive Option*. Champaign, Ill.: Research Press, 1978.
Keyes, K. Jr. *A Conscious Person's Guide to Relationships*. Marina Del Ray, Calif.: Living Love Publications, 1979.
Kirkpatrick, M., C. Smith, and R. Roy. "Lesbian Mothers and Their Children." *American Journal of Orthopsychiatry*, 51 (1981): 545-551.

Klein, F. and T.J. Wolf. *Two Lives to Lead: Bisexuality in Men and Women*. New York: Harrington Park Press, 1985.

Kritsburg, W. *The Adult Children of Alcoholics Syndrome: From Discovery to Recovery*. Pompano Beach, Fla.: Health Communications, Inc., 1985.

Kreston, J. and C.S. Besko. "The Problem of Fusion in the Lesbian Relationship." *Family Process* 19(3) (1980): 277-289.

Lakein, A. *How To Get Control of Your Time and Your Life*. New York: New American Library, 1973.

Lederer, W.J. *Creating a Good Relationship*. New York: W. W. Norton and Co., 1984.

Ledray, L.E. *Recovering from Rape*. New York: Henry Holt and Co., 1986.

Lerner, H. G. *The Dance of Anger: A Woman's Guide to Changing the Pattern of Intimate Relationships*. New York: Harper and Row, 1985.

Lesbian Mother's National Defense Fund. Personal communication, Sept. 30, 1986.

Levine, S. *Who Dies?* Garden City, N.Y.: Anchor Books, 1982.

Levine, S. *Healing into Life and Death*. Garden City, N.Y.: Anchor Press/Doubleday, 1987.

Lewis, E. and T. Lyons. "Everything in its Place: The Coexistence of Lesbianism and Motherhood." In *Homosexuality: Social, Psychological and Biological Issues*, edited by W. Paul, J. Weinrich, J. Gonsoriek, and M. Hotredt. Beverly Hills: Sage, 1982.

Lewis, K. "Children of Lesbians: Their Point of View." *Social Work* 25(3).(1980): 198-203.

Lewis, S.G. *Sunday's Women: A Report on Lesbian Life Today*. Boston: Beacon Press, 1979.

Lobel, K. *Naming the Violence: Speaking Out about Lesbian Battering*. Seattle: The Seal Press, 1986.

Loulan, J. *Lesbian Sex*. San Francisco: Spinsters Ink, 1984.

Loulan, J. "Psychotherapy with Lesbian Mothers." In *Contemporary Perspectives on Psychotherapy with Lesbians and Gay Men*, edited by T. S. Stein and C. J. Cohen. New York: Plenum Publishing Corp., 1986.

Loulan, J. *Lesbian Passion: Loving Ourselves and Each Other*. San Francisco: Spinsters/Aunt Lute, 1987.

MacDonald, B. with C. Rich. *Look Me in the Eye: Old Women,*

Aging, and Ageism. San Francisco: Spinsters Ink, 1983.

McWhirter, D.P., and M. Mattison. *The Male Couple: How Relationsips Develop*. Englewood Cliffs, N.J.: Prentice-Hall, 1984.

Maltz, W. and B. Holman. *Incest and Sexuality: A Guide to Understanding and Healing*. Lexington, Mass.: D.C. Heath and Co., 1987.

Mager, D. "Out in the Workplace." In *After You're Out: Personal Experiences of Gay Men and Lesbian Women*, edited by K. Jay and A. Young. New York: Links Books, 1975.

Mackoff, B. *Leaving the Office Behind*. New York: G.P. Putnam's Sons, 1984.

Martin, D. and P. Lyon. *Lesbian/Woman*. New York: Bantam Books, 1972; updated, revised ed., 1983.

McConnell, P. *Adult Children of Alcoholics: A Workbook for Healing*. San Francisco: Harper and Row, 1986.

McKay, M., M. Davis, and P. Fanning. *Messages: The Communication Book*. Oakland, Calif.: New Harbinger, 1983.

McNaron, T.A.H. and Y. Morgan. *Voices in the Night: Women Speaking about Incest*. Pittsburgh: Cleis Press, 1982.

Middleton-Moz, J. and L. Dwinell. *After the Tears: Reclaiming the Personal Losses of Childhood*. Pompano Beach, Fla.: Health Communications, 1986.

Miller, A. *Thou Shalt Not Be Aware: Society's Betrayal of the Child*. New York: Farrar, Straus, and Giroux, 1984.

Moses, A.E., and R.O. Hawkins. *Counseling Lesbian Women and Gay Men*. St. Louis: The C. V. Mosely Co., 1982.

Muller, A. *Parents Matter: Parents' Relationships with Lesbian Daughters and Gay Sons*. Tallahassee, Fla.: Naiad Press, 1987.

NiCarthy, G. *Getting Free: A Handbook for Women in Abusive Relationships*. Seattle: The Seal Press, 1982.

NiCarthy G. *The Ones Who Got Away*. Seattle: The Seal Press, 1987.

Nichols, M. "Lesbian Sexuality: Issues and Developing Theory." In *Lesbian Psychologies*, edited by The Boston Lesbian Psychologies Collective. Urbana, Ill.: University of Illinois Press, 1987: 97-125.

Norwood, R. *Women Who Love Too Much*. New York: Simon and Schuster, 1985.

Pagelow, M. "Heterosexual and Lesbian Single Mothers: A Comparison of Problems, Coping, and Solutions." *Journal of Homosexuality* 5 (1980): 189-204.

Paul,W., J. Gonsiorek, and M. Hotredt. *Homosexuality: Social, Psychological, and Biological Issues*. Beverly Hills, Calif.: Sage, 1982.

Phair, S. "Two Workshops on Homophobia." In *Naming the Violence: Speaking Out about Lesbian Battering*, edited by K. Lobel. Seattle: The Seal Press, 1986: 202-222.

Pies, C. *Considering Parenthood: A Work Book for Lesbians*. San Francisco: Spinsters Ink, 1985.

Pitzele, S.K. *We Are Not Alone: Learning to Live with Chronic Illness*. New York: Workman Publishing, 1986.

Pogrebin, L.C. *Among Friends: Who We Like, Why We Like Them, and What We Do With Them*. New York: McGraw-Hill, 1987.

Raphael, B. *The Anatomy of Bereavement*. New York: Basic Books, 1983.

Raphael, S. and M. Robinson. "The Older Lesbian: Love Relationships and Friendship Patterns." In *Women-Identified Women*, edited by T. Darty and S. Porter. Palo Alto, Calif.: Mayfield, 1984.

Richardson, D. "Lesbian Mothers." In *The Theory and Practice of Homosexuality*, edited by J. Hart and D. Richardson. London: Routledge and Kegan Paul, 1981.

Rofes, E. *I Thought People Like That Killed Themselves*. San Francisco: Grey Fox Press, 1983.

Rosenthal, L. *Partnering: A Guide to Owning Anything from Homes to Home Computers*. Cincinnati: Writer's Digest Books, 1983.

Rubin, L. *Worlds of Pain: Life in the Working-Class Family*. New York: Basic Books, 1977.

Rush, F. *The Best Kept Secret: Sexual Abuse of Children*. Englewood Cliffs, N.J.: Prentice-Hall, 1980.

Russell, D. H. *The Secret Trauma: Incest in the Lives of Girls and Women*. New York: Basic Books, 1986.

Samois. *Coming to Power*. 2nd. ed. Boston: Alyson Publications, 1982.

Sang, B. "Lesbian Relationships: A Struggle Toward Partner Equality." In *Women-Identified Women*, edited by T. Darty and S.

Porter. Palo Alto, Calif.: Mayfield, 1984.
Saslow, J.M. "Hear Oh Israel: We Are Jews, We Are Gay." *The Advocate* 465.(Feb. 3d) (1987): 38.
Sauerman, T.H. "Coming Out to Your Parents." Pamphlet published by Parents and Friends of Gays, 1984.
Scarf, M. *Intimate Partners: Patterns in Love and Marriage*. New York: Random House, 1987.
Schulenburg, J. *Gay Parenting*. Garden City, N.Y.: Anchor Press/Doubleday, 1985.
Sears, V.L. "Cross-cultural ethnic relationships." Unpublished manuscript, 1987(a).
Sears, V.L. "Disabilities and chronic illness." Unpublished manuscript, 1987(b).
Shaul, S., J.E. Bogle, J. Hale-Harbaugh, and A.D. Norman. *Toward Intimacy: Family Planning and Sexuality Concerns of Physically Disabled Women*. New York: Human Sciences Press, 1978.
Sheehy, G. *Passages: Predictable Crises of Adult Life*. New York: Bantam Books, 1974.
Silverstein, C. *A Family Matter: A Parent's Guide to Homosexuality*. New York: McGraw-Hill, 1978.
Smith, A. "Lesbian Battering." Paper presented at the 2nd National Lesbian Physicians Conference, Provincetown, Mass., 1985.
Stanley, J.P. and S.J. Wolfe. *The Coming Out Stories*. Watertown, Mass.: Persephone Press, 1980.
Stuart, R.B. and B. Jacobsen. *Second Marriage*. New York: W. W. Norton, 1985.
Swallow, J. *Out From Under: Sober Dykes and Our Friends*. San Francisco: Spinsters Ink, 1983.
Tanner, D. *The Lesbian Couple*. Lexington, Mass.: Lexington Books, 1978.
Tennov, D. *Love and Limerance: The Experience of Being in Love*. New York: Stein and Day, 1979.
Tessina, T.B. and R. Smith. *How To Be a Couple and Still Be Free*. North Hollywood, Calif.: Newcastle Publishing Co., 1980.
Ulrig, L. *The Two of Us: Affirming, Celebrating and Symbolizing Gay and Lesbian Relationships*. Boston: Alyson Publications Inc., 1984.
Vaughn, D. *Uncoupling: Turning Points in Intimate Relationships*. New York: Oxford University Press, 1986.

Vida, G. *Our Right to Love*. Englewood Cliffs, N.J.: Prentice-Hall, 1978.

Wanderer, Z. and T. Cabot. *Letting Go*. New York: Warner Books, 1978.

Wegscheider-Cruse, S. *Choicemaking: For Codependents, Adult Children, and Spirituality Seekers*. Pompano Beach, Fla.: Health Communications, 1985.

Weisinger, H. *Dr. Weisinger's Anger Work-Out Book*. New York: William Thurrow and Co., 1985.

Weisinger, H., and N.M. Lobseng. *Nobody's Perfect: How To Give Criticism and Get Results.* New York: Warner Books, 1981.

Woititz, J.G. *Adult Children of Alcoholics*. Hollywood, Calif.: Health Communications, 1983.

Woititz, J.G. *The Struggle for Intimacy*. Pompano Beach, Fla.: Health Communications, 1985.

Woodman, N.J., and H.R. Lenna. *Counseling with Gay Men and Women*. San Francisco: Jossey-Bass Publishers, 1980.

Worden, J.W. *Grief Counseling and Grief Therapy*. New York: Springer, 1982.

Zakarewsky, G.T. "Patterns of Support among Gay and Lesbian Deaf Persons." *Sexuality and Disability* 2(3) (1979): 178-191.

Other Resources

Films:

Choosing Children. Cambridge, Mass.: Cambridge Documentary.

In the Best Interests of the Children. Berkeley, Calif.: Iris Films.

Not All Parents Are Straight. K. White, Producer/Director. San Francisco: FullFrame Productions.

Parents Come Out. San Francisco: Parents and Friends of Lesbians and Gays.

National Organizations:

National Federation of Parents and Friends of Lesbians and Gays. Washington, D.C.

Lesbian Mothers National Defense Fund. Seattle, Wash.

About the Authors

D. Merilee Clunis, Ph.D., and G. Dorsey Green, Ph.D., are both psychologists in private practice in Seattle. Together they lead workshops for therapists who work with lesbian couples. Their papers on lesbian couples have been presented at the American Psychological Association's annual meetings.

OTHER LESBIAN TITLES FROM SEAL PRESS

BIRD-EYES by Madelyn Arnold. $8.95, 0-931188-82-8. A teenage runaway is institutionalized for her lesbianism in this powerful story of resistance and survival.

LOVERS' CHOICE by Becky Birtha. $8.95, 0-931188-56-3. Wonderful stories charting the course of women's lives by an important Black lesbian feminist writer.

GAUDÍ AFTERNOON by Barbara Wilson. $8.95, 0-931188-89-X. Amidst the dream-like architecture of Gaudí's city, this high-spirited comic thriller introduces amateur sleuth Cassandra Reilly as she chases people of all genders and motives.

OUT OF TIME by Paula Martinac. $8.95, 0-931188-91-1. A delightful and evocative ghost story exploring lesbian history and the power of memory.

GIRLS, VISIONS AND EVERYTHING by Sarah Schulman. $9.95, 0-931199-38-5. A funny, touching romp through New York's Lower East Side. By the author of *After Delores* and *People in Trouble.*

THE HAUNTED HOUSE by Rebecca Brown. $8.95, 0-9311888-1. This brilliant novel explores the psychic repercussions of growing up in an alcoholic family.

MISS VENEZUELA by Barbara Wilson. $9.95, 0-931188-58-X. A provocative collection of twenty-two new and previously published stories by a well-known lesbian author.

HALLOWED MURDER by Ellen Hart. $8.95, 0-931188-83-0. Featuring a memorable cast of characters, this page-turning mystery gives an intriguing inside view of the dark undercurrents of sorority and religious life.

CEREMONIES OF THE HEART *Celebrating Lesbian Unions* by Becky Butler .$14.95, 0-931188-92-X. An anthology of twenty-five personal accounts of ceremonies of commitment, from the momentous decision to the day of celebration.

NAMING THE VIOLENCE edited by Kerry Lobel. $10.95, 0-931188-42-3. This groundbreaking anthology deals with the problem of physical and emotional abuse in lesbian relationships.

SEAL PRESS, founded in 1976 to provide a forum for women writers and feminist issues, has many other titles in stock: fiction, self-help books, anthologies and translations. Any of the books above may be ordered from us at 3131 Western Ave., Suite 410, Seattle WA 98121 (add 15% of total book order for shipping and handling). Write to us for a free catalog or if you would like to be on our mailing list.